THE CONSTITUTION AS TREATY

The Constitution as Treaty transforms the conceptualization of U.S. constitutional law by exploring the interpretive implications of viewing the U.S. Constitution as a treaty. It argues that federal courts constitute an international tribunal system, and, as such, their jurisdiction is governed by international law enabling them to exercise judicial review authority and undercutting much of the judicial activist critique. *The Constitution as Treaty* continues with an examination of what international law is and its major interpretive principles in order to set the stage for examining how different sources and principles of international law are intrinsically integrated into U.S. constitutional law and, thereby, are available to federal courts for deciding cases. It addresses the *Charming Betsy* Rule, the non-self-execution doctrine, the last-in-time rule, and the proper use of customary international law and other international law not mentioned in Article III. *The Constitution as Treaty* concludes that federal courts generally must construe the United States' international legal obligations liberally.

Francisco Forrest Martin is the founder and president of Rights International, The Center for International Human Rights Law, Inc. He is also the former Ariel F. Sallows Professor of Human Rights at the University of Saskatchewan College of Law. Mr. Martin is the author of seven books and many articles on U.S. constitutional and international law, including *International Human Rights and Humanitarian Law* (Cambridge University Press 2006). He has litigated cases before U.S. and international courts, including the European Court of Human Rights, Inter-American Commission and Court of Human Rights, and the African Commission on Human and Peoples' Rights. He was the recipient of the American Civil Liberties Union's Anneta Dieckmann Award.

THE CONSTITUTION AS TREATY

THE INTERNATIONAL LEGAL CONSTRUCTIONALIST APPROACH TO THE U.S. CONSTITUTION

FRANCISCO FORREST MARTIN

President of Rights International,
The Center for International Human Rights Law, Inc.

CAMBRIDGE
UNIVERSITY PRESS

CAMBRIDGE UNIVERSITY PRESS
Cambridge, New York, Melbourne, Madrid, Cape Town, Singapore, São Paulo, Delhi

Cambridge University Press
32 Avenue of the Americas, New York, NY 10013-2473, USA

www.cambridge.org
Information on this title: www.cambridge.org/9780521881937

First published 2007

Printed in the United States of America

A catalog record for this publication is available from the British Library.

Library of Congress Cataloging in Publication Data

Martin, Francisco Forrest.
The Constitution as treaty : the international legal constructionalist approach
to the U.S. Constitution / Francisco Forrest Martin.
p. cm.
Includes bibliographical references and index.
ISBN 978-0-521-88193-7 (hardcover)
1. Constitutional law – United States – Interpretation and construction.
2. Judicial review – United States. I. Title.
KF4550.M268 2007
342.73–dc22 2007025861

ISBN 978-0-521-88193-7 hardback

This book is dedicated to the memories of William C. Martin and Stanley A. Teitler, and to their grandson, Jacob William Simon Teitler-Martin.

The author wishes to thank Bill Burke-White, James Sofka, Michael Lawrence, and John Berger for their very helpful and detailed comments on this book. The author also wishes to thank Geoffrey Hazard and those at the 2005 International Law Association Annual Weekend Conference who commented on earlier versions of parts of this book.

Contents

Prologue

In 1789, the First Congress gave custody and charge of the U.S. Constitution to the Department of Foreign Affairs – the predecessor to the State Department.[1] This bit of historical trivia may strike many as being somewhat odd. After all, why would Congress place the Constitution in the custody of a department charged with managing the foreign affairs of our country? Would it not have made more sense to place the Constitution with a department under the supervision of Congress or with the Supreme Court – the branches of our federal government that respectively make and interpret U.S. law? Only that part of U.S. law that concerns other nations – namely, treaties – should have been placed in custody of the Department of Foreign Affairs, and the Constitution is not a treaty. Or, is it?

[1] *See* "An act for establishing an executive department to be denominated the Department of Foreign Affairs," 1 Stat. 29, 1st Cong. 1st Sess., ch. 4, § 4, (July 27, 1789).

Introduction

This book explores further ramifications of International Legal Constructionism (ILC), a theory of U.S. constitutional interpretation first presented in the 2004 issue of the *Hastings Constitutional Law Quarterly*.[1] This interpretive theory argues that the U.S. Constitution is a treaty that must be construed in conformity with the United States' international legal obligations. One of ILC's claims is that the U.S. federal court system constitutes an international tribunal system. This book will elaborate on this claim and provide an international legal construction of different aspects of federal court jurisdiction, *viz.*, judicial review authority, the authority to use international law, and the appropriate manner of using such law.

A striking feature about the present international legal order is the great and growing number of international tribunals. Since the beginning of the twentieth century, numerous international tribunals of varying types have been created.[2] Although there were very few international

[1] *See* Francisco Forrest Martin, *Our Constitution as Federal Treaty: A New Theory of United States Constitutional Construction Based on an Originalist Understanding for Addressing a New World*, 31 HASTINGS CONST. L. QUART. 269 (2004) (describing ILC approach) [hereinafter, Martin, *Our Constitution as Federal Treaty*]; *see also* Francisco Forrest Martin, *The Constitution and Human Rights: The International Legal Constructionist Approach to Ensuring the Protection of Human Rights*, 1 FLA. INT'L. U.L. REV. 71 (2005) (same); *cf.* DAVID C. HENDRICKSON, PEACE PACT: THE LOST WORLD OF THE AMERICAN FOUNDING (2003) (arguing that Constitution is treaty from political science perspective); Torkel Opsahl, *An "International Constitutional Law"?* 10 INT'L. & COMP. L.Q. 760, 771 (1961) (arguing that Constitution was a treaty).

[2] *E.g.*, International Court of Justice (ICJ), International Military (Nuremberg) Tribunal (IMT), International Military Tribunal for the Far East (IMT-FE), International Criminal Court (ICC) and Tribunals for the former Yugoslavia (ICTY) and Rwanda (ICTR), UN Human Rights Committee (UNHRC), UN Committee to Eliminate Racial Discrimination

tribunals before the twentieth century,[3] two eighteenth-century international tribunal systems deserve special attention: the federal court systems respectively established under the Articles of Confederation[4] and the U.S. Constitution. Although the case law and academic literature providing an international legal construction of U.S. federal court jurisdiction is scarce,[5] it is not unknown. Indeed, "[f]rom the earliest days of the Republic, American courts and commentators have relied on principles of... international law to limit judicial jurisdiction."[6]

(CERD), UN Committee Against Torture (CAT), UN Working Group on Arbitrary Detention, European Court (and former Commission) of Human Rights, European Court of Justice, Inter-American Commission and Court of Human Rights, African Commission and Court of Human and Peoples' Rights, Human Rights Chamber for Bosnia and Herzegovina, International Criminal Tribunal for East Timor, World Trade Organization Panel and Appellate Body, North American Free Trade Agreement (NAFTA) Arbitral Tribunal, NAFTA Dispute Settlement Panels, International Tribunal for Law of the Sea (ITLOS), Benelux Court of Justice, Central American Court of Justice, Permanent Court of Arbitration, and Caribbean Court of Justice.

3 The earliest example of an international tribunal appears to be one established in 1474 by the Holy Roman Empire for trying Peter von Hagenbach for crimes committed by his troops. FRANCISCO FORREST MARTIN *ET AL.*, INTERNATIONAL HUMAN RIGHTS & HUMANITARIAN LAW: TREATIES, CASES & ANALYSIS 2 (2006).

4 July 9, 1778 (entered into force Mar. 1, 1781) [hereinafter ARTICLES OF CONFEDERATION]. The Articles of Confederation constituted a treaty. Martin, *Our Constitution as Federal Treaty*, *supra* note 1 at 278–79.

5 *See, e.g.*, HERBERT A. SMITH, THE AMERICAN SUPREME COURT AS AN INTERNATIONAL TRIBUNAL (1920) (arguing that U.S. Supreme Court is quasi-international court); Thomas H. Lee, *The Supreme Court of the United States as Quasi International Tribunal: Reclaiming the Court's Original and Exclusive Jurisdiction Over Treaty-Based Suits by Foreign States Against States*, 104 COLUM. L. REV. 1765 (2004) (providing international legal discussion of Supreme Court's original jurisdiction); Thomas H. Lee, *Making Sense of the Eleventh Amendment: International Law and State Sovereignty*, 96 NW. U. L. REV. 1027 (2001–2002) (providing international legal explanation of the Eleventh Amendment).

6 GARY B. BORN, INTERNATIONAL CIVIL LITIGATION IN UNITED STATES COURTS 70 (3d ed. 1997), *citing* Mason v. The Ship Blaireau, 6 U.S. 240 (1804); Rose v. Himely, 8 U.S. 241 (1808); D'Arcy v. Ketchum, 52 U.S. 165 (1850); The Bee, 3 Fed. Cas. 41, No. 1219 (D. Me. 1836); *see* Chisholm v. Georgia, 2 U.S. 419, 449 (1793) (Iredell, J., dissenting) (construction of Article III in conformity with conventional law of nations would be proper). In *Chisholm*, the Supreme Court examined whether Article III's diversity jurisdiction allowed the citizen of one state to sue another state. Iredell in his dissent stated that Article III must be construed in conformity with the conventional law of nations. He concluded that no norm under the conventional law of nations guaranteed the right of a citizen of one state to sue another state. However, in 1793, there was division among international legal

This book will explore the implications of providing an international legal construction to federal judicial power. However, before undertaking this exploration, let us first turn to the constitutional basis of International Legal Constructionism.

What Is Our Constitution?

What is our Constitution? What kind of legal instrument is it? It is not really that helpful to say that it is – well – a "constitution" because there a many different types of constitutions – state constitutions, corporate constitutions, intergovernmental constitutions, high school chess club constitutions. It certainly is not merely a statute. It could be a contract. Indeed, most folks wax theoretically and say that it is a social compact.[7] That's fair enough, but lawyers and judges tend to look for something a little bit less theoretical, and few politicians probably are very familiar with social compact theory. Yet, it's odd, but few judges, lawyers, or political leaders ever address what kind of legal instrument the Constitution represents. It certainly must be the case that determining the kind of legal instrument should be important to how one goes about interpreting it.

Instead, most constitutional interpretation does not begin with this fundamental threshold question but starts with examining only the text and moving outside it when the text is vague requiring the use of extraconstitutional authorities and most often making shortcuts by appealing to judicial precedents. However, the Constitution does not say what kind of extraconstitutional authorities are appropriate for construing it, and precedential shortcuts often beg the question by failing to address why earlier precedents using such extraconstitutional authorities are warranted. Consequently, one often ends up foundering on a Schylla of strict constructionism – desperately holding onto the rocks of a rigid textualism. Or, one descends into a Charibdis of judicial activism – swirled and sucked into the unfathomable depths of arbitrary authorities. One fails to safely navigate a constitutional course that is both loyal to the letter of the law, and responsive to new social and political realities such as globalization. Like the counsel given by Circe, it perhaps is best to

authorities over this issue. *See id.* at 425–26 (argument by U.S. Attorney General Randolph for the plaintiff).

[7] *See, e.g.*, Robert H. Bork, The Tempting of America: The Political Seduction of the Law 19 (1991).

navigate closer to the Schylla of strict constructionism because of the lesser danger that it poses. Constitutional text is limited, extraconstitutional authorities are not, and limited government generally is more protective of individual liberties. However, Circe was no sailor, and we should not be bewitched by such advice. Like a well-helmed ship that sometimes can slingshot itself around a whirlpool and gain greater speed, a loose construction of the Constitution sometimes can increase individual liberty.

But both monsters largely are creations of our own. Both are created by a failure to recognize what kind of legal vessel the Constitution is. Failing to understand what the Constitution is encourages constitutional expositors to become modern-day buccaneers, creating mayhem as they ply the high seas of international relations accountable to none. Like another vessel bearing the same name, the Constitution's mission should be to exterminate piracy – not to be pressed into its service.

Our Constitution Is a Treaty

To properly understand what the Constitution is, it is necessary to see what the Founders thought it was. For them, the Constitution was a treaty between the thirteen states. Mind you, it was a peculiar kind of treaty. It was a sort of *foedus* – a suzerainty-type treaty that created a central government that controlled the international affairs of its states-parties. Indeed, our word "federal" comes from the Latin word "*foedus*," and it is this meaning of "federal" that the Framers had in mind when they used the word.[8] The Framers drafted the Constitution in order to replace the Articles of Confederation and to create a stronger central government that could ensure that the individual states did not violate the United States' international legal obligations – a repeated problem faced by the U.S. government under the Articles of Confederation.[9]

When one looks at the ratification debates during the Constitutional Convention, it is clear that the Framers recognized that the law of nations

[8] *See* SAMUEL H. BEER, TO MAKE A NATION: THE REDISCOVERY OF AMERICAN FEDERALISM 315 (1993) (arguing that when Madison used "foederal" in context of compact federalism, he meant contemporary conventional sense of *foedus*, or treaty).

[9] *See* James Madison, *Vices of the Political System of the United States* [1787], eds. William T. Hutchinson, *et al.*, 9 THE PAPERS OF JAMES MADISON 348–57 (1962–77) [hereinafter Madison, *Vices*] (states violated treaties with Great Britain, France, and Holland).

governing treaties also governed the replacement of the Articles with the Constitution.[10] This was noncontroversial. Indeed, in settling on a nine-state ratification rule for the Constitution, the Framers adopted the same numerical rule for ratifying treaties under the Articles.[11] This only made sense because the Constitution was a treaty.

The use of treaties for uniting states and consolidating peoples was not unusual at the time of the Constitution's drafting. John Jay, Rufus King, and others used the example of the *Treaty of Union* (1707) that united the states of England and Scotland, and consolidated the British people, as an anology to the Constitution uniting the thirteen states and consolidating the American people.[12] As one Anti-Federalist put it, "Who is it that does not know, that by treaties in Europe the succession and constitution of

[10] *See, e.g.*, THE FEDERALIST No. 43 (Madison) at § 9 (1788) (establishment of Constitution governed by law of treaties); 1 THE DEBATES IN THE SEVERAL STATE CONVENTIONS ON THE ADOPTION OF THE FEDERAL CONSTITUTION 424 (Jonathan Elliot ed., 1968) (Madison arguing that "civil law of treaties" governed replacement of Articles of Confederation) [hereinafter ELLIOT'S DEBATES]; 1 THE RECORDS OF THE FEDERAL CONVENTION OF 1787 122–23 (Max Farrand ed., 1937) [hereinafter FARRAND'S RECORDS] (same); Madison, *Vices*, § 8 (same); 1 FARRAND'S RECORDS 122–23, 324–25 (Hamilton recognizing treaty law governed replacement of Articles). This is not to say that those provisions in the Articles that were not covered by the Constitution were eliminated. The Constitution's Supremacy Clause continued to recognize that pre-Constitution treaties were still part of federal law. *See infra* discussion in Subsection 1.1 accompanying notes 40–41.

[11] ARTICLES OF CONFEDERATION, art. IX (nine states needed for ratification of treaties); *see* United States Constitution, Sept. 17, 1787, art. VII (entered into force June 21, 1788) (nine of thirteen states needed for ratification of Constitution) [hereinafter U.S. CONST.]. Although the Articles of Confederation required unanimous state consent for the Articles to be altered, ratification by all thirteen states was not required under the law of treaties for establishing the Constitution because state-party violation of a treaty allowed other states-parties to not observe their treaty obligations in regard to those states violating a treaty. Many of the thirteen states had violated the Articles of Confederation; other states-parties did not have to comply with the Articles' unanimous consent rule. *See* Martin, *Our Constitution as Federal Treaty*, *supra* note 1 at 283–91.

[12] *See* THE FEDERALIST No. 5 (Jay) at ¶ 3 *et passim* (1787); 1 FARRAND'S RECORDS 492–93 ("Mr. King was for preserving the States in a subordinate degree.... He did not think a full answer had been given to those who apprehended a dangerous encroachment on their jurisdictions.... The articles of Union between Engld. & Scotland furnish an example of such a provision in favor of sundry rights of Scotland.").

many sovereign states, ha[ve] been regulated?"[13] This practice of using a treaty for creating a constitution has continued.[14]

Of course, one could say that the "states" of the United States are different from foreign "states" – such as France or Japan. However, the Framers made no such distinction. They understood the states of the United States to have the same legal status as foreign states. Indeed, James Patterson (the author of the New Jersey Plan) considered using another term – namely, "districts" – but he subsequently rejected this term.[15] The First Congress also shared this conception of the states. For example, the First Congress recognized that those states (*viz.*, North Carolina and Rhode Island) that had not ratified the Constitution were to be considered foreign states.[16] The Founders – being very familiar with the law of nations – knew the international legal significance of using the term "state," and they retained the use of this term in the Constitution.[17]

Most importantly, the Constitution's text discloses its status as a treaty. What is a treaty? The *Vienna Convention on the Law of Treaties* provides the customary definition of a treaty: a treaty is "an international agreement concluded between States in written form and governed by international law."[18] The first requirement is met in that the Constitution is written. The second requirement also is fulfilled in that Article VII of the Constitution says that "the Ratification of the Conventions of nine states,

[13] *See* The Anti-Federalist No. 75 (Hampden) at ¶ 2 (1788).

[14] *See, e.g.*, The General Framework Agreement for Peace in Bosnia and Herzegovina ("Dayton Agreement"), initialed Nov. 21, 1995, Annex IV (entered into force Dec. 14, 1995) (treaty establishing constitution for Bosnia and Herzegovina).

[15] "Notes Apparently Used by Patterson in Preparing the New Jersey Plan, June 13–15" in Notes of William Paterson in the Federal Convention of 1787, *available at* http://www.yale.edu/lawweb/avalon/const/patterson.htm (last visited Aug. 27, 2003).

[16] *See* Act of Sept. 16, 1789, 1 Stat. 69 (North Carolina and Rhode Island goods imported into United States considered to be goods imported from foreign state, country, or kingdom).

[17] Although the *Montevideo Convention on the Rights and Duties of States* establishes that a "federal state shall constitute a sole person in the eyes of international law," the states of the United States still meet the definition of states under the Convention in that they individually possess "(a) a permanent population; (b) a defined territory; (c) government; and (d) capacity to enter into relations with the other states." Montevideo Convention on the Rights and Duties of States, Dec. 26, 1933, arts. 1 and 2, 49 Stat. 3097, TS. 81, 165 L.N.TS. 19, 3 Bevans 145 (entered into force Dec. 26, 1934) [hereinafter *Montevideo Convention*].

[18] *See* Vienna Convention on the Law of Treaties, May 23, 1969, art. 2 (1) (a), 1155 U.N.T.S. 331 (entered into force Jan. 27, 1980) [hereinafter *Vienna Convention*].

shall be sufficient for the Establishment of this Constitution between the states so ratifying the same."[19] Note here the use of the word "ratification," which is how treaties come into force, but most importantly, also note that the Constitution is established "between the states" – that is, it is an agreement.

The third requirement for a treaty is that it must be governed by international law. The best way to ensure that a treaty is governed by international law is to incorporate international legal norms into the very treaty itself,[20] and the Constitution does that. For example, the Supremacy Clause ensures that treaties are part of the supreme law of the land,[21] including old treaties entered into by the Articles Congress because international law required the recognition of old treaty obligations by new governments.[22] Also, Article I ensures that Congress can clarify international legal norms.[23] Article IV ensures the observance of the international legal rules of the territorial inviolability of states[24] and state coequality,[25] respectively, by prohibiting annexation of state territory by other

19 U.S. CONST. art. VII.

20 *See, e.g.*, Statute of the International Criminal Court, July 17, 1998, art. 21, U.N. Doc. 2187, U.N.T.S. 90 (entered into force July 1, 2002) ("The Court shall apply . . . applicable treaties and the principles and rules of international law. . . . ") [hereinafter *ICC Statute*]; Hague Convention (IV) Respecting the Laws and Customs of War on Land, Oct. 18, 1907, pmbl., T.S. No. 539, 1 Bevans 631, 36 Stat. 2277 (entered into force Jan. 26, 1910) ("Until a more complete code of the laws of war has been issued . . . the inhabitants and the belligerents remain under the protection and the rule of the principles of the law of nations . . . . ").

21 *See* U.S. CONST. art. VI, § 2 ("all Treaties made, or which shall be made, under the Authority of the United States, shall be the supreme Law of the Land").

22 *Id.* at art. VI, § 2 ("all Treaties *made* . . . shall be the supreme Law of the Land" (emphasis provided)); *see, e.g.*, EMMERICH DE VATTEL, 2 THE LAW OF NATIONS OR PRINCIPLES OF THE LAW OF NATURE APPLIED TO THE CONDUCT AND AFFAIRS OF NATIONS AND SOVEREIGN, § 191 (1758) [hereinafter, VATTEL, LAW OF NATIONS]; SAMUEL PUFENDORF, 8 ON THE LAW OF NATURE AND OF NATIONS, § 8 (1672) (recognizing successor state responsibility for complying with treaties entered into by earlier state).

23 U.S. CONST. art. I, § 8, cl. 10 (Congress shall have the power "To define and punish . . . Offences against the Law of Nations").

24 *See, e.g.*, Charter of the United Nations, June 26, 1945, art. 51, 59 Stat. 1031, T.S. 993, 3 Bevans 1153 (entered into force Oct. 24, 1945) ("Nothing in the present Charter shall impair the inherent right of individual or collective self-defence if an armed attack occurs against a Member of the United Nations") [hereinafter *UN Charter*].

25 *See, e.g.*, VATTEL, THE LAW OF NATIONS, *supra* note 22, *Preliminaries*, at § 18 ("small republic is no less a sovereign state than the most powerful kingdom"); *UN Charter*, art. 2 (1) (recognizing sovereign equality of states).

states[26] and guaranteeing full faith and credit between states.[27] Article I also guaranteed that states retain their international legal personality and sovereignty by being able to enter into agreements with each other and with foreign nations (of course, subject to congressional approval *per* the "foederal" approach).[28] Even when the Constitution did not explicitly incorporate an international legal rule, the Framers recognized that the law of nations governed the Constitution's construction, as when there was no objection to Edmund Randolph's argument during the Virginia Constitutional Convention that Congress could not violate the law of nations governing navigational rights on the Mississippi – even if there was no explicit prohibition in the Constitution.[29]

It just was common sense to the Founders that a constitution governing a nation must itself be governed by the law of nations. James Madison,[30] John Jay,[31] Alexander Hamilton,[32] Edmund Randolph,[33] William Davie,[34] and others all recognized that the Constitution could not be interpreted to violate the United States' international legal obligations because of the Constitution's status as a treaty.

[26] *See* U.S. CONST. art. IV, § 3 ("[N]o new State shall be formed or erected within the Jurisdiction of any other State; nor any State be formed by the Junction of two or more States, or Parts of States, without the Consent of the Legislatures of the States concerned as well as of the Congress.").

[27] *See id.* at art. IV, § 1 ("Full faith and Credit shall be given in each State to the public Acts, Records, and judicial Proceedings of every other State.").

[28] *Id.* at art. I, § 10, cl. 3 ("No State shall, without the consent of Congress, . . . enter into any Agreement or Compact with another State, or with a foreign Power . . . ."); *see Vienna Convention*, art. 6 ("Every State possesses the capacity to conclude treaties.").

[29] 3 ELLIOT'S DEBATES 362.

[30] *See, e.g.*, THE FEDERALIST No. 43 (Madison) at § 9 (1788) (establishment of Constitution governed by law of treaties); 1 ELLIOT'S DEBATES 424 (Madison arguing that "civil law of treaties" governed replacement of Articles of Confederation); 1 FARRAND'S RECORDS 122–23 (same); James Madison, *Vices*, § 8 (same).

[31] *See* THE FEDERALIST No. 64 (Jay) at ¶ 12 (1788) (constitutional authority of Congress to make laws does not extend to breaking treaties).

[32] *See* 1 FARRAND'S RECORDS 324–25 (establishment of Constitution governed by treaty law).

[33] *See* 3 ELLIOT'S DEBATES 362 (congressional authority to control navigation on Mississippi River cannot violate law of nations).

[34] *See* 4 *ibid.* 119 (congressional authority to make laws does not extend to violating law of nations).

Therefore, even though most national constitutions are not treaties, both the text and original public understanding of the Constitution discloses the Constitution's legal status as a treaty.

Constitutional Canards

However, there are a number of old canards rejecting the idea that the Constitution is a treaty that have become embedded in our constitutional culture. For example, some folks argue that the Constitution is not a treaty because it was "ordain[ed] and establish[ed]" by the people, as its Preamble says.[35] This conclusion is incorrect. The Constitution was ratified by individual state conventions – not by the American people as a whole in a single convention. Indeed, the fact that the Constitution says that it is ordained and established by the people reconfirms its status as a treaty because the law of nations itself recognized in the eighteenth century that the original locus of sovereignty resided in the people – not states.[36]

Another myth is that James Madison – the "father of the Constitution" – stated that the Constitution was not a treaty. Actually, what Madison stated a couple of times is that our constitutional *system* was not a "mere league or treaty."[37] Madison was using the term "treaty" in its somewhat arcane

35 U.S. CONST. pmbl.

36 *See, e.g.*, J.J. BURLAMAQUI, 2 THE PRINCIPLES OF NATURAL AND POLITIC LAW, pt. II, ch. VI, § VI (1748) ("sovereignty resides originally in the people"); FRANCISCO DE VITORIA, ON THE LAW OF WAR (1557); *see* Ruben C. Alvarado, *Fountainhead of Liberalism*, 10 COMMON L. REV. (1994), *available at* http://www.wordbridge.net/ccsp/cm10_font.html (last visited Feb. 15, 2003) (sovereignty resides in peoples (*i.e.*, nations) – not states – under international law).

37 2 FARRAND'S RECORDS 93 (Madison "considered the difference between a system founded on the Legislatures only, and one founded on the people, to be the true difference between a league or treaty, and a Constitution."); James Madison to Daniel Webster (Mar. 15, 1833), *in* 1 THE FOUNDERS' CONSTITUTION, ch. 3, doc. 14 (ed. Philip B. Kurland & Ralph Lerner), *available at* http://press-pubs.uchicago.edu/founders/documents/v1ch3s14.html (last visited Feb. 15, 2003) ("[T]he Constitution was made by the people, but as imbodied into the several states, who were parties to it and therefore made by the States in their highest authoritative capacity. They [*i.e.*, the states] might, by the same authority & by the same process have converted the Confederacy into a mere league or treaty; or continued it with enlarged or abridged powers; or have imbodied the people of their respective States into one people, nation or sovereignty; or as they did by a mixed form make them one people, nation, or sovereignty, for certain purposes, and not so for others.").

sense of "league." And, he was right. Our constitutional system was not merely a league, which lacks a central government. He did not mean to say that the Constitution was not a treaty in sense of being a legal instrument. Indeed, during the Constitutional Convention, Madison recognized that the international law governing treaties also governed the establishment of the Constitution.

The claim that the Constitution was not a treaty received quite a bit of exposure in the early nineteenth century during the states' rights and federal law nullification controversy. The nationalists – such as John Marshall, Daniel Webster, and Joseph Story – argued that the Constitution was not a treaty on a number of grounds, all false. Webster and Story argued that the Constitution was not a treaty because a treaty allowed its individual states-parties unilaterally to construe the treaty that could lead to another state-party claiming a treaty violation and the latter's lawful withdrawal from the treaty.[38] However, this was not true. Treaties – such as the Articles of Confederation, the *Jay Treaty* (1794), and the *Treaty of Ghent* (1814) – had provisions, respectively, providing for the establishment of international courts and/or boards of commissioners to resolve treaty disputes between states-parties.[39] Indeed, under the Articles of Confederation, states repeatedly used federal courts to adjudicate disputes.[40] The

[38] *See* Daniel Webster, *Speech to Congress* (Jan. 26, 1830), *in* EDWIN P. WHIPPLE, THE SPEECHES AND ORATIONS OF DANIEL WEBSTER, WITH AN ESSAY ON DANIEL WEBSTER AS A MASTER OF ENGLISH STYLE (1879) (states are "own judges" in construing treaty because of absence of "superior" authority); JOSEPH STORY, COMMENTARIES ON THE CONSTITUTION OF THE UNITED STATES, bk. 3, ch. 3, § 321 *et passim* (1833) (each state allowed to construe treaty because of absence of "common arbiter").

[39] ARTICLES OF CONFEDERATION, art. IX (providing for court and boards of commissioners); Jay Treaty, Nov. 19, 1794, art. 6 (entered into force Oct. 28, 1795), *available at* http://www.yale.edu/lawweb/avalon/diplomacy/britian/jay.htm (last visited Oct. 5, 2003) (providing for board of commissioners); Treaty of Ghent, Dec. 28, 1814, art. 4, (entered into force Feb. 17, 1815), *available at* http://www.yale.edu/lawweb/avalon/diplomacy/britian/ghent.htm (last visited Oct. 5, 2003) (providing for board of commissioners).

[40] Connecticut v. Pennsylvania, 23 JOURNALS OF THE CONTINENTAL CONGRESS 1774–1789 6–32 (Worthington C. Ford *et al.*, eds., 1912) (1783 dispute over Wyoming Valley adjudicated by federal court established under Articles of Confederation); Massachusetts v. New York, 33 *ibid.* 617–29 (territorial dispute adjudicated by federal court established under the Articles and subsequently settled); Georgia v. South Carolina, 31 *ibid.* 651 (congressional resolution approving establishment of federal court for resolving territorial dispute).

Framers of the Constitution also established a similar international court for resolving interstate disputes – namely, the U.S. Supreme Court. Subsequently, the Supreme Court has adjudicated disputes between states of the Union.[41]

Marshall also argued that a confederation (unlike a constitutional government) generally could not independently execute its own resolutions.[42] This was not true. The Continental Army during the Revolutionary War executed the resolutions of the Articles Congress. Marshall also argued that unlike the Constitution that is formed by the whole people acting in convention, a league is formed by state legislatures who become members of the league.[43] Again, this was not necessarily true. The Constitution was not formed by the whole of the American people acting in single constitutional convention. It was formed by thirteen separate state conventions. And treaties can be ratified not only by legislatures but also by conventions and plebiscites. Finally, Marshall argued that unlike congressional representatives that are not constitutionally bound to act in conformity with instructions from their state legislatures, state representatives to a league act according to their state's instructions.[44] Again, this was not quite true. Delegates to intergovernmental organizations created by treaty are not necessarily prohibited from acting independently of their states – a present example being the European Union.[45] Indeed, there was nothing in the Articles of Confederation that prevented the delegates from voting in disregard of their instructions (if any) from their states – absent the possibility of recall after they had disregarded their instructions. Inversely, there was nothing in the Constitution that prevented state legislatures from ordering their senators to vote in conformity with their instructions.[46] Indeed, at least one senator in the early years of our constitutional

[41] *See, e.g.*, Kansas v. Colorado, 185 U.S. 125, 14 (1902) (Supreme Court sitting as international tribunal in dispute between Kansas and Colorado).

[42] John Marshall, *Friend of the Constitution* VII, *in* JOHN MARSHALL'S DEFENSE OF MCCULLOCH V. MARYLAND199 (ed. Gerald Gunther, 1969) ("A government, on the contrary, carries its resolutions into execution by its own means.").

[43] *Ibid.* at 202.

[44] *Ibid.*

[45] *See* Treaty Establishing the European Union, Feb. 7, 1992, art. 213 (2), 31 I.L.M. 247 (1992) (entered into force Nov. 1, 1993).

[46] However, it appears that the Framers understood that U.S. senators could not recalled by their state legislatures. Jay S. Bybee, *Ulysses at the Mast: Democracy, Federalism and the Sirens' Song of the Seventeenth Amendment*, 91 NW. U. L. REV. 500, 530 (1997).

government was censured by his state legislature for failing to obey its instructions.[47]

But if the Constitution is a treaty and the federal government violates this treaty by enacting unconstitutional federal statutes, can states lawfully nullify these statutes and/or unilaterally secede from the United States, as John Calhoun and other states' rights advocates respectively maintained? The answer is "no" because – as with the Articles of Confederation[48] – the Constitution does not provide for state withdrawal and provides a federal court system for addressing disputes that otherwise could serve as justification for state withdrawal. It is the constitutional duty of such federal courts to invalidate unconstitutional laws, and, of course, the U.S. Supreme Court often has invalidated unconstitutional federal legislation. The use of such a mechanism serves to obviate the apparent need for state secession and civil war. It was a failure of the Southern states in 1861 to use the federal courts to resolve any disputes with Northern states that led to secession and civil war – a rather ironic failure, given that the Supreme Court earlier had upheld the South's cherished institution of slavery in the *Dred Scott Case*.[49] Although perhaps unusual at the time of the Founding, it is now not unusual for international tribunals to find laws enacted by intergovernmental bodies to be unlawful because these laws violated the treaties that created these intergovernmental bodies. For example, the International Court of Justice (ICJ) and the European Court of Justice (ECJ), respectively, have done so with regard to the World Health Organization (WHO) and the European Union (EU).[50]

[47] *See* E. McPherson, *The Southern States and the Reporting of Senate Debates, 1789–1802*, 12 J. SOUTHERN HIST. 223, 228–235 (1946).

[48] *See* ARTICLES OF CONFEDERATION, art. IX (establishing federal court system) and art. XII ("that the Articles thereof shall be inviolably observed by the States we respectively represent, and that the Union shall be perpetual").

[49] Scott v. Sandford, 60 U.S. (19 How.) 393 (1857).

[50] *See, e.g.*, Federal Republic of Germany v. European Parliament & Council of the European Union, C-376/98, Eur. Ct. J. (2000) (annulling EU directive banning tobacco advertising as violation of European Community Treaty); Legality of the Use by a State of Nuclear Weapons in Armed Conflict, Advisory Opinion, 1996 I.C.J. 1 (July 8) (World Health Organization did not have authority to ask ICJ for advisory opinion under WHO's constitution).

Correctly Conceptualizing Our Constitutional System

Given that the Constitution is a treaty, the conception of our constitutional law changes. Constitutional law becomes a regional international law, like regional European or Inter-American law. Federal statutes are like European Union directives – law that is limited by a constitutive treaty and whose authority is derivative of such a treaty. As the Supremacy Clause puts it in the case of the U.S. Constitution, federal statutes only are made in "pursuance" of the Constitution. Reflecting this conception of federal statutory law, the U.S. Department of State in 1789 was given custody and charge of not only treaties but also other international legal instruments such as federal statutes.[51]

Furthermore, the United States becomes an intergovernmental organization – somewhat like the United Nations.[52] However, the United States has a strong central government, including a very strong executive. Furthermore, its Supreme Court becomes an international court for adjudicating disputes among states-parties to the Constitution and for determining whether the central government has exceeded its own authority, very much like the ICJ and the ECJ.[53] Indeed, the Supreme Court already has referred to itself as an international tribunal in interstate and other cases.[54] The federal court system also is an international tribunal system for ensuring the protection of individual rights and the prosecution of international crimes, somewhat like, respectively, the Inter-American Court of Human Rights, the European Court of Human Rights, the African Court of Human and Peoples' Rights, and the International Criminal Court.

[51] *See* "An act to provide for the safekeeping of the acts, records, and seal of the United States, and for other purposes," 1 Stat. 68, 1st Cong. 1st Sess., ch. xiv, § 2 (Sept. 15, 1789).

[52] The idea that the United States was a prototype of an intergovernmental organization similar to the League of Nations has been recognized earlier. *See* James Brown Scott, The United States of America: A Study in International Organization (1920).

[53] *See, e.g.*, Herbert A. Smith, The American Supreme Court as an International Tribunal (1920) (arguing that U.S. Supreme Court is quasi-international court).

[54] *See, e.g.*, Kansas v. Colorado, 185 U.S. 125, 14 (1902) (Supreme Court sitting as international tribunal in dispute between Kansas and Colorado). The Supreme Court also described itself an international court when sitting as a prize court because prize cases were determined by the law of nations. Penhallow v. Doane's Administrators, 3 U.S. (3 Dall.) 54, 91 (1795) ("A prize court is, in effect, a court of all the nations in the world, because all persons, in every part of the world, are concluded by its sentences.").

This conception of U.S. constitutional law has an interesting implication. As international law, some U.S. constitutional law could have substantially greater authority than other foreign national laws as evidence of international law. Indeed, this already has happened. The Universal Declaration of Human Rights – which reflects customary international legal obligations – was based in part on our own Bill of Rights.[55]

One needs to recognize that international law is not "foreign law" – as Mr. Chief Justice Rehnquist and Mr. Justice Scalia have argued[56] – any more than the Constitution is foreign law. If one does so, the conceptual conundrums that have been created by imposing legal dualism on our constitutional regime can be overcome. Indeed, this dualism is itself foreign, originating in a constitutional regime explicitly rejected by the Founders – namely, the British dualist constitutional system.[57] The issue of whether the United States' international legal obligations are incorporated into U.S. law is mooted because these obligations themselves are being used only to construe the Constitution.

Conclusion: Constitutional Coherence Constructed on International Law

Although the international community continues to make multilateral treaties governing a plethora of subjects, the United States increasingly has withdrawn from its international legal commitments or, at least, provided a strained, strict, and/or unilateral interpretation of such

[55] *See* Filártiga v. Peña-Irala, 630 F.2d 876, 882 (2d Cir. 1980) (Universal Declaration of Human Rights reflects customary international law); LOUIS HENKIN, THE AGE OF RIGHTS (1990) (modern manifestation of human rights drawn from Constitution and Bill of Rights).

[56] *See, e.g.*, Atkins v. Virginia, 536 U.S.304, 122 S.Ct. 2242, 153 L.Ed.2d 335 (2002) (Rehnquist, C.J., dissenting) ("the viewpoints of other countries simply are not relevant"); Antonin Scalia, Constitutional Relevance of Foreign Court Decisions, U.S. Association of Constitutional Law, American Univ. Washington College of Law, Jan. 13, 2005 (rejecting use of foreign law for interpreting Constitution), *available at* http://domino.american.edu/AU/media/mediarel.nsf/0/1F2F7DC4757FD01E85256F890068E6E0?OpenDocument.

[57] *See infra* Subsection 5.3 (discussing Last-in-Time Rule's basis in notion of Parliamentary Supremacy).

commitments.[58] This has created disruption in the global international legal order and provoked heated criticism from both within and without the United States.[59] This book will seek to demonstrate how this tension can be resolved by demonstrating that U.S. constitutional law is intrinsically integrated with international law and that international law is not foreign law alien to the interests and values of the American people. Indeed, this book will not alter many outcomes of constitutional analysis because most constitutional jurists have been doing international legal analysis without knowing it. Although this book will seek to alter some outcomes because of their incongruity with international law, its main objective is to *transform* the conceptualization of constitutional law.

Accordingly, Part I will explain how the federal courts constitute an international tribunal system established by a treaty with national and interstate dimensions. Therefore, their jurisdiction is governed by international law. An international legal construction of their competence to provide review of the compatibility of federal and state law with the Constitution provides a better justification of such authority. This book also will critically examine the relationship of such authority to a judicial activist critique based on the use of international law and will demonstrate that the *Non Liquet* Prohibition Principle in international law undercuts such a critique.

Part II examines what is international law and its major governing interpretive principles in order to set the stage for examining how United States law is international law in Part III. Readers not having a particular interest in U.S. law may find the discussion on emergence and crystallization of customary international law in Subsection 3.2 interesting because there appears to be no literature or legal authority addressing exactly when customary international legal norms emerge and crystallize for

[58] *See, e.g.*, Dana Priest, *Memo Lets CIA Take Detainees Out of Iraq: Practice is Called Serious Breach of Geneva Conventions*, Washington Post (Oct. 24, 2004), *available at* http://www.washingtonpost.com/ac2/wp-dyn/A57363-2004Oct23?language=printer (visited Jan. 25, 2006) (discussing U.S. Dept. of Justice Memo providing unconventional and strict reading of *Geneva Convention*).

[59] *See, e.g.*, Human Rights Watch, *The Road to Abu Ghraib, available at* http://www.hrw.org/reports/2004/usa0604/usa0604.pdf (last visited Jan. 26, 2005) (June 2004) (criticizing U.S. policy of avoiding its international legal obligations).

determining how long a state can avail itself of the Persistent Objector Rule. Perhaps also of interest to such readers is the discussion of general principles of law recognized by civilized nations in Subsection 3.3, in which this book provides a clearer understanding of what this traditionally amorphous international law consists.

Part III breaks down U.S. law into those international legal authorities explicitly mentioned in Article III of the U.S. Constitution and those that are not. In Chapter 5, this book will provide an international legal construction of U.S. federal law and its interpretive principles, and discuss the problems with some of these principles. In Chapter 6, this book will address the remaining sources of international law that are not mentioned in Article III as well as peculiarly American issues regarding their use by federal courts. An international legal construction of federal court jurisdiction reveals other aspects of judicial interpretation that otherwise would not be disclosed. Federal courts sometimes can use international legal authorities not expressly mentioned in Article III. Prominent among these extra–Article III international legal sources is customary international law. This book will discuss exactly when rules become and do not become customary international law binding on the United States. Furthermore, federal courts sometimes can decide cases *ex aequo et bono* and use such extra–Article III international law.

Most importantly, this book will demonstrate that federal courts often must use both Article III and extra–Article III international legal authorities that provide a liberal construction to the United States' and its member-states' federal and nonfederal legal obligations. These liberal construction rules are important to constitutional and other international legal adjudication in that they further integrate U.S. constitutional law with other international law – an important policy objective in a globalized world that seeks the uniformity of law and the reduction of transaction costs associated with nonuniformity. Because federal courts often have provided a strict interpretation of the United States' constitutional and other international legal obligations, these liberal construction rules could serve to change the United States' legal landscape because the U.S. Supreme Court has not been consistent in its international legal constructions.

One should not underestimate the importance of such liberal construction rules. The failure of judges to use international law as controlling authority has not been merely a failure to apply the United States' international legal obligations but – more often – the failure to construe these obligations properly, that is, liberally. Too many times, litigants properly have raised international legal claims and defenses only to have judges improperly construe the international law narrowly.

Some readers may find this book provocative or puzzling. At the least, I hope that readers will find this book interesting and informative.

PART ONE

UNITED STATES COURTS AS INTERNATIONAL COURTS

Tribunals (or courts) adjudicate disputes between two or more parties by applying laws and/or equity. They declare the legal obligations (if any) existing between the parties, sometimes issue reasoned opinions, and order remedies if such obligations are breached. Some tribunals need not even have an actual dispute to adjudicate to provide a declaration of the law. For example, some courts issue advisory opinions.[1]

Sometimes constitutions,[2] basic law,[3] or statutes[4] create tribunals. Sometimes, personal sovereigns[5] or communities[6] create tribunals. Most importantly, treaties also can create tribunals. For example, the *American Convention on Human Rights* created the Inter-American Court of

[1] For example, the English courts have issued advisory opinions. 3 K. Davis, Administrative Law Treatise 127–28 (1958).

[2] *See, e.g.*, Constitution of the Republic of South Africa (1996), art. 165 (1), *available at* http://concourt.law.wits.ac.za/constitution/ (last visited Nov. 11, 2005) ("The judicial authority of the Republic is vested in the courts.").

[3] *See, e.g.*, Basic Law for the Federal Republic of Germany (1949 as amended up to 1993), art. 92, *available at* http://www.iuscomp.org/gla/statutes/GG.htm (last visited Nov. 11, 2005) ("The judicial power shall be vested in the judges; it shall be exercised by the Federal Constitutional Court, by the federal courts provided for in this Basic Law, and by the courts of the Länder.").

[4] *See, e.g.*, Judiciary Act of 1789, 1 Stat. 73 (establishing judicial courts of the United States).

[5] *E.g.*, Henry II's "the bench" (*in banco residentes*). *See* J. H. Baker, An Introduction to English Legal History 16 (Butterworth's 2d ed. 1979) [hereinafter Baker] (discussing Henry II's transformation of the *curia regis* into an adjudicative court).

[6] *E.g.*, early Anglo-Saxon "hundreds" and religious courts. *Ibid.* at 6.

Human Rights,[7] and the U.S. Constitution created the Supreme Court.[8] Sometimes an institution operating under the authority of its constituent treaty creates a tribunal. For example, the UN Security Council operating under the authority of the *UN Charter* created the International Criminal Tribunal for the former Yugoslavia,[9] and Congress operating under the authority of the Constitution created the federal appellate and district courts.[10]

Because treaties are agreements between two or more states,[11] the tribunals established by these treaties can have jurisdiction over interstate disputes and operate as *interstate* tribunals. For example, the International Court of Justice (ICJ) sometimes exercises jurisdiction over disputes between states,[12] and the U.S. Constitution gives the Supreme Court jurisdiction over interstate disputes.[13] Given that the Constitution is a treaty

[7] American Convention on Human Rights, Nov. 22, 1969, ch. VII, 1144 U.N.T.S. 123 (entered into force July 17, 1978) [hereinafter *ACHR*].

[8] U.S. Const. art. III ("The judicial power of the United States, shall be vested in one supreme Court . . . .").

[9] Statute of the International Criminal Tribunal, pmbl. S/Res/808 (1993), U.N. Doc. S/25/704 (May 3, 1993) (tribunal established by UN Security Council acting under Chapter VII of *UN Charter*).

[10] *See* U.S. Const. art. I, § 8, cl. 9 (Congress shall have power to "constitute Tribunals inferior to the supreme Court") and art. III, § 1 ("The judicial power of the United States, shall be vested . . . in such inferior Courts as the Congress may from time to time ordain and establish."); Judiciary Act of 1789, Sept. 24, 1789, 1 Stat. 73 (establishing inferior federal courts).

[11] *See Vienna Convention*, art. 2 (1) (a) ("'treaty' means an international agreement concluded between States in written form and governed by international law . . . whatever its particular designation").

[12] Statute of the International Court of Justice, June 26, 1945, art. 35, 59 Stat. 1055, T.S. 993 ("1. The Court shall be open to the states parties to the present Statute. 2. The conditions under which the Court shall be open to other states shall, subject to the special provisions contained in treaties in force, be laid down by the Security Council, but in no case shall such conditions place the parties in a position of inequality before the Court. 3. When a state which is not a Member of the United Nations is a party to a case, the Court shall fix the amount which that party is to contribute towards the expenses of the Court. This provision shall not apply if such state is bearing a share of the expenses of the Court.") [hereinafter *I.C.J. Statute*].

[13] *See* U.S. Const. art. III, § 2 cl. 1 (judicial power extends "to Controversies between two or more States").

between states[14] governing their relations,[15] it should come as no surprise that the federal courts created by the Constitution have an interstate dimension.

Because treaties also can be made between a state(s) and an institution(s) created by a constituent treaty, the tribunals established by these treaties can have jurisdiction over disputes not only between states but also between a state(s) and the constituent institution(s), or between constituent institutions.[16] In such cases, the tribunal is operating as an *international* tribunal. For example, the European Court of Justice (ECJ) can exercise jurisdiction over disputes between a European state and a European Union (EU) institution.[17] The same is true for the U.S. federal court system: the federal courts have jurisdiction over controversies between states and federal agencies.[18] After all, even the word "federal"

[14] *See id.* at art. VII ("The Ratification of the Conventions of nine States shall be sufficient for the Establishment of this Constitution *between the States* so ratifying the Same." (emphasis provided)).

[15] *See, e.g., id.* at art. IV (provisions governing interstate relations regarding extradition, and state public acts, records, and judicial proceedings).

[16] *See* Vienna Convention on the Law of Treaties Between States and International Organizations or Between International Organizations, Mar. 21, 1986, art. 2 (1) (a), U.N. Doc. A/CONF.129/15, 25 I.L.M. 543 ("'treaty' means an international agreement governed by international law and concluded in written form: (i) between one or more States and one or more international organizations; or (ii) between international organizations") [hereinafter *Vienna Convention-SIO*].

[17] *See* Treaty Establishing the European Economic Community, Mar. 25, 1957, art. 175, 298 U.N.T.S. 11 (entered into force Jan. 1, 1958) *as amended by* Treaty on European Union, Feb. 7, 1992, 31 I.L.M. 253 (entered into force Nov. 1, 1993) [hereinafter *EU Treaty*] ("Should the European Parliament, the Council or the Commission, in infringement of this Treaty, fail to act, the Member States and the other institutions of the Community may bring an action before the Court of Justice to have the infringement established... Any natural or legal person may, under the conditions laid down in the preceding paragraphs, complain to the Court of Justice that an institution of the Community has failed to address to that person any act other than a recommendation or an opinion.").

[18] *See, e.g.,* U.S. Const. art. III, § 2, cl. 1 ("The judicial Power shall extend . . . – to Controversies to which the United States shall be a Party"); 28 U.S.C. § 1346 (vesting district courts with original jurisdiction, concurrent with the United States Court of Federal Claims, of certain civil actions against the United States).

comes from the word "*foedus*," which is a kind of treaty that gives a central government authority over states-parties to the *foedus*.[19]

Furthermore, the Supreme Court has described itself as an international court when sitting as a prize court[20] or when deciding interstate cases[21] because prize and interstate cases are decided according to international law.[22] When the Supreme Court decides a case brought by a state against a foreign nation or a case affecting a foreign nation's representative, the Court is sitting as an international tribunal. And, because Indian tribes constitute nations,[23] federal courts adjudicating cases between such nations and the American nation are sitting as international courts.[24]

[19] *See* SAMUEL H. BEER, TO MAKE A NATION: THE REDISCOVERY OF AMERICAN FEDERALISM 315 (1993) (arguing that when Madison used "foederal" in context of compact federalism, he meant contemporary conventional sense of *foedus*, or treaty).

[20] *See* Penhallow v. Doane's Administrators, 3 U.S. (3 Dall.) 54, 91 (1795) ("A prize court is, in effect, a court of all the nations in the world, because all persons, in every part of the world, are concluded by its sentences.").

[21] *See, e.g.*, Kansas v. Colorado, 185 U.S. 125, 146–47 (1902) (stating that the Supreme Court was sitting as international tribunal in dispute between Kansas and Colorado).

[22] *Cf.* JAMES BROWN SCOTT, JUDICIAL SETTLEMENT OF CONTROVERSIES BETWEEN STATES OF THE AMERICAN UNION: CASES DECIDED IN THE SUPREME COURT OF THE UNITED STATES (1918) (arguing that decisions from U.S. interstate cases could be used as law for international tribunal).

[23] *See, e.g.*, Treaty of Canandaigua, Nov. 11, 1794, pmbl., 7 Stat. 44, *reprinted in* 2 INDIAN AFFAIRS: LAWS AND TREATIES 34–37 (Charles J. Kappler, ed., 1904) ("A Treaty between the United States of America, and the Tribes of Indians called the Six Nations"); Worcester v. Georgia, 6 Pet. (31 U.S.) 515, 558 (1832) ("The Constitution, by declaring treaties already made, as well as those to be made, to be the supreme law of the land, had adopted and sanctioned the previous treaties with the Indian nations, and consequently admits their rank among those powers who are capable of making treaties. The words 'treaty' and 'nation' are words of our own language, selected in our diplomatic and legislative proceedings, by ourselves, having each a definite and well understood meaning. We have applied them to Indians, as we have applied them to the other nations of the earth. They are applied to all in the same sense.").

[24] Before 1871, the United States entered into numerous treaties with Indian nations. *See, e.g.*, Treaty with Arikara Tribe, July 18, 1825, 7 Stat., 259, *in* 2 INDIAN AFFAIRS: LAWS AND TREATIES (Charles J. Kappler ed., 1904) (treaty governing commerce with Indians). However with the enactment of the Indian Appropriation Act of March 3, 1871, Congress refused to recognize Indian tribes as nations:

> That hereafter no Indian nation or tribe within the territory of the United States shall be acknowledged or recognized as an independent nation, tribe, or power with whom the United States may contract by treaty: Provided, further, that nothing herein contained shall be construed to invalidate or impair the obligation of any treaty heretofore lawfully made and ratified with any such Indian nation or tribe.

Some international tribunals also can issue advisory opinions requested by a state[25] or constituent organization.[26] Other international tribunals cannot. For example, the U.S. federal courts probably cannot because their judicial power is limited to actual "cases" and "controversies."[27]

Furthermore, international tribunals often have jurisdiction over cases in which individuals are parties. For example, the appellate prize court established under the Articles of Confederation, the European Court of Human Rights, and the Inter-American Commission on Human Rights have exercised jurisdiction over cases brought by or against nonstate actors.[28] The same is true for the U.S. federal courts. Federal courts often exercise jurisdiction over nonstate actors in cases civil[29] and criminal.[30]

Furthermore, treaties also can constitute a national legal instrument. Although nationhood and statehood often are incorrectly conflated, a

16 Stat. 566, *now codified at* 25 U.S.C. § 71 (1988). The constitutionality of this federal statute is highly suspect in light of *Worcester v. Georgia.*

[25] *See, e.g., ACHR,* art. 64(2) ("The Court, at the request of a member state of the [Organization of American States], may provide that state with opinions regarding the compatibility of any of its domestic laws with the aforesaid international instruments.").

[26] *See, e.g., I.C.J. Statute,* art. 65 (1) ("The Court may give an advisory opinion on any legal question at the request of whatever body may be authorized by or in accordance with the Charter of the United Nations to make such a request.").

[27] U.S. Const. art. III, § 2, cl. 1; Nebraska Press Assn. v. Stuart, 427 U.S. 539, 546 (1976).

[28] *See, e.g.,* Articles of Confederation, art. IX, ¶ 1 ("establishing courts for receiving and determining finally appeals in all cases of captures"); Protocol No. 11 to the European Convention for the Protection of Human Rights and Fundamental Freedoms, May 11, 1994, art. 34, E.T.S. 155 (entered into force Nov. 1, 1998) ("The Court may receive applications from any person... claiming to be the victim of a violation by one of the High Contracting Parties of the rights set forth in the Convention or the protocols thereto."); *ACHR,* art. 44 ("Any person... may lodge petitions with the Commission containing denunciations or complaints of violation of this Convention by a State Party."); *see also* Optional Protocol to the International Covenant on Civil and Political Rights, Dec. 16, 1966, art. 2, 99 U.N.T.S. 171 (entered into force Mar. 23, 1976) ("individuals who claim that any of their rights enumerated in the Covenant have been violated... may submit a written communication to the Committee for consideration").

[29] *See, e.g.,* 28 U.S.C. § 1343 ("district courts shall have original jurisdiction of any civil action authorized by law to be commenced by any person" to recover damages for civil rights violations).

[30] *See, e.g.,* 18 U.S.C. § 3231 ("The district courts of the United States shall have original jurisdiction, exclusive of the courts of the States, of all offenses against the laws of the United States.").

treaty can be an agreement between two or more states that together represent a nation. For example, the *Treaty of Union* (1707) united the English and Scottish kingdoms while at the same time consolidating the English and Scottish peoples into one British nation. Accordingly, even a tribunal established by a treaty made between states also can be a *national* tribunal.[31] For example, the U.S. Constitution is not only a treaty but also a legal instrument creating a national government[32] with national courts that adjudicate cases between U.S. nationals of different states.[33]

Finally, international tribunals must enforce international law because the law governing international relations is international law.[34] However, not all national or state tribunals can or must enforce international law. There is nothing intrinsic to the concept of a national court system that requires it to enforce international law. One can imagine a totally isolated state that has no contacts with other states or their nationals. Such states would have no need and, hence, no requirement for their courts to enforce any international law. Also, some states do not allow their national courts to enforce certain species of international law. For example, the national courts in the United Kingdom cannot enforce treaties because U.K. law does not directly incorporate treaty obligations.[35] Furthermore, some[36] state courts in the United States before the Constitution's entrance

[31] And, sometimes a state and an international organization enter into a treaty establishing a national tribunal. For example, the UN and Sierra Leone established the Special Court for Sierra Leone. *See* Agreement between the United Nations and the Government of Sierra Leone on the Establishment of a Special Court for Sierra Leone, Jan. 16, 2002, *available at* www.specialcourt.org/documents/SpecialCourtAgreementFinal.pdf (last visited Aug. 1, 2005).

[32] *See* U.S. CONST. pmbl. ("We the People of the United States, in Order to form a more perfect Union . . . do ordain and establish this Constitution for the United States of America.").

[33] *See, e.g., id.* at art. III, § 2, cl. 1 ("The judicial Power shall extend . . . to Controversies . . . between Citizens of different States . . . . ").

[34] This is true even if the treaty requires the application of state law because such state law has become, in a sense, international law.

[35] Other examples of dualist legal regimes include those of Australia, India, and Sweden.

[36] *See* James Madison, *Vices of the Political System of the United States* [1787], eds. William T. Hutchinson, *et al.*, 9 THE PAPERS OF JAMES MADISON 348–57 (1962–77) [hereinafter Madison, *Vices*] (states violated treaties with Great Britain, France, and Holland). However, some state courts did enforce treaty and customary international law. *See, e.g.*, Rutgers v. Waddington (NYC Mayoral Ct. 1784), *reprinted in* 1 THE LAW PRACTICE OF ALEXANDER HAMILTON: DOCUMENTS AND COMMENTARY 392, 414–419 (eds. Julius Goebel, Jr., *et al.* 1964)

into force did not enforce treaties because they were operating under a dualist system like British courts, and the Articles of Confederation did not expressly require states to enforce treaties – unlike the Constitution's Supremacy Clause. However, U.S. federal courts even as national courts can enforce treaties and other international law.

This is not to say that all state or national courts that enforce international law are international tribunals. To be an international tribunal, the tribunal must have been created by a treaty or by a body with authority under a treaty to create a tribunal.

In conclusion, U.S. federal courts constitute an international tribunal system with interstate and national dimensions. In the next chapter, we will examine how the international legal character of the federal court system enables it to exercise judicial review authority.

(applying treaty and other law of nations norms); Respublica v. deLongchamps, 1 U.S. (1 Dall.) 120, 123 (Pa. Oyer and Terminer, 1784) (applying law of nations).

1

Final Judicial Review Authority of Federal and Other International Courts

Treaties are governed by international law; therefore, the jurisdiction of a tribunal created by or under the authority of a treaty is inherently governed by international law. A striking feature about U.S. federal courts is their authority to review the constitutionality of federal and state laws, and to nullify the legal effect of those laws. As demonstrated later, this feature is a result of the Constitution's legal status as a treaty. Although much has been written about the origins and justifications of final judicial review in U.S. courts,[1] no literature has addressed the origin and justification of judicial review from an international legal perspective. As argued later, the origin and justification of final judicial review authority can be based on the conventional law of nations governing tribunals. Treaties have recognized the competence of their tribunals to effectively nullify laws made by states, nations, and institutions created by constituent treaties respectively on the basis of their incompatibility with a nation's or state's international legal obligations and on the basis of the institution exceeding its authority under its constituent treaty. Although some have argued that the United States is the "home of judicial review,"[2] this chapter will demonstrate that a better understanding of the aetiology and legal justification of judicial review can be located in the law of nations governing tribunal practices.

[1] For a recent, fairly comprehensive survey of the historical and legal literature on judicial review, *see* Saikrishna B. Prakash and John C. Yoo, *The Origins of Judicial Review*, 70 U. Chi. L. Rev. 887 (2003) [hereinafter Prakash & Yoo].

[2] Geoffrey Marshall, Parliamentary Sovereignty and the Commonwealth 16 (1959).

1.1. JUDICIAL REVIEW

The notion of judicial review was not unknown to international law and international tribunal practice at the date of the Constitution's entrance into force in 1788. Since at least the beginning of modern international law (as dated from the 1648 *Treaty of Westphalia*), treaties often explicitly gave international and national tribunals the authority to enforce treaty provisions. For example, the *Treaty of Westphalia* required that its provisions were "perpetually to be follow'd, as well by the Imperial Counsellors and Officers, as those of other Lords, and all Judges and Officers of Courts of Justice."[3] Not only did the treaty require the national "Courts of Justice" of the states-parties to the *Treaty of Westphalia* to enforce the treaty's provisions, the treaty required two international courts – the Holy Roman Empire's Imperial Chamber Court (*Reichskammergericht*) and the Court Council of the Empire (*Reichshofrat*, also known as the "Aulic Council") – to enforce the treaty.

Most importantly, the *Treaty of Westphalia* gave national and international courts the authority to effectively nullify national, state, and some international law:

> That it never shall be alledg'd, allow'd, or admitted, that any Canonical or Civil Law, any general or particular Decrees of Councils, any Privileges, any Indulgences, any Edicts, any Commissions, Inhibitions, Mandates, Decrees, Rescripts, Suspensions of Law, Judgments pronounc'd at any time, Adjudications, Capitulations of the Emperor, and other Rules and Exceptions of Religious Orders, past or future Protestations, Contradictions, Appeals, Investitures, Transactions, Oaths, Renunciations, Contracts, and much less the Edict of 1629. or the Transaction of Prague, with its Appendixes, or the Concordates with the Popes,[4] or the Interims of the Year 1548. or any other politick Statutes, or Ecclesiastical Decrees, Dispensations, Absolutions, or any other Exceptions, under what pretence or colour they can be invented; shall take place against this Convention, or

[3] Treaty of Westphalia, Oct. 24, 1648, art. CXX, *available at* http://www.yale.edu/lawweb/avalon/westphal.htm (last visited Aug. 8, 2005) [hereinafter *Treaty of Westphalia*].

[4] "Concordates" are papal treaties.

> any of its Clauses and Articles neither shall any inhibitory or other Processes or Commissions be ever allow'd to the Plaintiff or Defendant.[5]

The *Treaty of Westphalia* required "Courts of Justice" at both national and international levels to enforce the treaty, and specifically prohibited the recognition and enforcement of a number of national (*e.g.*, civil law, decrees, judgments, statutes) and international (*viz.*, papal concordates) laws if such laws violated the treaty. The *Treaty of\ , Westphalia* is relevant to U.S. federal court jurisdiction in that the treaty as a widely adopted[6] multilateral treaty served as strong evidence of emerging customary international law[7] and general principles of law recognized by civilized nations that would have enabled U.S. federal courts to exercise judicial review authority. Albeit this was a *European* law of nations, it was a European law of nations with which the Founders and early federal courts were familiar and which effectively constituted the whole of their law of nations for the Founders.[8]

Most importantly, the Framers knew of these two international tribunals governed by the *Treaty of Westphalia*. For example, Alexander Hamilton and James Madison in *Federalist No. 19* mentioned the Imperial Chamber Court and the Aulic Council.[9] During the Constitutional Convention, Governeur Morris stated that "[w]e shall establish

[5] *Treaty of Westphalia*, art. CXXI.

[6] The treaty's parties included most European states because the treaty concluded a peace between the Kingdoms of France and Navarre (with its allies), and the Holy Roman Empire (with its allies). *Id.* at ¶ 1.

[7] Widely adopted multilateral treaties provide strong evidence of customary international law. ANTHONY D'AMATO, INTERNATIONAL LAW: PROSPECT AND PROCESS 123–47 (1987);CLIVE PARRY, THE SOURCE AND EVIDENCE OF INTERNATIONAL LAW 62–67 (1965); Richard R. Baxter, *Multilateral Treaties as Evidence of Customary International Law*, 41 BRIT. Y.B. INT'L L.275 (1965–66). There is a strong presumption that such customary norms have been accepted as legally binding by states unless a state has persistently objected to the norm during its emergence, and in such a case, the persistent objector state is not legally bound by the customary norm. *See* IAN BROWNLIE, PRINCIPLES OF PUBLIC INTERNATIONAL LAW 10 (4th ed. 1990) ("Evidence of objection [to an emerging customary international legal norm] must be clear and there is probably a presumption of acceptance [of the norm] which is to be rebutted.) [hereinafter, BROWNLIE, PRINCIPLES].

[8] *Cf.* The Antelope, 23 U.S. 66, 121 (1825) (applying European law of nations).

[9] THE FEDERALIST NO. 19 (Madison & Hamilton) at ¶ 3 (1787); *see also* Chisholm v. Georgia, 2 U.S. 419, 425 (1793) (Edmund Randolph arguing for petitioner mentioned Imperial Chamber and Aulic Council).

an Aulic Council without an Emperor to execute its decrees."[10] The Framers explicitly drew on the experience of previous international tribunals in drafting the Constitution's provisions governing federal courts.

International Judicial Review of National Law

As discussed earlier, the *Treaty of Westphalia* authorized international courts (*viz.*, the Aulic Council and Imperial Chamber Court) to nullify national law when such law violated the treaty. Although the Framers already were aware of the judicial review authority of these European tribunals, many of the Framers also earlier had approved the competence of their own international tribunals to nullify national law. The Articles of Confederation provided for the making of treaties with other nations, including Indian tribes.[11] One of these treaties provided for the establishment of an international criminal tribunal consisting of members of the American and Delaware nations. Most important, this treaty indicated that the tribunal could ignore and thereby effectively nullify national law, *viz.*, the laws of the United States:

> For the better security of the peace and friendship now entered into by the contracting parties, against all infractions of the same by the citizens of either party, to the prejudice of the other, neither party shall proceed to the infliction of punishments on the citizens of the other, otherwise than by securing the offender or offenders by imprisonment, or any other competent means, till a fair and impartial trial can be had by judges or juries of both parties, *as near as can be to the laws, customs and usages of the contracting parties and natural justice.*[12]

Although this treaty provision does not explicitly state that the tribunal must be international (as opposed to a U.S. or Delaware tribal tribunal),

[10] *See, e.g.*, James Madison, 1 The Debates in the Federal Convention of 1787 Which Framed the Constitution of the United States of America 98 (July 7, 1787) (Chicago: Albert, Scott & Co., 1893).

[11] Articles of Confederation, art. IX.

[12] Treaty with the Delawares, Sept. 17, 1778, art. IV, 7 Stat. 13, *in* 2 Indian Affairs: Laws and Treaties, (Charles J. Kappler, ed., 1904), *available at* http://www.yale.edu/lawweb/avalon/ntreaty/del1778.htm (last visited Aug. 8, 2005) (emphasis provided).

it is highly improbable that Delawares (or any other American Indians) could serve as U.S. judges or on a U.S. jury in 1778.

Since the Articles, other treaties have established international courts with authority that effectively allows judicial review of national laws.[13] Most importantly, the U.S. Constitution established federal courts with the authority to nullify federal statutory law, and the federal courts subsequently have nullified such federal law.[14]

International Judicial Review of Laws Promulgated by an Institution Vested with Lawmaking Authority under a Treaty

Federal statutory law is not merely national law. Federal statutory law also is a form of international law because it is made by an institution created by a treaty for the implementation of the treaty. International law also recognizes the authority of international tribunals to review such international law. The United States' *Treaty with the Delawares* (1778) appears to be the first treaty to provide for the establishment of an international court with competence to effectively nullify laws promulgated by an institution vested with such lawmaking authority under a treaty. This international tribunal had authority to effectively nullify the laws made by Congress – an institution vested with lawmaking authority by the Articles of Confederation. Although the authority of a tribunal to nullify international law had been known since the *Treaty of Westphalia*,[15] the *Treaty with the Delawares* may have been the first treaty to provide

[13] *See, e.g.*, *ACHR*, art. 63 (Inter-American Court of Human Rights has jurisdiction to rule that state measure found violative of *ACHR* be remedied); European Convention for the Protection of Human Rights and Fundamental Freedoms, Nov. 4, 1950, art. 50, 213 U.N.T.S. 221 (entered into force Feb. 3, 1953) (European Court of Human Rights has jurisdiction to provide satisfaction to party injured by state measure found incompatible with *ECHR*) [hereinafter *ECHR*].

[14] *See, e.g.*, Marbury v. Madison, 5 U.S. (1 Cranch.) 137 (1803) (invalidating federal statute). Although the first U.S. Supreme Court case to nullify federal statutes was *Marbury v. Madison*, an earlier U.S. Circuit Court had invalidated a federal statute. *See* Hayburn's Case, 2 U.S. (2 Dall.) 409 (1792) (invalidating federal statute that assigned arguably non-judicial duties to federal judges).

[15] For example, recall that the *Treaty of Westphalia* gave authority to "Courts of Justice" to enforce its provisions and nullify "Concordates with the Popes," which are treaties. *Treaty of Westphalia*, arts. CXX and CXXI.

for the establishment of an *international* tribunal with authority to effectively nullify such law. What is particularly remarkable about this treaty is that the Articles Congress – whose approval of the treaty was required under the Articles of Confederation[16] – appears to have confirmed that this international tribunal lawfully could effectively nullify Congress' own laws. Furthermore, given that the *Treaty with the Delawares* still constitutes federal law under the Constitution's Supremacy Clause, the treaty provides judicial review authority over federal statutory law in criminal cases concerning the Delaware Nation. The Constitution's Congress apparently confirmed this when it incorporated the treaty into its Statutes-at-Large.[17]

Judicial authority to nullify such law resonated with many of the Founders and the eighteenth-century positivist school of international law as exemplified by Emmerich Vattel[18] – who frequently was cited by the Founders.[19] The positivist school's claim that a state could only demand of other states that which it had accepted explicitly by treaty, implicitly

[16] *See* ARTICLES OF CONFEDERATION, art. IX, ¶ 6 ("The United States in Congress assembled shall . . . enter into any treaties or alliances . . . unless nine States assent to the same . . ."). However, a thorough search of the JOURNALS OF THE CONTINENTAL CONGRESS could not locate which nine or more states ratified the treaty. The probable reason for this is that the Articles of Confederation did not come into force until ten years later. Nevertheless, the Articles Congress still considered the treaty binding.

[17] *See* 7 Stat. 13.

[18] However, it should be noted that Vattel would not be considered a positivist today because of his recognition of the natural law of nations.

[19] Between 1789 and 1820, Vattel was cited thirty-eight times in U.S. Supreme Court opinions. *See* FRANCIS STEPHEN RUDDY, INTERNATIONAL LAW IN THE ENLIGHTENMENT: THE BACKGROUND OF EMMERICH DE VATTEL'S LE DROIT DES GENS 284 (1975) (citing Edwin Dickinson's research); *see also* JAMES KENT, COMMENTARY ON INTERNATIONAL LAW 36 (1878) ("[Vattel's book] has been cited more freely than that of any other public jurist, and is still the statesman's manual and oracle."); DANIEL GEORGE LANG, FOREIGN POLICY IN THE EARLY REPUBLIC: THE LAW OF NATIONS AND THE BALANCE OF POWER 95 (1985) (noting that Hamilton called Vattel "perhaps the most accurate and approved of the writers on the law of nations") (citation omitted); Stewart Jay, *The Status of the Law of Nations in Early American Law*, 42 VAND. L. REV. 819, 823 (1989) ("In ascertaining principles of the law of nations, lawyers and judges [in eighteenth-century America] relied heavily on continental treatise writers, Vattel being the most often consulted. . . . An essential part of a sound legal education consisted of reading Vattel, Grotius, Pufendorf, and Burlamaqui, among others.").

by custom, or presumptively by inference,[20] resonated with the Founders who believed that governing required the consent of the governed.[21]

A constituent treaty, such as the Constitution, only empowers the constituent government to make laws or undertake other actions that are allowed by the constituent treaty. The constituent government cannot make laws or undertake actions that exceed its powers granted by the constituent treaty.[22] When the same treaty establishes an international tribunal that has jurisdiction over disputes arising under the treaty and in which another constituent institution is a party, this other constituent institution cannot be a judge in its own cause. As Vattel stated, "whoever has submitted to the decision of a judge, is no longer capable of deciding his own pretensions."[23] Only the international tribunal is in the position of being a neutral party that can decide the dispute because it has not made the contested law. Accordingly, the international tribunal has competence to nullify such laws if they exceed the lawmaking institution's authority under the treaty.

This consent principle also extended to federal judicial review of federal statutes. For example, Alexander Hamilton believed that a federal court could nullify a federal statute if it were unconstitutional:

> where the will of the legislature, declared in its statutes, stands in opposition to that of the people, declared in the Constitution, the judges ought to be governed by the latter rather than the former. They ought to regulate their decisions by the fundamental laws, rather than by those which are not fundamental.[24]

Subsequently, the U.S. federal courts have nullified congressional legislation,[25] and the recognition of this international judicial review authority

[20] Emmerich de Vattel, The Law of Nations or Principles of the Law of Nature Applied to the Conduct and Affairs of Nations and Sovereign, *Preliminaries*, §§ 24 & 25 (1758) [hereinafter, Vattel, Law of Nations].

[21] *See, e.g.*, Declaration of Independence, July 4, 1776, ¶ 2 ("Governments are instituted among Men, deriving their just Powers from the consent of the governed").

[22] An arguable exception to this rule is when the constituent treaty also is a constituent national legal instrument and the national government exercises residual sovereign powers. For example, the Supreme Court has held that Congress has plenary authority to deport aliens. *See, e.g.*, Harisiades v. Shaughnessy, 342 U.S. 580 (1952).

[23] Vattel, 1 Law of Nations, *supra* note 20 at § 54.

[24] Federalist No. 78 (Hamilton) at 102 (1788).

[25] *See, e.g.*, Marbury v. Madison, 5 U.S. (1 Cranch.) 137 (invalidating federal statute).

has continued in other international legal systems both global and regional. For example, the ICJ opined that Inter-Governmental Maritime Consultative Organization's constitution did not authorize establishment of Maritime Safety Committee,[26] and the European Court of Justice nullified an EU directive banning tobacco advertising as violation of *European Community Treaty*.[27]

International Judicial Review of State Constitutional and Statutory Law

The Articles of Confederation also provided for the establishment of federal courts for deciding interstate disputes[28] and prize cases[29] that often addressed challenges to state constitutional and statutory law. For example, the federal Court of Appeals in Cases of Capture established under the authority of the Articles of Confederation reviewed 127 state court cases and reversed the state court judgments in forty-five of these cases.[30] The Court of Appeals in Cases of Capture is especially noteworthy because, like any international court, the Court of Appeals was governed by international law (specifically, the *jus in bello* relating to prizes[31]). Most

[26] *See* Constitution of the Maritime Safety Committee of the Inter-Governmental Maritime Consultative Committee, Advisory Opinion, 1960 I.C.J. 150 (June 8); *see also* Legality of the Use by a State of Nuclear Weapons in Armed Conflict, Advisory Opinion, 1996 I.C.J. 1 (July 8) (World Health Organization (WHO) did not have authority to ask the ICJ for advisory opinion under WHO's constitution).

[27] Federal Republic of Germany v. European Parliament & Council of the European Union, C-376/98, Eur. Ct. J. (2000).

[28] *See* Articles of Confederation, art. IX, ¶ 2 (establishing federal courts for interstate disputes).

[29] *Id.* at art. IX, ¶ 1 ("establishing courts for receiving and determining finally appeals in all cases of captures").

[30] William F. Swindler, *Evolution, Law and Order*, Yearbook 1976 Supreme Court Historical Society (1975), *available at* http://www.supremecourthistory.org/myweb/76journal/swindler.htm (last visited Aug. 1, 2005) [hereinafter Swindler].

[31] *See* 19 Journals of the Continental Congress 361 (1912). These instructions included not to kill, torture, or treat inhumanely persons "contrary to common usage, and the practice of civilized nations in war." *Ibid.* at 363; *see also* 21 *ibid.* at 1154. Congress also apportioned prizes for sea and land captures by privateers according to the law of nations. *Ibid.* at 1157–58; *see also ibid.* at 315 (prize courts governed by law of nations) and 364 (privateers violating laws of nations subject to forfeiture of commission and "liable to an action for breach of the condition of [privateer's] bond, [and] responsible to the party grieved for damages sustained by such malversation").

importantly, the Court of Appeals often reversed the state court orders based on jury findings[32] – notwithstanding the right to jury trial guaranteed by state constitutional law.[33]

Furthermore, one federal court established under the authority of the Articles for resolving interstate cases adjudicated a territorial dispute between Pennsylvania and Connecticut over the Wyoming Valley.[34] The federal court effectively invalidated earlier Connecticut statutory law giving title to certain Wyoming Valley inhabitants.[35]

Since the Articles of Confederation, other treaties have established courts for adjudicating not only interstate disputes[36] but also disputes between nonstate actors and states-parties that address the compatibility of state laws with the state-party's treaty obligations.[37] If a state law is incompatible with the state's treaty obligations, a competent international tribunal can effectively nullify the law – regardless if the state has a dualist legal system or its state courts do not have the authority to nullify such a law because the state, in exercising its sovereignty by

[32] Swindler, *supra* note 30 ("Specialists in admiralty law have concluded that the large numbers of reversals were due to a misunderstanding of the relevant evidence on the part of the juries at the trial level."); *see, e.g.*, Penhallow v. Doane's Administrators, 3 U.S. (Dall.) at 62 (discussing earlier decision by Court of Appeals in Cases of Capture that nullified a New Hampshire state court jury finding).

[33] *See, e.g.*, N.Y. CONST. OF 1777 art. XLI, *available at* http://www.yale.edu/lawweb/avalon/states/ny01.htm (last visited Aug. 1, 2005) ("And this convention doth further ordain, determine, and declare, in the name and by the authority of the good people of this State, that trial by jury, in all cases in which it hath heretofore been used in the colony of New York, shall be established and remain inviolate forever."). Admiralty courts, which were governed by the law of nations, did not employ juries.

[34] *See* Pennsylvania v. Connecticut, 23 JOURNALS OF THE CONTINENTAL CONGRESS 533–36 (Worthington C. Ford *et al.*, eds., 1912) (federal court established to resolve 1782 land dispute in Wyoming Valley); *see also* Georgia v. South Carolina, 31 *ibid.* 651 (congressional resolution approving establishment of federal court for resolving territorial dispute); Massachusetts v. New York, 33 *ibid.* 617–29 (territorial dispute adjudicated by federal court established under the Articles and subsequently settled).

[35] Pennsylvania v. Connecticut, 24 *ibid.* 6–32 (federal court effectively invalidated Connecticut legislation concerning land titles).

[36] *See, e.g.*, Decision of the Commissioners under Article 4 of the Treaty of Ghent, Nov. 24, 1817, 2 TREATIES AND OTHER INTERNATIONAL ACTS OF THE UNITED STATES OF AMERICA (ed. Hunter Miller 1931) (dispute over islands in Bays of Fundy and Passamaquoddy resolved by commission established under Treaty of Ghent).

[37] *See supra* Part I note 28.

undertaking to comply with an international legal norm, has waived any domestic legal impediments to its compliance with these obligations.[38] Most importantly, the U.S. Constitution incorporated this kind of judicial review authority in the Supremacy Clause, and the Supreme Court subsequently has nullified state law that is incompatible with the Constitution.[39] Indeed, insofar as Article IX of the Articles of Confederation still constitutes binding federal law under the Supremacy Clause because the Articles was a one of those "Treaties made [under the authority of the United States]," [40] the federal judicial review authority over state constitutional and statutory law in prize cases can be justified under the United States' early treaty obligations. Decrees from cases originally adjudicated by the Court of Appeals in Cases of Capture later were carried into effect by the federal courts created by the Constitution indicating that the federal courts could exercise jurisdiction established earlier by the Articles of Confederation for its Courts of Appeals.[41]

Final and Conclusive Authority of International Tribunals

The concept of judicial review authority does not necessarily entail final and conclusive authority. After all, one can imagine that a court could find a law unconstitutional, yet the legislative branch still may consider such a judicial determination merely an opinion that the legislative branch constitutionally could ignore. However, an international legal construction of the Supreme Court's jurisdiction under Article III requires that some of

38 For example, the *ACHR* expressly requires its federal state-parties to ensure that their federal governments "immediately take suitable measures" to ensure that their constitutive states comply with the *ACHR*. *ACHR*, art. 28 (2). And, the Supremacy Clause of the U.S. Constitution requires its states-parties (including their judges) to comply with the Constitution, federal statutory law, and U.S. treaties. U.S. Const. art. VI, cl. 2.

39 *See, e.g.*, Fletcher v. Peck, 10 U.S. (6 Cr.) 87 (1810) (Georgia statute annulling conveyance of public lands authorized by prior enactment held violative of Art. I obligation of contracts clause).

40 U.S. Const. art. VI. Article III refers to the United States in the plural by its use of "their" because federal question jurisdiction extends not only to treaties made with foreign states but also between all states of the United States, such as the Articles of Confederation.

41 *See* Penhallow v. Doane's Administrators, 3 U.S. (3 Dall.) 54 (federal court executing decree issued by Court of Appeals in Cases of Capture); United States v. Peters, 9 U.S. (5 Cranch.) 115 (1809) (same).

its judicial review authority also entail final and conclusive authority. For example, the Article IX of the Articles of Confederation (a treaty) authorized Congress to establish independent and impartial[42] federal courts "to hear and finally determine" interstate cases, whose judgments and sentences were to "be final and conclusive" and "lodged among the acts of Congress."[43] The Articles also established federal courts for "determining finally appeals in all cases of capture."[44] This treaty law may be the first explicit evidence in the law of nations of the final and conclusive authority of an international tribunal. Construing the Supreme Court's judicial power under Article III in conformity with this earlier treaty law ensures that the Supreme Court does have final and conclusive authority in some cases – otherwise, there is no final and conclusive authority because Article III does not state explicitly that the Supreme Court has such authority. Indeed, insofar as Article IX of the Articles of Confederation still constitutes binding federal law under the Supremacy Clause because the Articles was a one of those "Treaties made [under the authority of the United States],"[45] even the lower federal courts acquire such final and conclusive authority through an independent source of federal law that implements their Article III judicial power (subject to, of course, the Supreme Court's superior status over "inferior"[46] federal courts when Congress enables the Supreme Court to exercise its appellate jurisdiction by vesting original jurisdiction in inferior federal courts).

The reason why an international tribunal must have final and conclusive authority is based on the law of nations' rationale behind the establishment of international tribunals. States-parties to treaties that created tribunals wanted to establish neutral arbiters for settling interstate disputes that could fester into war, and only by guaranteeing the finality and conclusivity of international tribunal decisions could states prevent the outbreak of war and the attendant violation of natural law, specifically, the

[42] ARTICLES OF CONFEDERATION, art. IX, ¶ 2 ("every commissioner, before he sits in judgement, shall take an oath to be administered by one of the judges of the supreme or superior court of the State, where the cause shall be tried, 'well and truly to hear and determine the matter in question, according to the best of his judgement, without favor, affection or hope of reward'").

[43] *Id.*

[44] *Id.* at art. IX, ¶ 1

[45] U.S. CONST. art. VI.

[46] *See id.* at art. I, § 8, cl. 9 ("To constitute tribunals inferior to the supreme Court").

necessary law of nations[47] guarantees, such as the right to life.[48] Accordingly, Vattel thought that international tribunals should be established.[49]

The Founders also recognized the importance of tribunals in avoiding interstate conflicts. As Justice Wilson noted in *Chisholm v. Georgia*:

> A third declared object [in the Preamble] is "to ensure domestic tranquillity." This tranquillity is most likely to be disturbed by controversies between States. These consequences will be most peaceably and effectually decided by the establishment and by the exercise of a superintending judicial authority. By such exercise and establishment, the law of nations; the rule between contending States; will be enforced among the several States, in the same manner as municipal law.[50]

Justice Cushing also shared this view in *Chisholm v. Georgia*:

> As controversies between State and State, and between a State and citizens of another State, might tend gradually to involve States in war and bloodshed, a disinterested civil tribunal was intended to be instituted to decide such controversies, and preserve peace and friendship.[51]

Treaties continue to guarantee the finality and conclusivity of international tribunal decisions[52] – even to the exclusion of other international tribunals.[53] In conclusion, the origin and justification of the finality and conclusivity of the U.S. federal courts' judicial review authority in some

47 The necessary law of nations or "natural law of nations" forms part of the law of nations. *See* VATTEL, LAW OF NATIONS, *supra* note 20, *Preliminaries*, § 7 (describing necessary law of nations).

48 The right to life is a *jus cogens* norm, and *jus cogens* norms are strongly associated with natural law norms. *See, e.g.*, International Covenant on Civil and Political Rights, Dec. 16, 1966, art. 2, 999 U.N.T.S. 171 (entered into force Mar. 23, 1976) (right to life is nonderogable) [hereinafter *ICCPR*].

49 *See* VATTEL, 1 LAW OF NATIONS, *supra* note 20 at § 165 ("There ought to be established supreme courts of justice wherein causes should be finally determined.")

50 2 U.S. 419, 465 (1793) (Wilson, J.).

51 2 U.S. 419, 468 (1793) (Cushing, J.).

52 *See, e.g.*, *ACHR*, art. 67 ("The judgment of the Court shall be final and not subject to appeal.").

53 *See, e.g.*, Commission of the European Communities v. Ireland, Case-459/03, ECJ (Grand Chamber), *available at* http://eurlex.europa.eu/LexUriServ/LexUriServ.do?uri=CELEX:DKEY=426881:EN:NOT (2006) (*EC Treaty* establishes exclusive jurisdiction, and EC states-parties cannot submit case to ITLOS).

cases can be located in the United States' continuing treaty obligations under the Articles of Confederation.

However, it must be noted that the Articles of Confederation provided final and conclusive authority to federal courts *only* in cases between states of the United States and cases of capture. The Articles did not provide such authority in other cases. Although Article III of the Constitution establishes a "supreme" court suggesting to many jurists that the U.S. Supreme Court is supreme over all other courts – federal, state, and international – when it exercises jurisdiction over Article III cases and controversies, the Supreme Court has construed the Appellate Exceptions Clause[54] to give Congress the power to divest the Supreme Court of appellate jurisdiction in some cases, thereby making the Supreme Court *not* supreme in all Article III cases and controversies.[55] And even if the Supreme Court has been mistaken in its construction of the Appellate Exceptions Clause, as one commentator convincingly has demonstrated,[56] the decisions of the U.S. Supreme Court can only be "supreme" as to the decisions of inferior federal courts (and state courts indirectly through the Supremacy Clause) in the same manner that the decisions of a state supreme court can only be supreme as to those of inferior state courts.

Of course, the Constitution effectively does give the U.S. Supreme Court final and conclusive judicial review authority when there are no other international tribunals that can exercise such authority. In light of the Constitution's silence regarding the final and conclusive authority of the federal courts to decide cases and the Article of Confederation's

[54] *See* U.S. CONST. art. III, § 2, cl. 2 ("In all Cases affecting Ambassadors, other public Ministers and Consuls, and those in which a State shall be a Party, the supreme Court shall have original jurisdiction. In all other Cases before mentioned, the supreme Court shall have appellate jurisdiction . . . *with such Exceptions . . . as the Congress shall make.*" [Emphasis provided]).

[55] *See, e.g.*, Ex parte McCardle, 74 U.S. 506 (1869) (validating congressional divestment of Supreme Court's jurisdiction over habeas corpus petitions).

[56] *See* Laurence Claus, *The One Court that Congress Cannot Take Away: Singularity, Supremacy, and Article III*, San Diego Legal Papers No. 07–71 at 63–69, *available at* http://papers.ssrn.com/sol3/papers.cfm?abstract_id=935368 (last visited Nov. 21, 2006) (arguing that Congress cannot strip U.S. Supreme Court of jurisdiction when it makes exceptions to the Court's appellate jurisdiction).

explicit vestment of final and conclusive jurisdiction in only interstate and prize cases, the Supreme Court could only exercise final and conclusive authority in interstate and prize cases, and even in some prize cases, the Supreme Court's final and conclusive jurisdiction could be stripped by treaty. For example, shortly after the Constitution's entrance into force, a 1796 U.S.-Spain treaty gave final and conclusive authority to a board of commissioners in prize cases involving U.S. vessels and cargo taken by Spanish subjects.[57] In such cases, only the Supreme Court's final and conclusive authority over interstate disputes remains – subject to a new treaty between the states of the United States, that is to say, a new constitutional amendment.

The United States can continue to make treaties that vest final and conclusive authority in international tribunals. For example, consider the *I.C.J. Statute*. The United States is a party to the *UN Charter*, and the *UN Charter* makes all its states-parties *ipso facto* parties to the *I.C.J. Statute*[58] and requires all states-parties to comply with decisions of the ICJ in cases to which it is a party.[59] Most importantly, the *I.C.J. Statute* states that the ICJ's "judgment is final and without appeal."[60] If the Constitution were to have given final and conclusive authority to the U.S. Supreme Court in case over which the ICJ has jurisdiction, the United States constitutionally could not have become a party to the *UN Charter*.

57 *See* Treaty of Friendship, Limits, and Navigation Between Spain and The United States, Oct. 27, 1795, art. 21, 2 Treaties and Other International Acts of the United States of America (ed. Hunter Miller 1931) (entered into force Apr. 25, 1796):

> In order to terminate all differences on account of the losses sustained by the Citizens of the United States in consequence of their vessels and cargoes having been taken by the Subjects of his Catholic Majesty during the late war between Spain and France, it is agreed that all such cases shall be referred to the final decision of Commissioners. . . . [T]he three Commissioners so appointed shall be sworn impartially to examine and decide the claims in question according to the merits of the several cases, and to justice, equity, and the laws of Nations. . . . The award of the said Commissioners or any two of them shall be final and conclusive both as to the justice of the claim and the amount of the sum to be paid to the claimants . . . .

58 *UN Charter*, 93 (1).

59 *UN Charter*, art. 94 (1). After the ICJ's decision in *Case Concerning Avena and Other Mexican Nationals* (Mex.-U.S.), 2004 I.C.J. 128 (Mar. 31), the United States withdrew from the *Optional Protocol to the Vienna Convention on Consular Relations* that recognized the ICJ's competence to decide cases alleging violations of the Convention.

60 *I.C.J. Statute*, art. 60.

1.2. ONLY INTERNATIONAL LEGAL CONSTRUCTIONISM PROVIDES SUFFICIENT JUSTIFICATION OF FEDERAL JUDICIAL REVIEW

The U.S. Constitution does not explicitly state that federal courts have the authority to nullify state constitutional or statutory law that is incompatible with the Constitution. Starting with Chief Justice John Marshall, constitutionalists have construed the Judicial Power Clause in conformity with the Supremacy Clause to establish that the federal courts have the authority. In *Marbury v. Madison,* Chief Justice John Marshall took the route of construing Article III with the Supremacy Clause when he discussed the status of federal statutes as being inferior to the Constitution: "If then the courts are to regard the constitution; and the constitution is superior to any ordinary act of the legislature; the constitution, and not such ordinary act, must govern the case to which they both apply."[61] However, there is no language in the Constitution requiring such a construction. Most importantly, the Supremacy Clause only states that *state* judges must apply federal law notwithstanding conflicting state constitutional or statutory law.

The Constitution also does not explicitly state that federal courts have the authority to nullify federal statutory law that exceeds or violates the Constitution – a point made by many constitutionalists.[62] Again, constitutionalists historically have construed the federal courts' Article III judicial power in cases arising under the Constitution in conformity with, for example, the Supremacy Clause, Oaths Clause, or Treason Clause, in order to justify judicial review. Professors Prakash and Yoo elaborate on this theme by arguing that federal statutes are only made in *pursuance* of the Constitution. Any federal statute that is not made in pursuance of the Constitution is not part of the supreme law of the land, and federal courts exercising federal law claims jurisdiction under Article cannot give such "law" effect.[63] Again, however, there is no language in the Constitution requiring such a construction. Even if there were, the Supremacy Clause

[61] 5 U.S. (1 Cranch.) at 178.

[62] *See, e.g.*, Larry D. Kramer, *Foreward: We the Court*, 115 HARV. L. REV. 4 (2001); William Van Alstyne, *A Critical Guide to* Marbury v. Madison, 1969 DUKE L. J. 1, 16–29; ALEXANDER M. BICKEL, THE LEAST DANGEROUS BRANCH: THE SUPREME COURT AT THE BAR OF POLITICS 2–14 (1962).

[63] *See, e.g.*, Prakash & Yoo, *supra* note 1 at 907–09.

appears to be directed only to the states and only gives state courts judicial review. There arguably appears to be nothing that prevents one from using the Supremacy Clause to construe the Judicial Power Clause as not recognizing federal judicial review authority.

Marshall also employed the Oaths Clause in *Marbury*[64] to require federal judges to not enforce unconstitutional laws because the Oaths Clause required federal judges "to support this Constitution."[65] Again, there is no mention of federal judicial review authority in the Oaths Clause, and its construction with the Judicial Power Clause does not necessarily entail that federal judges must nullify unconstitutional laws because a federal judge can still "support" the Constitution by merely declaring the law unconstitutional but not enforcing the law's nullification.

Prakash and Yoo also argue that a construction of the Judicial Power Clause with the Treason Clause also supports the recognition of judicial review.[66] The Treason Clause appears to be directed toward the federal and state courts because it regulates treason trials: specifically, treason convictions can only be had on the testimony of two people.[67] If Congress were to enact a law allowing a treason conviction on the basis of the testimony of one witness, the federal court could not try the case without violating the Constitution even though federal courts must enforce all federal statutes. However, why could not such treason trials just take place in state courts that constitutionally can invalidate such unconstitutional federal law? After all, Congress for many years thought it appropriate that only state courts should have primary responsibility for federal question civil cases.[68]

Some constitutionalists rely on the original public understanding of judicial power in the eighteenth century by looking at, *inter alia*, the federal and state constitutional conventions, and the writings of the Framers and others.[69] However, there is no language in the Constitution requiring the interpretation of the federal courts' judicial power to conform with this original public understanding.

64 5 U.S. (1 Cranch.) at 180.

65 U.S. Const. art. VI, cl. 3.

66 *See, e.g.*, Prakash & Yoo, *supra* note 1 at 902.

67 U.S. Const. art. III, § 3, cl. 1.

68 Congress did not vest general federal question jurisdiction in the lower federal courts until 1875. *See* Act of March 3, 1875, 18 Stat. 470, *now codified at* 28 U.S.C. § 1331.

69 *See, e.g.*, Prakash & Yoo, *supra* note 1 at 927–75.

Furthermore, some have justified judicial review authority on the bases of natural law and/or early English case law. For example, many have pointed out that the earliest example of judicial review occurred in 1610 when Justice Coke decided *Dr. Bonham's Case* apparently on the basis of natural law. Justice Coke noted in *Dr. Bonham's Case* that:

> it appears in our books that in many cases the common law will control acts of parliament and sometimes adjudge them to be utterly void; for when an act of parliament is against common right and reason, or repugnant, or impossible to be performed, the common law will control it and adjudge such act to be void.[70]

However, there is some doubt as to whether Coke's conclusion "reflected the views of his brethren."[71] Indeed, Coke himself later appears to have withdrawn his conclusion.[72]

However, Coke may not have been appealing to natural law for his justification of judicial review. *Dr. Bonham's Case* concerned a situation in which a parliamentary act gave the Royal College of Physicians the authority both to impose and receive fines. Rather than appealing to a natural law principle that a judge cannot judge a case to which s/he is a party, Coke may have been noting the impossibility of the statute being performed.[73] It is physically impossible to argue one's case before a judge while at the same time sitting on the bench as the judge and deciding whether the argument is valid. Characterizing the principle that judges cannot be judges in their causes as naturalistic is an unnecessary invocation of a *deus ex machina* because one can easily characterize the principle as merely logical. If Coke had natural law in mind when he referred to "common right and reason," his statement was merely dicta.

Marshall himself appears to have borrowed Coke's "repugnant" and "void" language in *Dr. Bonham's Case* to justify federal judicial review in

[70] 8 Coke's Rep. 114, 118 (C.P. 1610).

[71] J.H. Baker, An Introduction to English Legal History 182 (Butterworth's 2d ed. 1979) [hereinafter Baker].

[72] *Ibid.* at 173.

[73] *See* S.E. Thorne, *Dr. Bonham's Case*, 54 L. Quart. L. Rev. 543 (1938) (arguing that Coke was engaging only in statutory interpretation – not natural law).

Marbury v. Madison.[74] However, it is not clear how an English case can be sufficient authority for U.S. federal courts to exercise judicial review over U.S. law – especially in light of the case's suspect authority or unclear meaning and the United States declaring its independence from Great Britain and its laws.

Although Marshall cited no authorities in support of judicial review, he also did borrow language from an earlier U.S. Circuit Court decision – *Vandorne's Lessee v. Dorrance*[75] – nullifying a Pennsylvania law.[76] The *Vanhorne* decision earlier had justified judicial review on the grounds of first principles sounding in natural law that purportedly were embodied in the Constitution.[77] Of course, Marshall could not cite *Vandorne* to justify judicial review of federal statutes because *Vandorne* only nullified state law.[78]

The only federal court case before *Marbury* that invalidated a federal statute was *Hayburn's Case* (1792),[79] and Marshall made an indirect reference to this case.[80] The Circuit Court for Pennsylvania opined that a

[74] Noah Feldman, *The Voidness of Repugnant Statutes: Another Look at the Meaning of* Marbury, 148(1) PROCEEDINGS OF THE AMERICAN PHILOSOPHICAL SOCIETY 27, 30–31 (March 2004). Given that *Dr. Bonham's Case* concerned the illegality of a judge judging his own cause, it was somewhat hypocritical of Marshall – whose failure to deliver Marbury's commission in a timely fashion gave rise to the litigation in *Marbury* – to not recuse himself. *See* Sanford Levinson & Jack M. Balkin, *What Are the Facts of* Marbury v. Madison, 20 CONST. COMMENTARY 255 (2003) (criticizing Marshall's failure to recuse himself). Therefore, *Marbury* represents poor precedent for judicial review authority.

[75] 2 U.S. (2 Dall.) 304 (C.C.D.Pa. 1795).

[76] William Michael Treanor, *Judicial Review before Marbury*, – STAN. L. REV. 1, 73 n.311 (forthcoming 2005), *available at* http://lsr.nellco.org/fordham/flfc/papers/13/ (last visited Sept. 22, 2005) [hereinafter Treanor].

[77] *See* 2 U.S. (2 Dall.) at 308–310.

[78] *Vandorne* was not the only federal court decision to invalidate state law before *Marbury*. A number of other U.S. Circuit Court decisions had invalidated state law. For a discussion of these cases, *see* JULIUS GOEBEL, HISTORY OF THE SUPREME COURT – VOLUME I: ANTECEDENTS AND BEGINNINGS TO 1801 (1971); Charles Warren, *Earliest Cases of Judicial Review of State Legislation by the Federal Courts*, 32 YALE L. J. 15 (1925). However, of these decisions, *Vanhorne's Lessee v. Dorrance* provided the most extensive pre-*Marbury* discussion of judicial review. 2 U.S. (2 Dall.) 304 (C.C.D.Pa. 1795). Citation of *Vanhorne* by other courts also indicates that it was the most influential of these decisions. Treanor *supra* note 76 at 73 n.311.

[79] 6 THE DOCUMENTARY HISTORY OF THE SUPREME COURT OF THE UNITED STATES 33–45 (Maeva Marcus ed. 1990) [hereinafter DHSC].

[80] Marbury v. Madison, 5 U.S. (1 Cranch.) at 170–72.

federal statute that required federal circuit courts to determine the eligibility of applicants seeking pensions was unconstitutional. Although the court only gave an oral decision, the judges later explained their decision in a letter to President George Washington. First, they claimed that the judicial power did not encompass such pension eligibility determinations, and, therefore, they had no constitutional authority to make such determinations. Second, they claimed that the statute violated the principle of judicial independence – which is purportedly, strictly observed by the Constitution – by making their determinations subject to review by the Secretary of War and by Congress.[81] However, *Hayburn's Case* is poor precedent for judicial review because the circuit court judges never explained how they lawfully could exercise judicial review. Instead, they only briefly addressed the merits of whether the federal statute was unconstitutional. A judge can opine that a federal law is unconstitutional, but such an opinion does not entail the authority to nullify the law.

Some constitutionalists also have justified federal judicial review authority on the basis that a number of state courts in America did exercise judicial review[82] before the Constitution's entrance into force in 1788,

[81] Letter from James Wilson, John Blair, and Richard Peters to George Washington (April 18, 1792), *reprinted in* 6 DHSC, *supra* note 79 at 53–54.

[82] *See, e.g.*, Josiah Philip's Case (Va. 1778), *in* St. George Tucker, 1 Blackstone's Commentaries: With Notes of Reference to the Constitution and Laws of the Federal Government of the United States and of the Commonwealth of Virginia, appendix at 293 (Lawbook Exchange 1996) (reprint of Birch and Small 1803) (refusing to enforce bill of attainder prohibited by state constitution); Holmes v. Walton (N.J. 1780), in Austin Scott, Holmes vs. Walton: *The New Jersey Precedent: A Chapter in the History of Judicial Review and Unconstitutional Legislation*, 4 Am. Hist. Rev. 456, 456–60 (1899) (holding state law allowing trial by jury of six persons violated state constitution); Commonwealth v. Caton, 8 Va. (4 Call.) 5, 20 (1782) (holding invalid pardon passed by one house of state legislature but not by the other house); Symsbury Case, 1 Kirby 444 (Conn. Super. Ct. 1785) (holding that state legislature cannot alter land grant without grantee's consent); Trevett v. Weeden (R.I. 1786), *in* James M. Varnum, The Case, *Trevett Against Weeden*: On Information and Complaint, for Refusing Paper Bills in Payment for Butcher's Meat, in Market at Par with Specie (John Carter 1787) (refusing jurisdiction where law required action to be tried by judge in face of fundamental law guaranteeing trial by jury); "Ten Pound Act" Cases (N.H. 1786), in William Winslow Crosskey, 2 Politics and the Constitution in the History of the United States 968–71 (1953) (holding statute that required small debt claims to be tried by justice of the peace violated state constitutional guarantee of trial by jury); Bayard v. Singleton, 1 N.C. (Mart.) 42, 45 (1787) (holding state statute directing courts to dismiss on party's motions actions brought to

before *Ware v. Hylton*[83] invalidated a state statute in 1796, and before *Marbury v. Madison*[84] invalidated a federal statute in 1803.[85] However, none of these pre-1788 state court decisions nullified state constitutional law or national law, including federal law, and it is doubtful whether they would have had lawful authority to do so absent a "supremacy clause" like that contained in the Constitution.[86] Moreover, these state courts were nullifying state law under the authority of their respective state constitutions. Federal courts cannot nullify state law under the authority of state constitutional law. Therefore, one cannot use such pre-1788 state court decisions *per se* in support of a federal judicial review authority over state constitutional and statutory law, and federal statutory law.

What is striking about these attempts to justify judicial review is that such justifications often rely on judge-made law. Such justifications have not relied on express recognition of judicial review authority in positive law enacted by the sovereign, that is, in the case of the United States, the American people or their democratically elected representatives. Consequently, whenever judges exercise judicial review and nullify a federal or state law, they become more easily susceptible to charges of judicial activism.

By contrast, International Legal Constructionism (ILC) provides a better justification of federal judicial review that is democratically accountable and less susceptible to charges of judicial activism. As a preface, it should be noted that the international law governing treaty interpretation

recover lands sold under another act violated state constitutional guarantee of trial by jury).

83 3 U.S. 199 (1796).

84 5 U.S. (1 Cranch.) 137.

85 *See, e.g.*, Prakash & Yoo, *supra* note 1 at 933 (using state case law to justify judicial review); Treanor *supra* note 76 at 46–67 (same).

86 The United States as a nation predated the Constitution's entrance into force in 1788. The Declaration of Independence earlier had declared the establishment of a new nation and new states in 1776. *See* Declaration of Independence, ¶ 5 ("We, therefore, the Representatives of the *United States* of America, in General Congress, Assembled, . . . do, in the Name, and by Authority of the good *People* of these Colonies. . . ." [emphasis added]); Articles of Confederation art. IV ("The better to secure and perpetuate mutual friendship and intercourse among the *people of the different States in this Union*, the free inhabitants of each of these States, paupers, vagabonds, and fugitives from justice excepted, shall be entitled to all privileges and immunities of free citizens in the several States. . . ." [emphasis added]).

requires that a treaty be interpreted in light of the other international legal obligations of the states-parties to the treaty. For example, the *Vienna Convention on the Law of Treaties* states that a treaty must be interpreted in light of "any rules of international law applicable in the relations between the parties."[87] The democratically accountable executive branch of the U.S. government has signed[88] the *Vienna Convention* and recognized the *Vienna Convention*'s substantive provisions "as the authoritative guide to current treaty law and practice."[89] Other such "rules of international law" include U.S. treaties, customary international law (evidence of which can be found in widely adopted treaties, general state practice, and judicial opinions), and general principles of law recognized by civilized nations.

As noted earlier, the *Treaty of Westphalia* represented strong evidence of customary international law or general principles of law recognized by civilized nations that could have been used to construe the Judicial Power Clause to include judicial review authority over federal statutory law, and state constitutional and statutory law. Indeed, the Framers may have had the Aulic Council and Imperial Chamber Court with their judicial review authority in mind when they provided for the establishment of federal courts in the Constitution. This international law authorizing judicial review was incorporated into the Articles of Confederation when the Articles expressly gave its federal courts final and conclusive adjudicative authority that was exercised by nullifying state constitutional and statutory law. Finally, the *Treaty with the Delawares* (which still represents binding federal law for the United States under the Supremacy Clause)

[87] *Vienna Convention*, art. 31 (3) (c).

[88] Vienna Convention on the Law of Treaties, UN website, *available at* http://untreaty.un.org/sample/EnglishInternetBible/partI/chapterXX/treaty1.asp).

[89] S. Exec. Doc. L. 92d Cong., 1st Sess. (1971) p. 1 (statement of U.S. Dept. of State); *see also* Weinberger v. Rossi, 456 U.S. 25, 29 (1982) (using *Vienna Convention*). Although the United States is not a party to the *Vienna Convention*, these two facts provide strong evidence that the *Vienna Convention* represents customary international law that is binding on the United States, and the Constitution as a treaty must be construed in conformity with the United States' customary international legal obligations. Although the *Vienna Convention* does not apply to treaties entered into force before the Convention's entrance into force in 1980, it is considered to reflect customary international law. *See Vienna Convention*, art. 4 (nonretroactivity of *Vienna Convention*); Libya v. Chad, 1994 I.C.J. 4, 21–22 at ¶ 41 (Feb. 3, 1994) (*Vienna Convention*'s rules of treaty interpretation reflect customary international law).

explicitly provided for the establishment of an international tribunal that effectively could nullify federal statutory law.

If a Judicial Power Clause construction with the *Treaty of Westphalia*, the Articles of Confederation, and the *Treaty with the Delawares* were not enough, ILC also can transform many of the aforementioned inadequate traditional justifications of federal judicial review into adequate ones providing even more authority for federal judicial review. For example, the aforementioned pre-1788 state court decisions can be used to justify federal judicial review of state statutory law through an international legal construction. These decisions reflected evidence of an American customary international law supporting judicial review of state statutory law that eventually would be codified in the Supremacy Clause. State courts in six of the thirteen original states-parties to the Constitution had exercised such judicial review,[90] and there is no evidence of a persistent objection[91] to such judicial review authority as evidenced in state constitutional and statutory law among any of the thirteen states. Indeed, the constitutions of Pennsylvania,[92] Vermont,[93] New York,[94] and Massachusetts[95] established

[90] One of these pre-1788 state cases is notable insofar as it suggests the relevance of international law to judicial review. In *Rutgers v. Waddington*, the New York City Mayoral Court nullified a state statute (*viz.*, the Trespass Act) in 1784 on the basis of the statute's conflict with a U.S. treaty and the law of nations. The U.S. Supreme Court twelve years later in *Ware v. Hylton* would for the first time nullify a state law also on the basis that the law violated a U.S. treaty.

[91] A state's persistent objection to an emerging customary international legal norm exempts the state from being bound to the norm once the norm crystallizes. This is known as the "Persistent Objector Rule." *See* Fisheries Case (U.K. v. Norway), 1951 I.C.J. 116, 131 (recognizing Norway's persistent objection to customary international legal norm governing territorial fishing zone); Asylum Case (Colombia v. Peru), 1950 I.C.J. 266, 272–78 (Nov. 20) (recognizing Peru's persistent objection to purported customary international legal norm governing asylum).

[92] *See* Penn. Const. of 1776 § 47, *reprinted in* William F. Swindler, ed., 8 Sources and Documents of United States Constitutions 277, 285 (Oceana 1979) (establishing Council of Censors whose role was to determine "whether the legislature and executive branches of government have . . . exercised other or greater powers than they are intitled [*sic*] to by the constitution.").

[93] *See* Vt. Const. of 1777 ch. 2, § 44, 9 *ibid.* 487, 495 (establishing Council of Censors in nearly identical language to Pennsylvania's constitution).

[94] *See* N.Y. Const. of 1777 art. III, 7 *ibid.* 168, 172 (created council of revision consisting of the governor, chancellor, and supreme court judges who had veto authority over legislation).

[95] *See* Mass. Const. of 1780 ch. 1, § 1, art. III, 5 *ibid.* 96 n. 153 (vesting veto authority over legislation in governor).

devices for review of unconstitutional legislation, and when state courts did exercise judicial review, the legislatures often supported this exercise (or at least acquiesced).[96] The federal courts' judicial review authority over state law can be recognized by construing the Constitution in conformity with this American customary international law because the conventional law of nations required (and still requires) that treaties be construed in conformity with the customary international legal obligations of its parties. Such a judicial construction justifying judicial review is based not merely on judge-made law but on the customary international law reflected in the widespread acceptance by, respectively, the state constitutions and state legislatures.

Moreover, ILC allows the use of the Framers' statements made at the Constitutional Convention and state constitutional conventions to be used to construe the Judicial Power Clause. Such statements represent the *travaux préparatoires* and circumstances surrounding the conclusion of the Constitution, and the *Vienna Convention* allows the use of such preparatory works for interpreting treaties.[97]

Furthermore, an international legal construction of the leading federal circuit case before *Ware v. Hylton* that nullified a state law appears to provide a better justification of judicial review – one based on the explicit text of the Articles of Confederation and other international law. *Vandorne's Lessee v. Dorrance* appears to have effectively enforced the decision reached earlier by a federal interstate court (in *Pennsylvania v. Connecticut*) established under a treaty (*viz.*, the Articles of Confederation) that explicitly gave the court final review authority.[98] Recall that the federal court in *Pennsylvania v. Connecticut* earlier had held that the Wyoming territory belonged to Pennsylvania, thereby nullifying Connecticut law. However, the court also had recognized the individual land claims of the Connecticut settlers in the Wyoming Territory (although it should be

[96] *See* Prakash & Yoo, *supra* note 1 at 937 nn. 193–98 (2003) (discussing different state legislature responses to state court judicial review decisions).

[97] *See Vienna Convention*, art. 32 ("Recourse may be had to supplementary means of interpretation, including the preparatory work of the treaty and the circumstances of its conclusion. . . .").

[98] Articles of Confederation, art. IX, § 2 ((federal courts authorized "to hear and finally determine the controversy" and "the judgement and sentence of the court . . . shall be final and conclusive").

noted that there is a difference of opinion among scholars as to whether the federal judges' recognition of the individual land claims was made in their official capacity[99]). In a similar manner to the execution of decrees of the U.S. Courts of Appeals in Cases of Capture by federal courts later established under the Constitution, the federal circuit court in *Vandorne* effectively enforced the earlier decision of the federal court in *Pennsylvania v. Connecticut*. The international legal rule of continuity of treaty obligations[100] required that the new federal courts established under the Constitution enforce the decisions of the old federal courts established under the Articles.[101]

Even *Dr. Bonham's Case* in its natural law casting can be used to justify federal judicial review of national law when given an international legal construction – notwithstanding that it is an English case. One dimension of the law of nations was the "necessary law of nations," which is also called the "natural law of nations." The purportedly natural law rule in *Dr. Bonham's Case* could have been used as evidence of a natural law of nations norm that in turn could have been used to construe the Judicial Power Clause to include federal judicial review of national law.

In conclusion, a sufficient and better justification of federal judicial review authority can be located only in the law of nations.

[99] Treanor, *supra* note 76 at 77 n.330.

[100] *See, e.g.*, VATTEL, 2 LAW OF NATIONS, *supra* note 20 at § 191 ("Since public treaties... concluded by... any... sovereign... are treaties of the state, and obligatory on the whole nation... real treaties, which were intended to subsist independently of the person who has concluded them, are undoubtedly binding on his successors ...."); SAMUEL PUFENDORF, 8 ON THE LAW OF NATURE AND OF NATIONS, § 8 (1672) (recognizing successor state responsibility for complying with treaties entered into by earlier state).

[101] This international legal rule was incorporated into the Constitution. U.S. CONST. art. VI, § 2 ("[A]ll Treaties *made*... shall be the supreme Law of the Land.") (emphasis added).

2

The Fallacy of Federal Judicial Activism in Light of International Law's *Non Liquet* Prohibition Principle

According to Francis Bacon, judges are not appointed to make or change the law: "their office is *jus dicere* and not *jus dare*."[1] Such Legal Formalism claims that judges may only apply the law and only interpret it when it is vague. Judges are not sovereigns capable of making positive law.

The general constitutional corollary to this doctrine is that the authority to make positive law only resides in the political branches, and their constituent courts only have limited jurisdiction.[2] Judicial review authority available under some constitutional legal regimes often – but not necessarily – creates conditions that generate charges of judicial activism. Charges of judicial activism do not occur in all constitutional legal regimes that authorize judges to review the constitutionality of laws. For example, charges of judicial activism are infrequent in most states having constitutions in Europe, Africa, and the Americas. Judicial review authority *per se* does not create sufficient conditions for maintaining the judicial activist critique. An explanation for why the U.S. constitutional regime has been subjected to the judicial activist critique probably is a result of the Constitution's very brief,[3] often vague[4] text characterized by arcane

[1] Francis Bacon, The Essayes 316 (1625).

[2] *See* Turner v. Bank of North America, 4 Dall. (4 U.S.) 8 (1799) (Congress sets federal court jurisdiction and federal courts do not have general jurisdiction). However, Congress cannot limit the Supreme Court's original jurisdiction over cases in which states are parties and cases affecting foreign state representatives. U.S. Const. art. III § 2, cl. 2.

[3] For example, consider the U.S. Constitution is approximately twelve pages long, whereas the *European Constitution* is approximately 450 pages.

[4] *See, e.g.*, U.S. Const. amend. XIII (prohibition of "cruel and unusual punishments").

syntax and drafted sometimes in secrecy[5] coupled with the numerous changes in American political, economic, and cultural life over the last two hundred–plus years unforeseen and unforeseeable by the Framers. This situation has required federal and state courts to provide interstitial interpretations of the constitutional text in order to adapt to new situations that, in turn, have provided fertile ground in which the judicial activist critique has taken root.

Judicial activism occurs when judges make positive law. Judicial review authority enables judicial activism to occur by allowing courts either to void laws as purportedly unconstitutional or uphold laws as purportedly constitutional. Judicial activism occurs when a court improperly voids or upholds the law, thereby effectively making law without proper authority. Directly applying improper normative authorities as law and failing to use proper normative authorities in the construction of constitutional text are two kinds of judicial activism.

Different schools of constitutional theory have formulated different methods of determining whether courts have exceeded their authority by improperly making law. Textualists generally scorn interpretation of constitutional text because it leads to judicial lawmaking. Only when the constitutional text is vague does Textualism allow the use of extraconstitutional authorities and usually only insofar as they can shed light on the original public understanding of the Constitution.

However, even judicial interpretation of positive law can generate secondary rules that acquire their own legally binding authority, and Legal Realists have long argued that judges make law,[6] as especially evidenced in the common law. State courts having general jurisdiction often formulate such secondary legal rules in the absence of positive law. Even federal courts sometimes are common law courts.[7] For example, there is judge-made law in the law of nations that federal courts often

[5] For example, although there was much public discussion regarding the need for further rights guarantees in the Constitution, the Bill of Rights itself was drafted in secrecy, and there are no *travaux préparatoires* to consult as to the drafters' original understanding.

[6] *See, e.g.*, Karl Llewellyn, The Bramble Bush: On Our Law and Its Study (1930).

[7] *See* Sosa v. Alvarez-Machain, 542 U.S. 692, 124 S. Ct. at 2764, 159 L. Ed. 2d at 9H (2004) (federal courts retain jurisdiction for some common law claims notwithstanding *Erie Railroad Co. v. Tompkins*).

apply.[8] Although Legal Realists accept that judges often make law, some Realists call for judges to restrain themselves when doing so.[9]

Critical Legal Studies (CLS) proponents sometimes go further. One CLS analysis maintains that even arguably clear and specific rules are indeterminate; therefore, judicial activism is always present in the adjudicative process.[10] By examining the judicial interpretive process as one that often deconstructs a legal instrument's language to obtain certain politically desirable ends resulting in the creation of new law, this CLS analysis accepts judicial activism as a given – not a practice to be scorned always. Judicial activism is only to be scorned when it results in an outcome that is politically or economically unfavorable to a particular audience (usually one that has been oppressed), and cherished when politically or economically favorable to the audience.

However, if a legal instrument tasks its court with adjudicating disputes but does not mention what law to apply, the court lawfully can apply whatever legal authorities it wishes to apply in adjudicating the dispute. Indeed, the court need not apply any legal authorities. It lawfully could decide the dispute according to what it considered equitable and not even provide any reasons. For example, the federal court in *Pennsylvania v. Connecticut* did not provide any reasons for its decision.[11] And, if the court's constituent legal instrument gives the court review authority, the court effectively could nullify a law – as the federal court in *Pennsylvania v. Connecticut* did when it effectively nullified Connecticut law.[12] In these situations, the court is not being judicially activist because it is not *making* law in the sense of legislation that is legally binding on all persons regardless of whether they are parties to a case before the court. The court is just making a decision that is *legally enforceable* under its

[8] *See id.* at 542 U.S. 692, 124 S. Ct. at 2756–57,159 L. Ed. 2d at **743 ("The law of nations included a second, more pedestrian element, however, that did fall within the judicial sphere, as a body of judge-made law regulating the conduct of individuals situated outside domestic boundaries and consequently carrying an international savor.").

[9] *See, e.g.*, Southern Pacific Co. v. Jensen, 244 U.S. 205, 221 (1917) (Holmes, J., dissenting) ("[J]udges do and must legislate, but they can do so only interstitially; they are confined from molar to molecular motions.").

[10] *See, e.g.*, Mark V. Tushnet, *Following the Rules Laid Down: A Critique of Interpretivism and Neutral Principles*, 96 HARV. L. REV. 781 (1982).

[11] *See* Pennsylvania v. Connecticut, 24 JOURNALS OF THE CONTINENTAL CONGRESS 31–32 (1912).

[12] *Ibid.*

constituent legal instrument. Another example is when the U.S. Supreme Court exercises its original jurisdiction in cases affecting foreign state representatives or cases to which states are parties. Congress cannot limit the Court's jurisdiction, and the Constitution does not mention what law – if any – the Court is to apply directly in such cases.

The only potential legal limit on the court's decision making is if its constituent legal instrument is of a certain genre that requires the application of normative authorities belonging to that genre. For example, a labor statute that vests a tribunal with jurisdiction over workmen's compensation claims most often would require the tribunal to apply only labor law. Another example is if a court is established by a treaty, then the court's decision making is limited to applying the law of nations (including the necessary law of nations if the parties so agree[13]) because treaties are by definition governed by international law, and, therefore, so are their constituent tribunals. Therefore, even in the example of the U.S. Supreme Court exercising its original jurisdiction, its jurisdiction still would be limited to the application of international legal norms.

Furthermore, the *Charming Betsy* Rule requires that federal statutes be construed in conformity with the law of nations,[14] suggesting that even federal statutes vesting appellate jurisdiction in the Supreme Court and jurisdiction in the inferior federal courts must be construed in conformity with international law. If judicial activism is to be avoided, only international legal norms could be used to construe such jurisdiction-vesting statutes. This conclusion may appear to be alarming to many – especially those who disdain the use of international law – because some statutes are vague arguably requiring construction with other extrainternational legal authorities in order to ensure the statutes' adaptability to new circumstance political, economic, or social. However, as shall be seen in the following chapters, this alarm is not merited because there is an enormous reservoir of international legal norms from which to draw in the

[13] *See, e.g., I.C.J. Statute*, art. 38 (2) ("This provision shall not prejudice the power of the Court to decide a case *ex aequo et bono*, if the parties agree thereto."); Agreement Establishing the Caribbean Court of Justice, Feb. 14, 2001, art. 17 (3) (entered into force July 23, 2003) (Caribbean Court of Justice has jurisdiction "to decide a dispute *ex aequo et bono* if the parties so agree.") [hereinafter *CCJ Agreement*].

[14] *See* Murray v. Schooner Charming Betsy, 6 U.S. (2 Cranch.) 64, 118 (1804) (federal statutes must be construed in conformity with the United States' law of nations obligations).

construction of federal statutory law, and these norms either have been accepted by the political branches as conventional or customary international legal norms, or the Constitution – which the states accepted as law – gives such federal courts the authority to use such norms. However, before examining this reservoir, let us turn to the relevance of the *Non Liquet* Prohibition Principle to the judicial activist critique in order to demonstrate the lawfulness of using this reservoir.

An international tribunal that has competence to adjudicate an admissible dispute cannot issue a *non liquet* ("it is not clear") judgment on the merits. This is called the "*Non Liquet* Prohibition Principle." The Principle is well-established positive law based on "uninterrupted continuity of international arbitral and judicial practice."[15] A recent example is the *Agreement Establishing the Carribean Court of Justice* that explicitly requires that the Court "may not bring in a finding of *non-liquet* on the ground of silence or obscurity of the law."[16] As Judge Lauterpacht stated, "[i]t is not easy to conceive of a rule or principle of international law to which the designation 'positive" could be applied with greater justification than the prohibition of *non liquet*."[17]

[15] *See, e.g.*, Hersch Lauterpacht, *Some Observations on the Prohibition of "Non Liquet" and the Completeness of the Law*, *in* Hersch Lauterpacht, 2 International Law: Collected Papers 216, 217 (Elihu Lauterpacht ed. 1975) [hereinafter Lauterpacht].

[16] *CCJ Agreement*, art. 17 (2).

[17] Lauterpacht, *supra* note 15 at 223; *see* 1 Oppenheim's International Law, § 3, 12–13 (Robert Jennings and Arthur Watts eds. 9th ed. 1996) (international law should be regarded as a complete system in that every international conflict can be resolved by the application of law and, hence, international tribunals can not pronounce a *non liquet* judgment). However, some writers have cast doubt on whether international law any longer reflects a prohibition on *non liquet* judgments after the International Court of Justices' *Advisory Opinion on the Legality of the Use or Threat of Use of Nuclear Weapons* in which the Court did pronounce a *non liquet* opinion. For example, Judge Vereshchetin notes the following:

> there is a strong doctrinal view that the alleged "prohibition" on a declaration of a *non liquet* "may not be fully sustained by any evidence yet offered" (J. Stone, *"Non Liquet* and the Function of Law in the International Community," *The British Year Book of International Law*, 1959, p. 145). In his book devoted specifically to the problems of lacunae in international law, L. Siorat comes to the conclusion that in certain cases a court is obliged to declare a *non liquet* (L. Siorat, *Le problème de lacunes en droit international*, Paris, 1958, p. 189).

Advisory Opinion on the Legality of the Threat or Use of Nuclear Weapons, 1996 I.C.J. 341 (1996) (separate opinion by Vereshchetin, J.). However, Judge Vereshchetin notes further that "[i]n the present case, however, the Court is engaged in advisory procedure. It is

The importance of the Principle becomes clear when one examines the structure of disputes *vis-à-vis* the international legal principle of state reciprocity and equality. The crux of a dispute inherently centers on the parties' conflicting notions of whether the respondent has a duty or not. A complainant argues that there exists law imposing a duty on the respondent, and the respondent argues that there does not exist law imposing a duty – albeit both parties may concede that the duty is ambiguous. The *Non Liquet* Prohibition Principle operates under the initial assumption that the duty is ambiguous and effectively requires the tribunal to undertake a comprehensive survey of international legal authorities to find rules applicable to the facts in the dispute in order to provide clarification of the arguably vague duty and to ensure that a reasoned decision made on the basis of law can be reached.[18] International tribunals undertake such a survey in order to prevent a state-respondent from unjustly enriching itself at the expense of the state-complainant (and other states) who had reasonably construed their mutual duty liberally by using other international legal duties that had provided a liberal interpretation of the duty.

The international legal system generally[19] operates on the principle of reciprocity and equality. When the state-respondent to a dispute has

requested not to resolve an actual dispute between actual Parties, but to state the law as it finds it at the present stage of its development." *Id.* Moreover, the authorities that Judge Vereshchetin cited are somewhat dated. Some have pointed out the advantages of the *Non Liquet* Prohibition Principle. For example, Professor Bodansky supports the *Non Liquet* Prohibition Principle because its application can serve to put the international community on notice that it needs to articulate a new rule. *See* Daniel Bodansky, *Non Liquet and the Incompleteness of International Law*, 153, 170, *in* International Law, the International Court of Justice and Nuclear Weapons (Laurence Boisson de Chazournes & Philippe Sands eds. 1999).

18 The Principle's operative presumption resonates with CLS' claim that rules are indeterminate. However, the *Non Liquet Prohibition* Principle operates on the presumption that even vague rules can become defined and determinate through their construction with other rules.

19 However, the principle of state reciprocity and equality cannot serve as a justification for state withdrawal from its international human rights and humanitarian legal obligations. *See, e.g.*, UN Hum. Rts. Ctte., General Comment No. 24 (52), General comment on issues relating to reservations made upon ratification or accession to the Covenant or the Optional Protocols thereto, or in relation to declarations under article 41 of the Covenant, § 17, U.N. Doc. CCPR/C/21/Rev.1/Add.6 (1994) ("The principle of inter-State reciprocity has no place, save perhaps in the limited context of reservations to declarations on the Committee's competence" to consider inter-state complaints.); *cf. ibid.* at ¶ 8 ("Although treaties that are mere exchanges of obligations between States allow them

acquired an advantage at the expense of the state-complainant by strictly construing its own duty and yet relying on other states' liberal construction of the duty, the state-respondent has become a "free-rider."[20] The "free-rider" state has unjustly enriched itself at the expense of other states who have observed a liberally construed duty in regard to the "free-rider" state. In doing so, the "free-rider" state has not only violated the principles of state reciprocity and co-equality,[21] but it also has violated the prohibition of unjust enrichment, which is a general principle of law recognized by civilized nations.[22] A tribunal created by a treaty that fails to apply these applicable international legal authorities risks giving one state-party an unfair advantage over the other.

The Principle can be justified further as a means of preventing wars because interstate or international (or even sometimes intranational[23]) conflicts whose resolution is difficult because of the ambiguity or absence of applicable law can fester into war, which undermines the very international legal order by not only allowing the suspension or termination of many rules of the positive law of nations but also encouraging the violation of natural law as reflected in *jus cogens*[24] norms, such as the

to reserve *inter se* applications of rules of general international law, it is otherwise in human rights treaties, which are for the benefit of persons within their jurisdiction . . . "); *Vienna Convention*, art. 60 (5) (termination or suspension of humanitarian treaty not justified by breach).

[20] *See* Anthony D'Amato, The Concept of Custom in International Law 201 (1971) (discussing "expectation-reliance" complex of customary international law's operation).

[21] *See, e.g.*, Emmerich de Vattel, The Law of Nations or Principles of the Law of Nature Applied to the Conduct and Affairs of Nations and Sovereign, *Preliminaries*, at § 18 (1758) ("small republic is no less a sovereign state than the most powerful kingdom") [hereinafter, Vattel, Law of Nations]; *UN Charter*, art. 2 (1) (recognizing sovereign equality of states).

[22] *See, e.g.*, Case T-171/99, Corus UK Ltd. v. Commission, ECR 2001, II-02967, ¶ 55 (recognizing prohibition of unjust enrichment as "general principle of [European] Community law"); Case C-259/87, Greece v Commission, ECR 1990, I-2845 (same); Beyeler v. Italy, Appl. No. 33202/96, Eur. Ct. H.R. (Jan. 5, 2000) (recognizing unjust enrichment violated right to enjoyment of property in violation of *ECHR, Prot. No. 1*); Archawski v. Hanioti, 350 U.S. 532 (1956) (recognizing prohibition against unjust enrichment).

[23] In cases in which a nation is divided into states, interstate conflicts become national conflicts that can result in war. A good example of such a nation is the United States, and an example of an interstate/national conflict that erupted into war was the Civil War.

[24] *Jus cogens* "is a norm accepted and recognized by the international community of States as a whole as a norm from which no derogation is permitted and which can be modified

right to life and humane treatment.[25] The Principle ensures that a peaceful resolution is made and war is avoided.

The Principle makes available the lawful use of applicable international legal norms and destroys the judicial activist critique insofar as the use of such international legal norms might otherwise would constitute judicial activism. Furthermore, if the treaty's tribunal applies noninternational legal authorities, this would constitute judicial activism because treaties are only governed by international law. In the case of U.S. federal courts, the same conclusions would follow. Federal courts lawfully can tap into this reservoir of international legal norms, and federal courts cannot constitutionally apply authorities other than international legal ones; otherwise, they would be making law. Although the Constitution only mentions international certain legal authorities (*viz.*, treaties,[26] interstate and foreign compacts or agreements,[27] and the law of nations[28] generally) and, more important, the Judicial Power Clause in Article III only mentions treaties (and the Constitution and the laws of the United States), the Constitution's status as a treaty in conjunction with an international

only by a subsequent norm of general international law having the same character." *Vienna Convention*, art. 53. Such norms can be established by treaty if the treaty is widely accepted and the norm cannot be suspended. C.L. Rozakis, The Concept of *Jus Cogens* in the Law of Treaties 71 (Amsterdam: North-Holland, 1976).

25 The rights to life and humane treatment are peremptory and nonderogable. *ICCPR*, art. 4 (2). Therefore, they constitute *jus cogens* norms. *Cf.* Domingues v. United States, Report No. 62/02, Case 12.285, Inter-Am. Comm. H.R., at § 49 ("It has been suggested that a reliable starting point in identifying those international legal proscriptions that have achieved *jus cogens* status is the list of rights that international human rights treaties render non-derogable") (2002).

26 *See* U.S. Const. art. I, § 10, cl. 1 ("No State shall enter into any Treaty, Alliance, or Confederation ..."); art. II, § 2, cl. 2 (President "shall have Power, by and with the Advice and Consent of the Senate to make Treaties, provided two thirds of the Senators present concur"); art. III, § 2, cl. 1 ("The judicial Power shall extend to all Cases, in Law and Equity, arising under this Constitution, the Laws of the United States, and Treaties made, or which shall be made, under their Authority..."); art. VI, § 2 ("This Constitution, and the Law of the United States which shall be made in Pursuance thereof, and all Treaties made, or which shall be made, under the Authority of the United States, shall be the supreme Law of the Land; and the Judges in every State shall be bound thereby, any Thing in the Constitution or Laws of any State to the Contrary notwithstanding.").

27 *See id.* at art. I, § 10, cl. 3 ("No State shall, without the Consent of Congress, ... enter into any Agreement or Compact with another State, or with a foreign Power... ").

28 *See id.* at art. I, § 8, cl. 10.

legal construction of the Judicial Power Clause that conforms to the *Non Liquet* Prohibition Principle ensures that federal courts have the constitutional authority to apply or use in the construction of federal constitutional or statutory law, a number of international legal authorities not expressly mentioned in the Constitution. When federal courts are reviewing the constitutionality of federal and state law, their use of such international legal authorities cannot be viewed as judicial activism because the Constitution is a treaty whose provisions (including the Judicial Power Clause) must be construed in conformity with the United States' international legal obligations *per* the international law governing treaty interpretation.

In the following chapters, this book will examine what these international legal authorities are and how the federal courts must use such authorities. Most importantly, this book will demonstrate that those international legal authorities that provide the most liberal construction to the federal and state governments' duties are the appropriate authorities to use.

PART TWO

INTERNATIONAL LAW

The "law of nations" (*jus gentium*) is what is now called "international law." Unfortunately, the phrase "international law" is misleading because it suggests a kind of law that only governs the relations *between* nations – something that jurists used to call "*jus inter gentes.*" However, the law of nations always has governed not only international matters but also many intranational matters. The fact that the law of nations also governed many intranational matters comes out clearly in Vattel's discussion of the justification under the law of nations for members of a state dissolving their relations with their prince if the prince failed to protect them, and establishing an independent state:

> The state is obliged to defend and preserve all its members. . . ; and the prince owes the same assistance to his subjects. If, therefore, the state or the prince refuses or neglects to succour a body of people who are exposed to imminent danger, the latter, being thus abandoned, become perfectly free to provide for their own safety and preservation in whatever manner they find most convenient, without paying the least regard to those who, by abandoning them, have been the first to fail in their duty. The country of Zug, being attacked by the Swiss in 1352, sent for succour to the duke of Austria, its sovereign; but that prince, being engaged in discourse concerning his hawks, at the time when the deputies appeared before him, would scarcely condescend to hear them. Thus abandoned, the people of Zug entered into the Helvetic confederacy.[1]

[1] EMMERICH DE VATTEL, THE LAW OF NATIONS OR PRINCIPLES OF THE LAW OF NATURE APPLIED TO THE CONDUCT AND AFFAIRS OF NATIONS AND SOVEREIGN, *Preliminaries*, § 3 (1758) [hereinafter, VATTEL, LAW OF NATIONS].

James Wilson, a Framer of the Constitution, recognized that the law of nations governed not only relations between nations but also relations between the state and its citizens.

> Some seem to have thought, that [the law of nations] respects and regulates the conduct of nations only in their intercourse with each other. A very important branch of this law – that containing the duties which a nation owes itself – seems to have escaped their attention. "The general principle ... of the law of nations, is nothing more than the general law of sociability, which obliges nations to the same duties as are prescribed to individuals."[2]

Wilson may have had Jeremy Bentham in mind in 1791 when he stated that "some seem to have thought that [the law of nations] respects and regulates the conduct of nations only in their intercourse with each other." Two years earlier, Bentham had published his PRINCIPLES AND MORALS OF LEGISLATION in which he was the first to coin the phrase "international law" to refer to the "[p]rinciples of legislation in matters betwixt nation and nation."[3] However, "international law" (*jus inter gentes*) is only a subset of the law of nations (*jus gentium*). Indeed, a large segment of the law of nations was the *lex mercatoria* that governed private commercial transactions.[4] The Founders would not have viewed the law of nations as

[2] JAMES WILSON, LECTURES ON LAW, *Of the Law of Nations*, ¶ 1 (1791); *see also* VATTEL, 1 LAW OF NATIONS, *supra* note 1 at ch. 2 ("General Principles of the Duties of a Nation towards herself").

[3] JEREMY BENTHAM, PRINCIPLES AND MORALS OF LEGISLATION, *Preface*, at Part the Seventh (1789).

[4] *See* Sosa v. Alvarez-Machain, 542 U.S. 692, 124 S. Ct. at 2756–57,159 L. Ed. 2d at **743 (2004) ("The law of nations included a second, more pedestrian element, however, that did fall within the judicial sphere, as a body of judge-made law regulating the conduct of individuals situated outside domestic boundaries and consequently carrying an international savor. ... There was, finally, a sphere in which these rules binding individuals for the benefit of other individuals overlapped with the norms of state relationships. Blackstone referred to it when he mentioned three specific offenses against the law of nations addressed by the criminal law of England: violation of safe conducts, infringement of the rights of ambassadors, and piracy. [citation omitted]); *see also* Hilton v. Guyot, 159 U.S. 113 (1895) ("International law – in its widest and most comprehensive sense – including not only questions of right between nations, governed by what has appropriately been called the 'law of nations' but also what is usually called 'private international law' ... and concerning the rights of persons within the territory and dominion of one nation, by reason of acts, private or public, done within the dominions of another nation – is part of our law.").

a body of law governing only international subjects.[5] In the next chapter, we will examine the positive law of nations.

[5] After reading above passage from Vattel, one can see why the Founders – who had dissolved their ties with King George – were so enamored of Vattel's view of the law of nations, and it is Vattel's inclusion of domestic matters in the law of nations that the Founders embraced, as evidenced by Wilson's observation.

3

The Positive Law of Nations and Its Interpretive Principles

Vattel defined the law of nations (*jus gentium*) as "the science which teaches the rights subsisting between nations or states, and the obligations correspondent to those rights."[1] The U.S. Supreme Court in *Sosa v. Alvarez-Machain* recently reaffirmed this definition.[2] Vattel discussed the various dimensions of the law of nations. One dimension is the "necessary law of nations" that is immutable and identified with natural law.[3] Nations are required to observe the necessary law of nations as a matter of conscience.[4] (We will address the necessary law of nations jurisdictions of international courts in Chapter 4.) This necessary law of nations establishes that states are free and independent; therefore, states are free

[1] Emmerich de Vattel, The Law of Nations or Principles of the Law of Nature Applied to the Conduct and Affairs of Nations and Sovereign, *Preliminaries*, § 3 (1758) [hereinafter, Vattel, Law of Nations].

[2] Sosa v. Alvarez-Machain, 542 U.S. 692, 124 S. Ct. at 2756 159 L. Ed. 2d at 8C (2004).

[3] Vattel, Law of Nations, *supra* note 1 at *Preliminaries*, §§ 7 and 8 ("Since therefore the necessary law of nations consists in the application of the law of nature to states, – which law is immutable, as being founded on the nature of things, and particularly on the nature of man, – it follows that the *Necessary* law of nations is *immutable*." [emphases in original]); *see also* J.J. Burlamaqui, 1 The Principles of Natural Law, pt. II, ch. VI, § IX (1748) (one kind of law of nations is "universal, necessary, and self-obligatory . . . [and] differs in nothing from the law of nature, and is consequently immutable") [hereinafter Burlamaqui, Principles].

[4] Vattel, Law of Nations, *supra* note 1 at *Preliminaries*, § 28 ("as the Necessary law is always obligatory on the conscience, a nation ought never to lose sight of it in deliberating on the line of conduct she is to pursue in order to fulfil her duty; but when there is question of examining what she may demand of other states, she must consult the Voluntary law, whose maxims are devoted to the safety and advantage of the universal society of mankind.").

to create a "positive law of nations."[5] Within the positive law of nations is the voluntary law of nations, the conventional law of nations (or law of treaties), and the customary law of nations.

Article 38 of the *Statute of the International Court of Justice* [hereinafter *I.C.J. Staute*] generally is considered to list the sources of positive international law. Article 38 states:

> 1. The Court, whose function is to decide in accordance with international law such disputes as are submitted to it, shall apply:
>   a. international conventions, whether general or particular, establishing rules expressly recognized by the contesting states;
>   b. international custom, as evidence of a general practice accepted as law;
>   c. the general principles of law recognized by civilized nations;
>   d. subject to the provisions of Article 59,[[6]] judicial decisions and the teachings of the most highly qualified publicists of the various nations, as subsidiary means for the determination of the rules of law.[7]

Section 1 establishes the International Court of Justice's (ICJ) positive law of nations jurisdiction. The first three sources of law (*viz.*, treaties, customary international law, and general principles) constitute the positive law of nations, and the fourth source (*viz.*, judicial decisions and publicist teachings) constitute secondary sources for construing the previous three sources.

Although Article 38 probably does not set out a formal hierarchy of international legal sources,[8] Article 38 does effectively sets out a method "for technical legal reasoning in international law, proceeding from the specific to the general."[9] First, an international tribunal looks at treaties that provide express and often specific rules. If the treaty rules are vague or there are no applicable treaties between the parties, the Court then turns

[5] *Ibid.* at § 21.

[6] Article 59 states: "The decision of the Court has no binding force except between the parties and in respect of that particular case."

[7] *I.C.J. Statute*, art. 38.

[8] *See* Ian Brownlie, Principles of Public International Law 4 (4th ed. 1990) ("it is probably unwise to think in terms of hierarchy dictated by order (a) to (d) in all cases").

[9] Stephen Hall, *The Persistent Spectre: Natural Law, International Order and the Limits of Legal Positivism*, 12 E.J.I.L 269, 297 (2001).

to the customary international legal obligations of the parties either to construe the vague treaty rules or to apply this other positive law to which the parties have assented. If the treaty or customary international legal rules are vague or non-existent, the Court then turns to general principles of law recognized by civilized nations in order to construe these treaty and customary rules or to apply this other positive law.[10] This is consonant with the U.S. Supreme Court's holding in *Geofroy v. Riggs* that the words of a treaty are "to be taken in their ordinary meaning, as understood in the public law of nations"[11] in that customary international law and general principles constitute parts of the public law of nations. Finally, judicial decisions and teachings of the most highly qualified publicists can be used as subsidiary interpretive sources.

3.1. TREATIES

Vattel describes the conventional law of nations as follows:

> The several engagements into which nations may enter produce a new kind of law of nations, called Conventional, or of Treaties. As it is evident that a treaty binds none but the contracting parties, the conventional law of nations is not a universal but a particular law. All that can be done on this subject, in a treatise on the Law of Nations, is to lay down those general rules which nations are bound to observe with respect to their treaties. A minute detail of the various agreements made between particular nations, and of the rights and obligations thence resulting, is matter of fact, and belongs to the province of history.[12]

It is important to note that Vattel viewed treaties *per se* as dealing only with particular obligations between states-parties that did not necessarily create general legal obligations for all states, which was Vattel's primary concern with writing a treatise on the law of nations. However, the conventional law of nations also sometimes addressed general legal obligations

[10] *See Vienna Convention*, art. 31 (using other international legal obligations for interpreting treaty).

[11] Geofroy v. Riggs, 133 U.S. 258, 271 (1890).

[12] VATTEL, LAW OF NATIONS, *supra* note 1, *Preliminaries* at § 24.

regarding the interpretation of treaties. One such treaty interpretive rule is the *Namibia Rule*.

The *Namibia Rule*

In its *Namibia Advisory Opinion*, the ICJ opined that "an international instrument must be interpreted and applied within the *overall* framework of the [international] juridical system in force."[13] Subsequently, Inter-American Court of Human Rights[14] and the Inter-American Commission on Human Rights[15] have confirmed this treaty interpretive rule. The *Namibia Rule* can be justified on the basis that many treaties codify customary international law even for states that are not parties to these treaties[16] and many treaties codify general principles of law recognized by civilized nations.[17] Indeed, what is particularly striking about the present international legal order is the growing acceptance among states that many rules are binding on states that did not accept such rules as originally stated in treaties, and the use of these rules by international tribunals for construing these treaties – although there remains considerable resistance to this development in some quarters. International courts sometimes construe a treaty in conformity with other treaties that do not share any states-parties with the treaty being construed and, hence strictly speaking, do not constitute binding treaty law for a party to the treaty being construed. For example, the Inter-American Court of Human

[13] Legal Consequences for States of the Continued Presence of South Africa in Namibia (South West Africa) notwithstanding Security Council Resolution 276 (1970), Advisory Opinion, 1971 I.C.J. 16, 31 (1971) (emphasis provided).

[14] *See* Interpretation of the American Declaration of the Rights and Duties of Man within the Framework of Article 64 of the American Convention on Human Rights, Advisory Opinion OC-10/89, Inter-Am. Ct. H.R. Ser. A, No. 10, at ¶ 37 (1989) (quoting language from above Namibia advisory opinion);

[15] *See* Coard v. United States, Inter-Am. Cm. H.R., No. 109/99 at ¶ 40 (1999), *available at* http://www.cidh.oas.org/annualrep/99eng/Merits/UnitedStates10.951.htm (last visited Feb. 15, 2003) (quoting above language in the Namibia advisory opinion).

[16] *See, e.g., Vienna Convention*, art. 38 (rules in a treaty become binding on third States through international custom).

[17] For example, the *pacta sunt servanda* rule is a general principle of law recognized by civilized nations, and it is codified in the *Vienna Convention on the Law of Treaties. Vienna Convention*, art. 26.

Rights has recognized that even non-Inter-American treaties properly can be used to complement and construe Inter-American treaties:

> The need of the regional system to be complemented by the universal finds expression in the practice of the Inter-American Commission on Human Rights and is entirely consistent with the object and purpose of the Convention, the American Declaration and the Statute of the Commission. The Commission has properly invoked in some of its reports and resolutions "other treaties concerning the protection of human rights in the American states," regardless of their bilateral or multilateral character, or whether they have been adopted within the framework or under the auspices of the inter-American system.

The apparent reason for this change is that the international legal order is now populated with multilateral treaties that have created regional and global intergovernmental organizations with international tribunals tasked with the responsibility of making the positive law of nations operate coherently and effectively for states whose treaty obligations often overlap with those of other states that may not be parties to the treaty being construed. Most importantly, the application of such international legal authorities serves to prevent international tribunals from being forced to issue *non liquet* pronouncements.

The U.S. Supreme Court's observation in 1825 that because "no nation can prescribe a rule for others, none can make a law of nations" is somewhat inaccurate in some cases.[18] For example, regional customary international law can be used to construe treaties with extraregional states because a regional state also might be a party to the treaty being construed. Furthermore, a nation sometimes is shared among states whose practices often constitute a regional customary law of nations. A perfect example is the United States.[19] Hence, one nation-state[20] effectively can

[18] The Antelope, 23 U.S. 66, 122 (1825).

[19] *See infra* Subsection 6.2. (discussing regional federal, American customary international).

[20] It is important to recall that, strictly speaking, nations are peoples, and states are bodies politic. Although the two often are conflated into nation-states, the two often are distinct. For example, a nation may be shared by different states, as is the case with the American people in the United States. In the case of the United States, it is more accurate to refer to it as a "nation-state." Sometimes nations are not organized into states (as is the case

prescribe a rule for other states by making regional customary international law.

This propensity for a treaty rule to become binding on all states regardless of whether they have explicitly consented to the rule is found in the nature of the international legal process. As discussed in the following subsections, in the case of customary international law, states by their mere failure to object to an emerging rule in a timely fashion can become legally bound to the norm. No positive act demonstrating consent to the rule is required for states to become bound to the norm. In the case of general principles of law recognized by civilized nations, the state need never have even complied with the general principle if it merely recognized it. As the U.S. Supreme Court noted in *The Schooner Exchange v. McFaddon*, "[t]his consent [to a law of nations rule] may be either express or implied. In the latter case, it is less determinate, exposed more to the uncertainties of construction; but, if understood, not less obligatory."[21]

Aside from requiring that a treaty be interpreted in conformity with the overall international juridical system, the *Namibia Rule* also requires that a treaty be interpreted in conformity with the international juridical system *presently* in force. The *Nambia Rule* takes into account the fact that there may be other international legal obligations that require a new interpretation of a treaty that was entered into by the parties before they acquired new international legal obligations. In order to ensure that their international legal obligations do not conflict, the treaty must be construed in conformity with these new international legal obligations.

The *Namibia Rule* effectively incorporates also the European Court of Human Rights' "evolutive technique" which the Court has used for interpreting the *European Convention on Human Rights* (*ECHR*).[22] The evolutive technique requires that the *ECHR* be interpreted in light of present-day conditions. In determining what are present-day conditions, the Court turns to the national laws of the states-parties to the *ECHR* to determine if a new consensus among European national laws has

of the Kurdish people in Turkey and Iraq). Also, a state may include multiple nations. For example, Florida includes both the American and Seminole nations.

21 7 Cranch. 116, 136 (1812).

22 *See, e.g.*, Bankovic and Others v. Belgium and Others, Application No. 52207/99 (2001) (discussing evolutive technique for interpreting *ECHR*).

crystallized regarding the interpretation of a human right. If it has, the Court will use this interpretation for interpreting the relevant human right guaranteed by the *ECHR*. What this evolutive interpretive technique may reflect is the use of customary international law for interpreting treaties that requires only a consensus of state-party practices, which in some cases can represent a departure from the Persistent Objector Rule. To discover whether this evolutive technique does depart, let us now turn to customary international law and its interpretation.

3.2. CUSTOMARY INTERNATIONAL LAW

As discussed earlier, customary international law is a subset of the law of nations. It was traditionally called the "customary law of nations"[23] and is now defined as "international custom, as evidence of a general practice accepted as law." It consists of two elements: (i) general state practice and (ii) a sense of necessary and legal obligation (*opinio juris et necessitatis*).[24]

For a rule to be *customary*, states must practice the rule because custom is constituted by practice. Such practice is represented either (i) by performance of an overt act when the rule prescribes performance, or (ii) by nonperformance of an overt act when the rule proscribes performance. In the case of legal rules requiring nonperformance of an overt act, it is almost always the case that at least one official from a state recognizing the legal rule has complied with the rule – notwithstanding that another official from the same state is acting *ultra vires* and violating the legal rule. Most importantly, the requisite showing of state practice for a customary international legal norm need not be a practice that is performed by *all* state officials because some state officials may not have the lawful capacity to perform the practice (as in the inverse case that *not all* state officials must commit an international legal violation for the state to incur liability[25]). Only some state practice must be shown, and only that state

[23] VATTEL, LAW OF NATIONS, *supra* note 1 at *Preliminaries*, § 25.

[24] IAN BROWNLIE, PRINCIPLES OF PUBLIC INTERNATIONAL LAW 7 (4th ed. 1990) [hereinafter Brownlie].

[25] *See* International Law Commission, *Responsibility of States for Internationally Wrongful Acts*, art. 4, OFFICIAL RECORDS OF THE GENERAL ASSEMBLY, 56th Sess., Supp. No. 10, UN Doc. A/56/10 [hereinafter ILC Draft Articles] ("(1) The conduct of any State organ shall

practice which has a sense of legal obligation. Otherwise, no state could actually ever commit or refrain from committing an act that violated its customary international legal obligation. The concept of customary international law would be superfluous. Furthermore, only rule compliance by state actors can be evidence of state practice. Although nonstate actors can contribute to the articulation and interpretation of customary international legal norms through the submission of, *inter alia*, legal briefs and scholarly articles, these materials only may represent "subsidiary means for the determination" of customary international legal norms.[26] These nonstate actor practices do not represent state practice by definition.

For a rule to be *international*, the rule must govern the relation between at least two states. Under international law, a state cannot unilaterally impose a legal rule on another state(s)[27] unless the rule already reflects an

be considered an act of that State under international law, whether the organ exercises legislative, executive, judicial or any other functions, whatever position it holds in the organization of the State, and whatever its character as an organ of the central Government or of a territorial unit of the State. (2) An organ includes any person or entity which has that status in accordance with the internal law of the State.").

26 *I.C.J. Statute*, art. 38 (1) (d).

27 *See* The Antelope, 23 U.S. at 122 ("[N]o [state] can rightfully impose a rule on another. Each legislates for itself, but its legislation can operate on itself alone."); JOSEPH STORY, COMMENTARIES ON THE CONFLICT OF LAWS 19, 21–22 (2d ed. 1841) ("no state or nation can, by its laws, directly affect, or bind property out of its own territory, or persons not resident therein"); ULRICH HUBER, DE CONFLICTU LEGUM *in* E. LORENZEN, SELECTED ARTICLES ON THE CONFLICT OF LAWS 136 (1947) ("Every state's laws apply within the state's territory, but not beyond.").

U.S. federal courts have vacillated between recognizing the extraterritoriality of certain federal statutes. *Compare* American Banana Co. v. United Fruit Co., 213 U.S. 347 (1909) (refusing to recognize extraterritorial application of Sherman Act), *with* Hartford Fire Insurance Co. v. California, 509 U.S. 764 (1993) (recognizing extraterritorial application of Sherman Act). Federal court interpretations of the Sherman Act recognizing extraterritorial application frequently have been met with foreign state declarations of objection. GARY B. BORN, INTERNATIONAL CIVIL LITIGATION IN U.S. COURTS 584–87 (1996). Therefore, if such foreign state declarations are timely and persistently made, the Sherman Act does not represent a customary international legal obligation for these states because the declaration represents a persistent objection. However, other states have adopted competition laws that are broadly similar to the U.S. antitrust laws that may indicate declarations of the Sherman Act representing a customary international legal norm for these states. *See* J. ATWOOD & K. BREWSTER, ANTITRUST AND AMERICAN BUSINESS ABROAD § 3.01 et seq. (2d ed. 1985 & Cum. Supp.).

international legal rule binding on the other state.[28] Although a customary international legal norm must reflect sufficient general practice, evidence of such generality may be established by the practice of only two states. For example, two bordering states can recognize a custom having *opinio juris* governing their boundaries that only binds them. Although the ICJ in its 1969 *North Sea Continental Shelf Cases* held that state practice must be extensive, the Court did not define with any specificity how extensive the state practice must be.[29] Given that international law has long recognized that customary international law can be regional, there appears to be no principled reason why such regional law could not govern only two states. Indeed, the ICJ already had recognized in 1960 that customary international law could govern only two states:

> It is difficult to see why the number of States between which a local custom may be established on the basis of long practice must necessarily be larger than two. . . . Where therefore the Court finds a practice clearly established between two States which was accepted by the parties as governing the relations between them, the Court must attribute decisive effect to that practice for the purpose of determining their specific rights and obligations.[30]

Although the rule must govern international relations, this does not entail that the rule govern only international matters. The law of nations – including its customary aspects – also governs intranational subjects. This is important in the context of the United States' constitutional

[28] For example, states often must enforce international legal rules extraterritorially in cases of piracy on the high seas, international airspace, international armed conflicts, or human rights. *See, e.g.*, Bankoviç and Others v. Belgium and Others, Application, No. 52207/99, Eur. Ct. H.R. (2001) (recognizing extraterritorial application of the right to life under the *ECHR* in areas under "effective overall control" of state party during international armed conflict); Alejandre *et al.* v. Cuba, Case 11.589, Report No. 86/99, OEA/Ser.L/V/II.106 Doc. 3 rev. at 586 (1999) (recognizing extraterritorial application of right to life under the *ACHR* in international airspace); *see also* Saldías de López v. Uruguay, Comm. No. 52/1979, U.N. Doc. CCPR/C/OP/1 (1985) (views adopted July 29, 1981) (recognizing extraterritorial application of right to life under the *ICCPR* in another state);

[29] North Sea Continental Shelf Cases (Germany v. Denmark, Germany v. The Netherlands), 1969 I.C.J. 3, 43 ¶ 74.

[30] Case Concerning Rights of Passage Over Indian Territory (Merits), 1960 I.C.J. Reports 39–44 (Apr. 13).

arrangement with the states. The United States is both a nation and an intergovernmental organization of several states.[31] Because the Constitution represents a treaty between states that customarily have the capacity to be persistent objectors, and at the same time creates a government for one nation, states still can be persistent objectors notwithstanding the sometime intranational effect of objecting to an emerging customary international legal norm.

Finally, for a customary rule to be *legal*, the custom instantiating the rule must have a sense of legal obligation (*opinio juris*) for the states practicing the custom. A rule becomes a legal rule once a state has recognized the rule as having *opinio juris*. Conclusive evidence of a state's recognition of the rule as having *opinio juris* can be established by, for example, a constitutional or statutory provision (or its interpretation by the state's tribunal), an international agreement to which the state is a party (or an interpretation of the agreement by an international tribunal whose competence the state recognizes), another customary international legal norm that the state recognizes (or an interpretation of the norm by an international tribunal whose competence the state recognizes), a general principle of law recognized by civilized nations (or an interpretation of the principle by an international tribunal whose competence the state recognizes), or common law if the state has a common law system. Furthermore, the rule must not violate the state's own fundamental domestic law. For example, if the state or a branch of its government were to overreach its domestic legal authority by adopting a rule that violates the state's own fundamental domestic law, the rule cannot be considered to have *opinio juris*.

Furthermore, for a state to be bound by a customary international legal rule, it is not necessary that there is evidence that the state explicitly accepted the rule: evidence of the consent can be implied from surrounding circumstances.[32] Most importantly, the practice instantiating the emerging customary international legal rule can acquire a sense of

[31] For the classical exposition of the United States' status as an intergovernmental organization, *see* JAMES BROWN SCOTT, THE UNITED STATES OF AMERICA: A STUDY IN INTERNATIONAL ORGANIZATION (1920).

[32] *See* The Schooner Exchange v. McFaddon, 11 U.S. (7 Cranch) 116, 136 (1812) (sovereign's consent to customary international legal norm can be implied).

legal obligation for another state that has not performed the practice by virtue of the fact that this other state must perform the practice in order that it is not unjustly enriched at the expense of a state that already has performed the practice. The general principle of law recognized by civilized nations that prohibits unjust enrichment provides the requisite *opinio juris*. In the same way that the general principle of law recognized by civilized nations requiring that promises be observed (*pacta sunt servanda*) provides the primary positive international law basis for the conventional law of nations,[33] the general principle of law recognized by civilized nations prohibiting unjust enrichment provides the primary positive international law basis for the customary law of nations.

However, the concept of implicit consent can be troubling because it sometimes relies on a legal fiction, namely, that mere refusal to respond to a state's claim entails another's acceptance of the state's claim. A state cannot logically conclude from another state's silence that the other state has accepted the claim. To do so is fallacious reasoning – a form of an *argumentum ad ignoratiam*.

Nonetheless, a state can acquire advantages (*i.e.*, rights) *vis-à-vis* other states that have acquiesced to customary international legal norms. Even when a state has not expressly accepted the norm or not expressly rejected it, the state often relies on the fact that the customary international legal norm is binding on other states to its own benefit. In order to avoid the scenario of a state becoming a "free-rider," this effective state reliance operates to impose a reciprocal obligation upon the state to observe the norm in its relations to other states that have acquiesced to the customary international legal norm. In order to ensure that a state is not unjustly enriched by receiving benefits at the expense of another state's recognition of the customary international legal duty and to ensure finality of international legal relations, international courts have recognized the Acquiescence Principle as a general principle of law: a state cannot challenge another state's claim if the state has failed to object to the claim

[33] *See, e.g., Study on treaties, agreements and other constructive arrangements between States and indigenous populations,* Final Report of the Special Rapporteur, UN Commission on Human Rights (Sub-Commission on Prevention of Discrimination and Protection of Minorities) ¶ 277, E/CN.4/Sub.2/1999/20 (1999) (treaty compliance represents *jus cogens* norm); Hans Wehberg, *Pacta Sunt Servanda,* 53 AM. J. INT'L L. 775, 782 (1959) (treaty compliance represents genera principle of law recognized by civilized nations).

before a reasonable time has passed.[34] For example, in *Temple of Preah Vihear*, the ICJ refused to recognize Thailand's territorial claim against Cambodia on two bases: (i) Thailand's objection to Cambodia's territorial claim, which was made fifty years earlier, was not timely made and (ii) Thailand had enjoyed benefits resulting from Cambodia's reliance on the earlier claim.[35]

Most importantly, it is the Acquiescence Principle that often provides the *opinio juris* necessary for establishing a norm's customary international legal status by imposing a legal deadline for making a persistent objection to an emerging customary international legal norm. Unfortunately, the ICJ or any other international legal authority never has provided a bright line rule for timely objections. However, a set of Objection Deadline Rules will be presented later in this section.

The Persistent Objector Rule

A state that persistently, consistently, clearly, and expressly objects to a customary international law norm during the norm's emergence is not bound by the norm when the norm finally crystallizes. After the norm has crystallized, the state lawfully cannot exempt itself from being bound by the norm, unless the norm is superseded by a new customary international legal norm or *jus cogens* norm.[36] This rule is known as the "Persistent Objector Rule" [hereinafter "the Rule"]. Professor Ian Brownlie has noted the following about the Rule:

> *The persistent objector.* The way in which, as a matter of practice, custom resolves itself into a question of special relations is illustrated further by the

34 *See* Thomas M. Franck and Dennis M. Sughrue, *The International Role of Equity-as-Fairness*, 81 GEO. L. J. 563, 568 (1993) (articulating Acquiescence Principle as a general principle of law that holds that silence or absence of protest may preclude a state from later challenging another state's claim).

35 *See* Temple of Preah Vihear (Cambodia v. Thail.), 1962 I.C.J. 6, 34 (June 15) ("[W]hen two countries establish a frontier between them, one of the primary objects is to achieve stability and finality. This is impossible if the line so established can, at any moment . . . be called in question . . . .").

36 *See* Aloeboetoe *et al.* v. Suriname, Inter-Am. Ct. H.R. (Ser. C) No. 15, at §§ 56–57 (1994) (recognizing that 1762 Netherlands-Saramaka treaty allowing sale of slaves – which had been protected by contemporary customary international law – "would be today null and void" because treaty violates present *jus cogens*).

> rule that a state may contract out of a custom in the process of formation. Evidence of objection must be clear and there is probably a presumption of acceptance which is to be rebutted. Whatever the theoretical underpinnings of the principle, it is well recognized by international tribunals, and in the practice of states. Given the majoritarian tendency of international relations the principle is likely to have increased prominence.[37]

Persistent objections operate on customary international law in a similar way as reservations operate on treaty law – except that reservations cannot always exempt the reserving state from its other international legal obligations and persistent objections are not only expressed through international mechanisms, such as treaties. There is a presumption that an extant customary international legal norm is binding on a state absent (i) express, (ii) persistent, and (iii) consistent evidence of an objection to the norm.

The objection to the rule must be *express*. As in the case of the law of treaties, customary international law requires that the objection – the customary international legal analogue to a treaty reservation – be explicit. This requirement may seem inconsistent given that states can only undertake treaty obligations explicitly, whereas states can undertake customary international legal obligations implicitly. As noted earlier, for a state to be bound by a customary international legal norm, it is not necessary that there is evidence that the state explicitly has accepted the norm. However, if the state's objection is not express, other states will have no notice that the state does not consider itself also bound to comply with the rule and, consequently, still will consider themselves to be bound to comply with the rule, thereby providing a benefit to the nonexpress objector state. This would constitute unjust enrichment. Therefore, mere physical acts – not verbal or written declarations – cannot constitute objections.

This is not to say that the express objection to the rule must be articulated as an express objection to the rule as a customary international legal rule *per se*. As evidence of a rule having *opinio juris* can be established by a number of state acts (*e.g.*, statute, treaty), so too can the state's express objection to the rule having *opinio juris* be established by such

[37] Brownlie, *supra* note 24 at 10.

acts – even if not expressly described as a customary international legal objection.

The objection also must be *persistent* and *consistent*. If a nonobjector state were to subsequently object to the norm after it had crystallized, this subsequent objector state could unfairly benefit from the other nonobjector states' observance of the customary norm in regard to the subsequent objector state. This constitutes "unjust enrichment" at the expense of nonobjector states, and the prohibition of unjust enrichment is a general principle of law recognized by civilized nations.[38]

The objection must be *clear*. It is not necessary for a state to expressly accept an emerging customary international legal norm as such for the norm to become binding on the state. It is sufficient that the state acquiesces to the emerging norm. This dynamic is important to determining what kind of objection is needed for the state to exempt itself from a customary international legal norm. As with reservations,[39] persistent objections cannot be general or vague because, otherwise, it is not possible for other states to know which customary international legal obligations that the objector state has not undertaken and to which other states are not bound in their relations with the objector state.

An analysis of the Rule is essential to the concept and operation of customary international law because it defines which and when particular norms have become legally binding on a state through its consent. Although some academics have disputed the existence of the Persistent Objector Rule in positive law and practice,[40] both the International Court

[38] *See, e.g.*, Case T-171/99, Corus UK Ltd. v. Commission, ECR 2001, II-02967, ¶ 55 (recognizing prohibition of unjust enrichment as "general principle of [European] Community law"); Case C-259/87, Greece v Commission, ECR 1990, I – 2845 (same); Beyeler v. Italy, Appl. No. 33202/96, Eur. Ct. H.R. (Jan. 5, 2000) (recognizing unjust enrichment violated right to enjoyment of property in violation of *ECHR, Prot. No. 1*); Sea-Land Serv., Inc. v. Iran, 6 Iran-U.S. C.T.R. 149, 168 (1984 II) (unjust enrichment "is codified or judicially recognized in the great majority of the municipal legal systems of the world, and is widely accepted as having been assimilated into the catalogue of general principles of law available to be applied by international Tribunals.").

[39] *See* Belilos v. Switzerland, 132 Eur. Ct. H.R. (ser. A) § 60 (1988) (Swiss reservation found invalid because of general and vague language).

[40] *See, e.g.*, Anthony D'Amato, The Concept of Custom in International Law 201 (1971) (no example of state protest operating to prove illegality of protested act by other states)

of Justice in the *Asylum Case*[41] and the *Fisheries Case*,[42] and the Inter-American Commission on Human Rights in *Domingues v. United States*[43] have recognized the Rule. Furthermore, the U.S. Supreme Court in *The Antelope* appears to have recognized the Rule.[44] Indeed, Emmerich Vattel provided a statement of the Rule as early as 1758:

> When a custom or usage is generally established, either between all the civilized nations in the world, or only between those of a certain continent, as of Europe, for example, or between those who have a more frequent intercourse with each other; if that custom is in its own nature indifferent, and much more, if it be useful and reasonable, it becomes obligatory on all the nations in question, who are considered as having given their consent to it, and are bound to observe it towards each other, as long as they have not expressly declared their resolution of not observing it in future.[45]

[hereinafter, D'AMATO, CUSTOM]; Jonathan I. Charney, *Universal International Law*, 87 AM. J. INT'L. L. 529, 540 (1993) ("state practice and other evidence do not support the existence of the persistent objector rule").

[41] Asylum Case (Colombia v. Peru), 1950 I.C.J. 266, 272–78 (Nov. 20) (recognizing Peru's persistent objection to purported customary international legal norm governing asylum).

[42] Fisheries Case (U.K. v. Norway), 1951 I.C.J. 116, 131 (recognizing Norway's persistent objection to customary international legal norm governing territorial fishing zone).

[43] Report No. 62/02, Case 12.285, Inter-Am. Comm. H.R., at § 49 (2002) ("as customary international law rests on the consent of nations, a state that persistently objects to a norm of customary international law is not bound by that norm"); *see* Pinkerton and Roach v. United States, Inter-Am. Comm. H.R. No. 3/87, ANNUAL REPORT OF THE INTER-AMERICAN COMMISSION ON HUMAN RIGHTS: 1986–87, OEA/Ser.L/V/II.71/doc.9 147 (1987) (effectively recognizing United States' persistent objection to the emerging customary international legal norm prohibiting execution of persons committing capital crimes under the age of eighteen).

[44] *See* The Antelope, 23 U.S. 66, 121 (1825) (African slaves cannot avail themselves of European law of nations prohibition of slave trade given that African nations had not assented to prohibition).

Furthermore, the RESTATEMENT (THIRD) OF FOREIGN RELATIONS LAW OF THE UNITED STATES, ¶ 102 comment b (1987) [hereinafter RESTATEMENT], recognizes the Rule – albeit somewhat incongruently with its claim that the United States can void its customary international legal obligations at any time.

[45] VATTEL, LAW OF NATIONS, *supra* note 1, *Preliminaries*, § 26. Note that Vattel in this passage recognizes that there can be regional customary international law, such as a European customary international law. *See also* Asylum Case (Colombia v. Peru), 1950 I.C.J. at 276–77 (Nov. 20) (recognizing regional customary international law).

Emergence and Crystallization Rules

Exactly when does a norm emerge and crystallize into customary international law? This question is important to the Persistent Objector Rule because a state or intergovernmental organization can persistently object only before the norm crystallizes, and knowing exactly when the norm will crystallize enables the state or intergovernmental organization to know how long it has to object before it becomes bound by the norm. However, there appears to be no established global test in either law or literature for determining *exactly* when crystallization occurs for a couple of reasons. First, the requirement that a customary international legal norm reflect "general state practice" entails that evidence of crystallization must be reflected in the practices of a sufficient number of states, but *exactly* how many states observing the norm (as legally binding) are sufficient? Compounding this problem is that the law of nations has recognized the existence of customary international law norms that exist only on the regional level[46] and a region arguably could consist of only a handful of states. For example, the Benelux Economic Union consists only of three states (*viz.*, The Netherlands, Belgium, and Luxembourg)[47] out of a total of over 190 states worldwide. Accordingly, the general practice of a very few number of states could be sufficient for establishing their legal norms as regional customary international law, and even a regional customary international law constituted by the general practice of a handful of states can impose international legal obligations on extraregional states.[48] Therefore, evidence of general state practice

[46] *See, e.g., id.* (recognizing regional customary international law); The Antelope, 23 U.S. at 121 (recognizing European law of nations).

[47] Treaty Establishing the Benelux Economic Union, Feb. 3, 1958, art. 1, *available at* http://www.benelux.be (entered into force Nov. 1, 1960).

[48] *See* Legal Consequences for States of the Continued Presence of South Africa in Namibia (South West Africa) notwithstanding Security Council Resolution 276 (1970), Advisory Opinion, 1971 I.C.J. 16, 31 (1971) ("an international instrument has to be interpreted and applied within the framework of the entire [international] legal system prevailing at the time of the interpretation"); Interpretation of the American Declaration of the Rights and Duties of Man within the Framework of Article 64 of the American Convention on Human Rights, Advisory Opinion OC-10/89, Inter-Am. Ct. H.R. Ser. A, No. 10, at ¶ 37 (1989) (same); Coard v. United States, Inter-Am. Cm.H.R., No. 109/99 at ¶ 40 (1999), *available at* http://www.cidh.oas.org/annualrep/99eng/Merits/UnitedStates10.951.htm (last visited Feb. 15, 2003) (same); Geofroy v. Riggs, 133 U.S. at 271 (meaning of treaty language "to be taken in their ordinary meaning, as understood in the public law of nations"); *cf. Vienna*

often does not offer much analytical help in establishing a norm's customary international legal status. Although one could argue that the generality problem can be solved by limiting the pool of states from which the requisite generality of state practice can be established, to those states that have participated, could participate, or merely possess a special interest in the activity governed by the norm, this approach not only arguably violates the principle of state coequality,[49] it still does not provide a means of establishing a specific number of states whose practices reflect a sufficient generality. This approach only works if the practices of *all* such states are consistent with the norm, but then the complete uniformity of such state practices would moot the relevance of the Persistent Objector Rule because no state has persistently objected.[50]

Second, another crystallization problem is that the general state practice requirement suggests that state acts must be overt, but some customary international legal norms prohibit practices; therefore, general state practice also must include non-performance, and a state often is silent as to whether it considers its non-performance as having *opinio juris*. Accordingly, the ICJ in *Military and Paramilitary Activities in and against Nicaragua (Nicar. v. U.S.)* – a case concerning a norm requiring nonperformance of overt acts – has noted that evidence of *opinio juris* should be emphasized over evidence of general state practice.[51]

Convention, art. 31 (3)(c) (treaty must be interpreted in light of "any rules of international law applicable in the relations between the parties"); *Vienna Convention-SIO*, art. 31 (3)(c) (treaty between intergovernmental organization and state must be interpreted in light of "any relevant rules of international law applicable in the relations between the parties").

[49] *See, e.g., UN Charter*, art. 2 (1) (recognizing sovereign coequality of states); VATTEL, THE LAW OF NATIONS, *supra* note 1, *Preliminaries*, at § 18 ("small republic is no less a sovereign state than the most powerful kingdom").

[50] The ICJ has not helped matters much. In the *Asylum Case*, the ICJ required each state's practice to be "constant and uniform." Asylum Case (Colombia v. Peru), 1950 I.C.J. at 277 (Nov. 20). Such a requirement makes a state's arguable violation of its customary international legal obligations impossible.

[51] *See* Military and Paramilitary Activities in and against Nicaragua (Nicar. v. U.S.), Merits, 1986 I.C.J. 4, 106–110, ¶¶ 202–209 (June 27) (deemphasizing evidence of general state practice and emphasizing evidence of *opinio juris* for establishing customary international legal status of norm prohibiting state intervention in another state's affairs).

This subsection will provide a set of rules based on an analytical framework that does *not* begin with establishing the generality of state practice (and *opinio juris*) and ends with establishing whether or not there has been a specific instance of persistent objection. Rather, this subsection will approach the subject from examining specific, bilateral interstate relations. Although under this analytical framework a norm may crystallize at different times for different states, there appears to be no legal reason why such a norm cannot do so. After all, a regional norm may crystallize earlier than a global norm, and this time differential has not served as a barrier to the recognition of the regional norm's customary international legal status. Indeed, the ICJ in the *Case Concerning Rights of Passage Over Indian Territory* already has recognized that only two states can make customary international law and that this special customary international law trumps general customary international law and general principles of law recognized by civilized nations, because specific rules prevail over general rules.[52]

Furthermore, this subsection will approach the issue by bifurcating customary international legal norms into ones that prescribe performance of overt acts and ones that prohibit performance of overt acts. This set of rules is as follows:

(i) *Prescribed Acts Rule*: When a state performs an overt act, the overt act begins to emerge as potential customary international law for the state at the moment the state performs the act. The performance of the act represents the emergence of a potential customary international law for another state at the moment it becomes aware of the other state performing the act. When both states perform the same overt acts that produce mutual benefits, their performances represent the crystallization of a customary international legal rule if neither state makes a persistent objection within a timely period. The rule crystallizes at the moment when this timely period is exhausted *per* the Objection Deadline Rules that are set out later.

(ii) *Prohibited Acts Rule*: When a state refrains from performing an overt act, the nonperformance of the overt act begins to emerge as potential customary international law for the state at the moment the state refrains

[52] Case Concerning Rights of Passage Over Indian Territory (Merits), 1960 I.C.J. 39–44 (Apr. 13).

> from performing the act. The nonperformance of the act represents the emergence of a potential customary international law for another state at the moment it becomes aware of the other state's nonperformance. When both states refrain from performing the same overt acts that produce mutual benefits, their nonperformances represent the crystallization of a customary international legal rule if neither state makes a persistent objection within a timely period. The rule crystallizes at the moment when this timely period is exhausted *per* the Objection Deadline Rules that are set out later.

When states practice a custom that produces mutual benefits, this custom acquires *opinio juris* by virtue of their respective recognitions of the Unjust Enrichment Prohibition Principle. The Unjust Enrichment Prohibition Principle provides the requisite *opinio juris* to the state practices forming the custom. The Unjust Enrichment Prohibition Principle also makes it reasonable for a state to expect that if it engages in the practice that produces a benefit for another state, the other state also must engage in the practice to the original state's benefit. Most importantly, the application of the international legal principle of *restitutio in integrum* ensures that the other state must engage in the specific practice (not merely compensate the benefactor state for its loss) because the benefited state must engage in the practice to ensure that benefactor state is returned to its *status quo ante*. Consider the following hypothetical case. States A and B have exclusively public educational systems and no available private tutors. States A and B have been providing free education to each other's nationals, thereby ensuring their nationals are literate. If State A were to stop providing free education to State B's nationals resulting in their illiteracy but continues to take advantage of State B's free educational program, State A would owe State B full restitution that could only take the form of resuming the free educational program for State B's nationals to ensure their literacy.

It also must be noted that a benefit may accrue not only to the state *per se* but also to its nationals/citizens, and the state will acquire the customary international legal obligation through the benefit given to its national/citizen. Customary international legal norms often protect only individuals acting in their non–state-actor capacities – not states (*i.e.*, governments) themselves. For example, the *Universal Declaration of Human Rights*, which is considered to codify customary international law,[53] guarantees individuals the right to marry.[54] Most importantly, this right "is entitled to protection by . . . the State."[55] States *per se* have no right to marry; they only have duties to guarantee observation of the right. Therefore, a state, whose nationals/citizens enjoy the benefit of the customary international legal right to marry from another state, also receives the benefit and also must observe the same customary international legal right in regard to the other state's nationals/citizens. Consistent with this conclusion, the *Universal Declaration of Human Rights* also guarantees the right to marry "without any limitation due to . . . nationality."[56]

53 *See, e.g.*, Advisory Opinion on the Continued Presence of South Africa in Namibia (S.W. Africa), 1971 I.C.J. 16, 76 (1971) (separate opinion by Vice President Ammoun) (*Universal Declaration of Human Rights* (*UDHR*) reflects customary international law); Filártiga v. Peña-Irala, 630 F.2d 876, 882 (2d Cir. 1980) (*UDHR* reflects customary international law); Richard Bilder, *The Status of International Human Rights Law: An Overview*, 1978 INT'L & PRACTICE 1, 8 (same).

54 *UDHR*, art. 16 (1).

55 *Id.* at art. 16 (3).

56 *UDHR*, art. 16(1).

This raises a question. What if a state were to stop complying with its customary international legal obligation toward its own nationals/citizens but continues to comply with its obligation toward another state's nationals/citizens? In such a case, the benefit enrichment basis on which the obligation acquired customary international legal status for the state drops away in regard to the state's own nationals/citizens. It is perhaps somewhat strange that a state should choose to discriminate against its own nationals/citizens, but states sometimes have done so. Nevertheless, the manner in which an international legal norm comes into being does not undercut the legal obligation of the norm. *See, e.g.*, ILC Draft Articles, *supra* note 25, at art. 12 ("There is a breach of an international obligation by a State when an act of that State is not in conformity with what is required of it by that obligation, *regardless of its origin or character*." [emphasis provided]). "In the international law field, there is no distinction between contractual and tortious responsibility." *The Rainbow Warrior* (New Zealand v. France), 20 UNRIAA 217, 251 (1990). The mutual observation of a rule by states is not a necessary *defining* condition for establishing the rule's customary international legal status. Mutual state observation is only an *aetiological* explanation of the rule acquiring customary international legal status.

Only other states can refrain from observing their customary international legal obligations in such a case and only as a countermeasure to induce the state to recommence its compliance with its customary international legal obligation. *See* ILC Draft Articles, *supra* note 25 at art. 22 ("The wrongfulness of an act of a State not in conformity with an international obligation towards another state is precluded if and to the extent that the act constitutes a countermeasure taken against the latter State in accordance with chapter II of part three [governing countermeasures].") Even in such a case, such a countermeasure cannot violate the customary international legal norm if it is human rights related. *Ibid.* at art. 50 (1) ("Countermeasures shall not affect: (a) The Obligation to

Generally speaking, for purposes of establishing customary international law, it is easier to establish evidence of a state not performing an overt act than evidence of a state performing an overt act because it is highly likely that the state (or one of its officials) at some time is not performing the act, whereas state performance of an overt act often requires the state to commit resources and it may be reluctant to do so. Therefore, in cases involving state nonperformance practices, the custom already has begun to emerge. This explains the ICJ's emphasis on evidence of *opinio juris* rather than state practice in cases where the rule prohibits performance of an overt act, such as aggression. In the *Case Involving Military and Paramilitary Activities in and against Nicaragua*, the ICJ deemphasized evidence of general state practice and emphasized evidence of *opinio juris* for establishing customary international legal status of norm prohibiting state intervention in another state's affairs.[57] Although many states had committed acts of aggression suggesting that a rule prohibiting such aggression did not have the status of customary international law, these states had recognized the rule as having *opinio juris* by virtue of, *inter alia*, their ratification/accession to the *UN Charter* and, specifically, its prohibition of aggression.[58] Unless a state had been continuously committing acts of aggression since the aggression prohibition norm had emerged, the norm already had crystallized as customary international law for the state. It is doubtful that any state – including the United States – had continuously committed such acts. Therefore, there was a customary international legal norm binding on the United States prohibiting it from committing acts of aggression against Nicaragua.

By contrast, mere acceptance of a rule prescribing performance of an overt act is insufficient for establishing a customary international legal norm. When a state has not performed an overt act required by a rule to

refrain from the threat or use of force as embodied in the Charter of the United Nations; (b) Obligations for the protection of fundamental human rights; Obligations of a humanitarian character prohibiting reprisals; (c) Other obligations under peremptory norms of general international law.").

57 Case Involving Military and Paramilitary Activities in and against Nicaragua (Nicar. v. U.S.), Merits, 1986 I.C.J. 4, 106–110, ¶¶ 202–209 (June 27).

58 *See UN Charter*, art. 2 (4) ("All Members shall refrain in their international relations from the threat or use of force against the territorial integrity or political independence of any state . . . .").

which it has consented, the rule does not bind the state as a matter of customary international law because there is no state practice to which the *opinio juris* could adhere. For example, a state that merely has signed – not ratified – a treaty with another state is only under an international legal obligation to refrain from the commission of overt acts that "would defeat the object and purpose" of the treaty.[59]

If a benefited state chooses to object to the emerging customary international legal norm, such objection must be timely in order that the benefactor state – that otherwise would be acting in reasonable reliance on the benefited state's failure to make a timely objection – does not have to continue to provide a benefit to the benefited state. However, if the benefited state fails to immediately object on learning that it has received a benefit, the following Objection Deadline Rules apply:

> (iii) (a) Starting from the moment of the rule's emergence, the other state has that amount of time equal to the amount of time set by its domestic law to make an objection to the emerging norm and/or to the practice's characterization as a benefit.

It is proper to apply the benefited state's own domestic because it is the benefited state's exclusive prerogative to consent or object to the rule having *opinio juris*. Although the domestic laws of different states may impose different deadlines whose applications arguably may violate the international legal principles of equality of arms or state coequality, these principles are irrelevant because it is the benefited state's prerogative to object – not the benefactor state's. The use of the potential objector's own law represents a self-imposed deadline for the potential objector that it must meet in all cases involving customary international law or related claims.

In many cases, the other state will have that amount of time equal to the amount set by its domestic procedural law in responding to a case filed with its domestic tribunal with compulsory jurisdiction over claims against the state that can be characterized as customary international law violations (notwithstanding whether in fact a case has been filed with such a tribunal or the tribunal does not have jurisdiction over customary international law claims *per se*). A state first must be

[59] *Vienna Convention*, art. 18.

given an opportunity to exhaust its own domestic remedies before a complaint can be submitted to an international tribunal; therefore, it would be improper to look first to the procedural law of an international tribunal.[60]

In cases in which the United States has received a benefit from a foreign state, U.S. federal procedural law would apply.[61] For example, the Alien Tort Statute vests jurisdiction over torts committed in violation of the law of nations (which includes customary international law) in the U.S. district courts.[62] The *U.S. Federal Rules of Civil Procedure* [FRCP] generally require U.S. officials to answer a civil complaint (including a ATS complaints) within sixty days.[63] Therefore, under this Objection Deadline Rule, the United States must make a persistent objection within sixty days of becoming aware of receiving the benefit.

In cases in which an intergovernmental organization has received a benefit from a foreign state (or another intergovernmental organization), the intergovernmental organization's constituent treaty's procedural law would apply. For example, the *EU Treaty* establishes a two-month deadline for EU organs to respond to an alleged violation of the *EU Treaty*.[64] Therefore, if the EU wished to make an objection to an emerging customary international legal norm, it would have two months to do so after becoming aware of receiving a benefit from a state's observance of the norm.

[60] *See, e.g.*, *ICCPR*, art. 5 (2) (b) (UN Human Rights Committee shall not consider communications from individuals who have not exhausted domestic remedies).

[61] Recall that Article 2 of the *Montevideo Convention* establishes that a "federal state shall constitute a sole person in the eyes of international law." Therefore, the United States would be treated as a sole person in such a case.

[62] 28 U.S.C. § 1350.

[63] FRCP 12 (a) (3) (A).

[64] *See EU Treaty*, art. 232:

> Should the European Parliament, the Council or the Commission, in infringement of this Treaty, fail to act, the Member States and the other institutions of the Community may bring an action before the Court of Justice to have the infringement established. The action shall be admissible only if the institution concerned has first been called upon to act. If, within two months of being so called upon, the institution concerned has not defined its position, the action may be brought within a further period of two months. Any natural or legal person may, under the conditions laid down in the preceding paragraphs, complain to the Court of Justice that an institution of the Community has failed to address to that person any act other than a recommendation or an opinion.

However, some domestic courts may not have compulsory jurisdiction over customary international legal claims *per se*. For example, the U.S. Supreme Court in dicta has suggested that federal question jurisdiction under 28 U.S.C. § 1331[65] might not be available for customary international law claims.[66] Therefore, U.S. district courts that otherwise would have jurisdiction over customary international law claims if submitted by alien plaintiffs under the Alien Tort Statute, do not have jurisdiction over such claims when submitted by U.S. nationals. However, 28 U.S.C. § 1331 vests jurisdiction in U.S. district courts for all civil actions arising under federal statutory law, and the *Charming Betsy* Rule requires such law to be construed in conformity with the United States' customary international legal obligations. Therefore, parties still could use the FRCP governing such civil suits for determining when a customary international legal norm crystallizes. Again, the FRCP generally require U.S. officials to answer a civil complaint (including other federal question complaints) within sixty days.[67] Therefore, under this Objection Deadline Rule, the United States must make a persistent objection within sixty days of becoming aware of receiving the benefit.

A sixty-day deadline may appear to be very short given how long it usually takes the bureaucratic processes of government to operate. However, a state can temporarily express its objection upon notification of receiving a benefit. The state always can withdraw its objection at a later time after it has sufficient time to consider the matter. The cost of an arguably short deadline time period to a state must be balanced against the expense another state incurs when it provides a benefit to the state in order to ensure state coequality and reciprocity.

However, if there is no domestic law setting a deadline, then the following Objection Deadline Rule applies:

> (iii) (b) In the case that there is no such domestic law, the benefited state has that amount of time equal to the amount set by international law in responding to a case filed with an international tribunal with compulsory jurisdiction over claims against the state that can be char-

[65] 28 U.S.C. § 1331 states: "The district courts shall have original jurisdiction of all civil actions arising under the Constitution, laws, or treaties of the United States."

[66] *See, e.g.*, Sosa v. Alvarez-Machain, – U.S. – n.19, 124 S.Ct. 2739, 159 L. Ed. 2d 718 (2004).

[67] FRCP 12 (a) (3) (A).

acterized as customary international law violations (notwithstanding whether in fact a case has been filed with such a tribunal or the tribunal has jurisdiction over customary international law claims *per se*) to make an objection to the emerging norm and/or to the practice's characterization as a benefit.

If the benefited state has no applicable domestic law, then it still must accept the applicability of the international procedural law because the state still must comply with the international procedural law of an international tribunal whose compulsory jurisdiction it already recognizes. Also, in many cases (such as human rights cases), international law guarantees a right to an effective domestic judicial remedy[68] and the benefited

[68] International human rights law guarantees that individuals have a remedy enforceable in domestic courts. For example, the *ICCPR* states:

> 2. Where not already provided for by existing legislative or other measures, each State Party to the present Covenant undertakes to take the necessary steps, in accordance with its constitutional processes and with the provisions of the present Covenant, to adopt such legislative or other measures as may be necessary to give effect to the rights recognized in the present Covenant.
> 3. Each State Party to the present Covenant undertakes:
>   a. To ensure that any person whose rights or freedoms as herein recognized are violated shall have an effective remedy, notwithstanding that the violation has been committed by persons acting in an official capacity;
>   b. To ensure that any person claiming such a remedy shall have his right thereto determined by competent judicial, administrative or legislative authorities, or by any other competent authority provided for by the legal system of the State, and to develop the possibilities of judicial remedy;
>   c. To ensure that the competent authorities shall enforce such remedies when granted.

ICCPR, art. 2 (2)-(3); *see* UN Hum. Rts. Ctte., General Comment No. 24 (52), General comment on issues relating to reservations made upon ratification or accession to the Covenant or the Optional Protocols thereto, or in relation to declarations under article 41 of the Covenant, §§ 3 and 12, U.N. Doc. CCPR/C/21/Rev.1/Add.6 (1994) (state-party cannot make reservation denying remedy – including judicial remedy – for human rights violations); *see also ACHR*, art. 25 (right to judicial protection). Although generally speaking, international law often allows states to exercise a certain amount of discretion in fashioning how they provide a domestic remedy for international legal violations, international human rights tribunals have strictly limited this deference and have required a *judicial* remedy because other remedies (such as those provided by the political branches) are most often ineffective and/or inadequate and a judicial remedy is the only remedy that can provide complete restitution. *See, e.g.*, Anguelova v. Bulgaria, Application No. 38361/97, Eur. Ct. H.R. at § 161 (2002) (states allowed "some discretion" as to how they provide remedy to individuals for international law violations); M. J. Bossuyt, Guide to the "Travaux Préparatoires" of the International Covenant on Civil and Political Rights 67 (1987); Darmburg v. Suriname, Case No. 10.117, Res. No.

state still is legally accountable at the international law level for providing a remedy notwithstanding that its domestic law does not provide a judicial remedy for violations of customary international law or related claims.[69]

For example, the *Statute of the [European] Court of Justice* establishes a two-month deadline for a states-party to the *EU Treaty* to respond to a preliminary ruling by the ECJ in a case regarding an interpretation of the *EU Treaty* requested by the court of the state-party to the *EU Treaty*.[70] Therefore, if an EU member wished to express an objection to an emerging customary international legal norm, it must do so within two months of becoming aware of receiving a benefit from another state's observance of the norm.

19/89, Inter-Am. Cm. H.R. 138, OEA/ser.L/V.II.76, doc. 10 (1988–89); Tumilovich v. Russia, Application No. 47033, Eur. Ct. H.R. (1999) (domestic remedy depending on discretionary powers do not constitute effective domestic remedy).

Other areas of international law also guarantee the right to a domestic remedy. *See, e.g.*, China-Argentina Agreement on Promotion and Reciprocal Protection of Investments, May 11, 1992, art. 8, *available at* http://www.unctad.org/sections/dite/iia/docs/bits/argentina_china.pdf ("(1) Any dispute which arises within the terms of this Agreement concerning an investor between an investor of one Contracting Party and the other Contracting Party shall . . . be settled amicably . . . (2) If the dispute cannot be settled through negotiations within six month . . . either party to the dispute shall be entitled to submit the dispute either to the competent court of the Contracting Party accepting the investment or to international arbitration according to the following conditions."); International Convention on Civil Liability for Bunker Oil Pollution Damage, Mar. 23, 2001, art. 9, *available at* http://www.official-documents.co.uk/ document/cm66/6693/6693.pdf ("1. Where an incident has caused pollution damage in the territory, including the territorial sea, or in an area referred to in article 2(a)(ii) of one or more States Parties, or preventive measures have been taken to prevent or minimise pollution damage in such territory, including the territorial sea, or in such area, actions for compensation against the shipowner, insurer or other person providing security for the shipowner's liability may be brought only in the courts of any such States Parties. 2. Reasonable notice of any action taken under paragraph 1 shall be given to each defendant. 3. Each State Party shall ensure that its courts have jurisdiction to entertain actions for compensation under this Convention.").

[69] *See, e.g.*, *Vienna Convention*, art. 27 ("A party may not invoke the provisions of its internal law as justification for its failure to perform a treaty."); *cf.* ILC Draft Articles, art. 3 ("The characterization of an act of a State as internationally wrongful is governed by international law. Such characterization is not affected by the characterization of the same act as lawful by internal law.").

[70] Statute of the Court of Justice, art. 23, *available at* http://curia.europa.eu/en/instit/txtdocfr/index.htm (Nov. 2005).

Sometimes there is no international tribunal procedural law setting clear deadlines for state responses. For example, the ICJ leaves it to the discretion of the President of the Court to set countermemorial deadlines for state-respondents.[71] Furthermore, an international tribunal may not have competence to adjudicate customary international law claims *per se* because it only has jurisdiction over violations of a treaty that has vested the tribunal with its jurisdiction. However, treaty norms often must be construed in conformity with the states-parties' customary international legal obligations. Therefore, it often becomes a moot issue whether the claims are customary international law claims *per se* because the tribunal still must apply this customary international law in adjudicating the treaty claims over which it exercises compulsory jurisdiction.

On the other hand, the treaty vesting compulsory jurisdiction in the tribunal may not have provisions that need construction with customary international law or that have applicable customary international legal norms. For example, a treaty provision may be very clear, thereby not needing any construction. Also, a treaty provision may not have any analogous customary international legal norms that can be applied in the construction of the provision.[72] Therefore, as we shall see, Rule No. (iii) (c) (*infra*) would apply in such cases.

Exactly how much time a benefited state has on receiving notice of the benefit will turn on the kind of benefit. For example, in human rights cases, the appropriate international tribunal procedural law to use is that governing international human rights tribunals whose compulsory jurisdiction the benefited state recognizes. In the case of the United States, the *ICCPR* gives states-parties three months to respond to a complaint made by another state-party that also recognizes the UN Human Rights Committee's competence to examine interstate complaints.[73] Therefore,

[71] *I.C.J. Statute*, art. 44 (1).

[72] If there is more than one international tribunal with compulsory jurisdiction, then the international tribunal procedural law governing the response deadline is that which provides the shortest time because the international procedural law still governs the arguably benefited state.

[73] *ICCPR*, art. 41 (1) (a). The United States recognizes the competence of the UN Human Rights Committee to examine interstate complaints against it. U.S. Reservations, Declarations, and Understandings to the International Covenant on Civil and Political Rights,

the United States must make san objection within three months after becoming aware of the benefit. For other kinds of benefits, the governing procedural law is that of the international tribunal having compulsory jurisdiction over the kind of benefit.[74]

If there is no international law or benefited state law, then it is proper to use the domestic law of the other state's tribunal if the benefited state recognizes the compulsory jurisdiction of that state's tribunal.[75]

> (iii) (c) In the case that there is no such domestic or international procedural law, the benefited state has that amount of time equal to the amount set by the domestic law of another state in responding to a case filed with that state's domestic tribunal with compulsory jurisdiction over claims against the state that can be characterized as customary international law violations (notwithstanding whether in fact a case has been filed with such a tribunal or the tribunal has jurisdiction over customary international law claims *per se*) to make an objection to the emerging norm and/or to the practice's characterization as a benefit. The benefited state must recognize the compulsory jurisdiction of the other state's domestic tribunal.

In some cases, neither the law of the benefited state or of an international tribunal is available. In such a case, the domestic tribunal procedural law of another state can be used if the benefited state recognizes the compulsory jurisdiction of the other state's tribunal.[76] For

at § III (3), 138 Cong. Rec. S4783–4 (daily ed., April 2, 1992). This three-month deadline rule also comports with the *Rules of Procedure of Inter-American Commission on Human Rights* that require the United States as an OAS member state to respond to a complaint alleging a violation of the *American Declaration of the Rights and Duties of Man* within two months (or no more than three months for good cause). Rules of Procedure of the Inter-Am. Comm. H.R., art. 30 (3) (2003). Although the Inter-American Court of Human Rights requires that states respond within four months, respondent states already have been given notice by the Inter-American Commission on Human Rights when the Commission refers the complaint to the Court. *See* Rules of Procedure of the Inter-Am. Ct. H.R., art. 38 (1) (Nov. 25, 2003) (state has four months to respond).

[74] *See, e.g.*, Rules of the Tribunal, ITLOS, art. 59 (1), U. N.Doc. ITLOS/8, 27 Apr. 2005 (no more than six months).

[75] *Cf.* ILC Draft Articles, art. 52 (3) (b) ("Countermeasures may not be taken . . . if . . . [t]he dispute is pending before a court or tribunal which has authority to make decisions binding on the parties").

[76] Although the domestic laws of different states may have different deadlines that can encourage forum shopping, there appears to be no legal reason preventing such forum shopping subject to the state's own domestic law governing forum shopping.

example, the United States' Foreign Sovereign Immunities Act sets a sixty-day deadline for foreign states (or their agents) to answer a complaint.[77] Therefore, under this Objection Deadline Rule, the benefited state must make a persistent objection within sixty days of becoming aware of receiving the benefit.[78] However, the foreign state must recognize the jurisdiction of the U.S. federal courts. It is not necessary that the foreign state recognizes the jurisdiction of the U.S. federal courts over the state itself as a party. It is sufficient if the state recognizes the jurisdiction of the federal courts over one of its nationals as a party. Such recognition already is available under international law: "[E]very State possesses exclusive jurisdiction and sovereignty over persons and property within its jurisdiction."[79] However, in such cases, the U.S. federal courts must allow the foreign state to introduce evidence of its persistent objection.

However, in the context of nonfederal, American customary international law, a state of the United States cannot avail itself of the Objection Deadline Rules if it continues to provide the benefit to its own citizens while denying the benefit to citizens of other states because the Privileges and Immunities Clause guarantees that "[t]he Citizens of each State shall be entitled to all Privileges and Immunities of Citizens in the several States."[80] However, the Privileges and Immunities Clause does not require a state to observe rights possessed by citizens of another state by

[77] 28 U.S.C. § 1698 (d) ("In any action brought in a court of the United States or of a State, a foreign state, a political subdivision thereof, or an agency or instrumentality of a foreign state shall serve an answer or other responsive pleading to the complaint within sixty days after service has been made under this section."). However, U.S. courts sometimes still cannot exercise jurisdiction over a foreign state because of foreign state immunity. *See id.* at § 1605 (a) (5) (immunity recognized for claims based on discretionary acts, and claims arising out of malicious prosecution, abuse of process, libel, slander, misrepresentation, deceit, and interference with contract rights).

[78] Although the fact that U.S. federal courts are international courts with ATS jurisdiction over customary international law claims suggests that their procedural law must be used before turning to a benefactor state's law, the U.S. Supreme Court has suggested that foreign domestic legal remedies may have to be exhausted in ATS cases before coming into U.S. courts. Sosa v. Alvarez-Machain, 542 U.S. 692, n. 21 (2004).

[79] Pennoyer v. Neff, 95 U.S. 714, 722 (1877).

[80] U.S. Const. art. IV, § 2, cl. 1; *see* Paul v. Virginia, 75 U.S. (8 Wall.) 168 (1869) (state cannot discriminate against citizen of another state if it provides benefit to own citizens).

virtue of his/her state citizenship.[81] Nevertheless, the benefited state still would be subject to the Objection Deadline Rules.

These Objection Deadline Rules serve the interests of both the benefactor state and the benefited state, as well as the interests of tribunals. The Rules provide the benefited state a means of knowing how long it has to object without incurring legal liability as well as provide the benefactor state a means of knowing how long it could incur an expense by complying with the customary international legal rule. The Rules also serve to save a tribunal's time and resources by giving a bright-line crystallization test to states, thereby discouraging their submission of contentious cases.

Finally, a note about customary international law binding more than two states. Although this subsection has examined customary international law in terms of bilateral state relationships, the conclusions drawn from such an examination also apply to customary international law binding more than two states. To determine whether a rule has emerged and crystallized for another state(s), one need only apply the aforementioned rules in regard to the other state(s). Whether the rule has emerged and crystallized for a greater number of states will depend on a case-by-case analysis using these rules. Although this task may at first glance appear to pose tremendous research challenges, two modern developments make this task less onerous. First, state recognition of a rule having *opinio juris* and sufficient specificity now can be more easily established by virtue of the rule's codification in widely adopted multilateral treaties that increasingly have populated the international law arena. One need not try to delve into peculiar and/or obscure domestic legal sources that often are difficult to access or to understand in order to determine whether a rule has acquired *opinio juris* for a state. One need only see if the rule is guaranteed by a widely adopted multilateral treaty to establish whether the rule has *opinio juris*.

Second, modern international migration has resulted in the large presence of numerous nationalities in almost all states globally (especially the United States), and these states often provide benefits to and receive benefits from other states through the media of their nationals/citizens.

[81] City of Detroit v. Osborne, 135 U.S. 492 (1890).

Therefore, state accrual of foreign state benefits is widely and often present, and these states incur international legal liabilities through the Unjust Enrichment Prohibition Principle and sometimes in combination with the Objection Deadline Rules. Therefore, one need only establish that all states (or any of their officials) have ever complied with the rule during its emergence to establish state practice sufficient for describing it as global customary international law. Making such a determination is made all the easier when the rule prohibits the commission of an overt act because it is highly likely that some state official in all states have not committed the overt act.

Let us now turn to the next source of international law: general principles recognized by civilized nations.

3.3. GENERAL PRINCIPLES OF LAW RECOGNIZED BY CIVILIZED NATIONS

If there is no customary international law to apply directly or to use in the construction of a treaty norm, the international tribunal often turns to general principles of law that are recognized by civilized peoples. Although many of these principles also reflect customary international law because they reflect practices among states, it is important to note that this source of law is not state-centered, as the previous two sources of law (*viz.*, treaties and international legal custom) are. These general principles are those recognized by "nations," that is, "peoples." Such general principles of law are those "*recognized* by the peoples of the world, without necessarily being recognized or enacted into law by states"[82] – although most of these principles originate in national legislation. There may be a people whose government has not been recognized by other states (*e.g.*, a provisional revolutionary government) or who are incapable of entering into relations with other states (*e.g.*, a geographically isolated people).[83] Also, many such general principles of law are

[82] Stephen Hall, *The Persistent Spectre: Natural Law, International Order and the Limits of Legal Positivism*, 12 E.J.I.L 269, 293 (2001).

[83] *See* Montevideo Convention on Rights and Duties of States, Dec. 26, 1933, art. 1, 49 Stat. 3097, T.S. 881, 3 Bevans 145 (entered into force Dec. 26, 1934) ("capacity to enter into relations with the other states" required for statehood).

located in the *lex mercatoria* that emerged from private, international, commercial transactions. Such transactions were conducted by nonstate actors in the shadow of customary expectations, many of which have not been codified into domestic statutes but have been enforced by courts as general principles of law. Absent such general principles of law, these nations would have no other international legal obligations governing them. It also is important to note that unlike customary international law, general principles need be only "recognized" by civilized nations. Such nations need not observe these general principles *all* the time or even *some* of the time. Such principles sound in natural law, and Judge Schwebel has noted that general principles were included in Article 38 of the Statute of the Permanent Court of Justice by its drafters as a source of law to avoid "especially the blind alley of *non liquet*."[84]

Related to the recognition issue is whether *all* or merely *some* nations must recognize the principle to be a general principle of law recognized by civilized nations. Clearly the recognition of all nations is not required because some nations may be disabled from recognizing principles of law. For example, one can imagine a small group of people whose daily interactions are completely controlled by an absolute monarch. The group also is internationally isolated, thereby mooting the issue of whether the absolute monarch can enter into relations with other states. In this scenario, there is no rule of law – just the rule of one person exercising his/her personal predilections. This nation could not recognize general principles of law. Insofar as some national observance of the rule of law is a necessary condition for establishing the nation's civilized status because the absence of rule of law – anarchy – would make civilization impossible, the civilization requirement for general principles of law is reasonable. Although the civilization requirement initially will strike many as anachronistic or even racist, it is not inconceivable that there are or have been "uncivilized" peoples insofar as they have been disabled from recognizing general principles of law. Therefore, not all nations must recognize a general principle of law for it to have the status as a general principle of law recognized by civilized nations – only civilized nations.

[84] Advisory Opinion on the Legality of the Threat or Use of Nuclear Weapons, 1996 I.C.J. 311, 323 (1996) (Schwebel, J., dissenting) (quoting President of the Advisory Committee of Jurists).

Must *all* civilized nations recognize such general principles? Is it necessary to undertake a comprehensive survey of national laws in order to discern whether a particular principle has been universally recognized? Article 38 of the *I.C.J. Statute* is not clear (as it also is not clear under Article 38 how "general" a state practice must be to constitute customary international law) – it only says that the general principle must be "recognized by civilized nations." Because such general principles of law sound in natural law and natural law is universally obligatory, then it appears that such principles must be recognized by all civilized nations. Supporting this conclusion is that norms *erga omnes* and *jus cogens* norms legally bind all nations, and these norms represent such general principles of law. Most importantly, the ICJ still can apply such general principles in adjudicating cases in the absence of conventional or customary international legal obligation that do not necessarily bind all nations. If such general principles were not recognized by all civilized nations, then the ICJ could not apply such principles because the ICJ cannot impose its own notion of what is legally obligatory (unless the states-parties have agreed to allow the Court to decide the case *ex aequo et bono* under Article 38 (2)).[85] If a nation in fact does violates a general principle which also happens to represent a conventional or customary international legal obligation, other nations still must observe the principle as a matter of international law obligation towards all persons everywhere that nations otherwise lawfully could stop observing if the principle only reflected a conventional or customary international legal obligation.[86] General principles of law recognized by civilized nations are transnational legal norms that often serve to protect nations and their members from harms perpetrated by states or powerful non-state actors, as in the case of *jus cogens* norms whose violations often are identified as gross human rights violations and international crimes (*e.g.*, genocide, war crimes, crimes against

[85] *I.C.J. Statute*, art. 38 (2) ("This provision shall not prejudice the power of the Court to decide a case *ex aequo et bono*, if the parties agree thereto.").

[86] *Vienna Convention*, art. 60 (material breach of treaty by one party entitles the other party to suspend or terminate treaty).

humanity) and are not subject to reprisals[87] or the defense of *tu quoque*.[88] Because of their importance to the international community as a whole, such general principles of law are presumed by international law to be recognized by all civilized nations effectively making them norms *erga omnes*.[89] Therefore, for a norm to be such a general principle, it must be recognized or presumed to be recognized by all civilized nations – even if one or more nations have failed to comply with the principle.

However, practically speaking, the extrapolation of general principles from national laws most often will necessarily require interpretation given the enormous diversity of national laws and legal cultures in which these laws are embedded – unless all civilized nations have recognized the general principle in a multilateral treaty that they have signed and/or ratified. In the absence of such a universally adopted treaty, general principles must be extrapolated from the laws of civilized nations by means of interpretation. In the next subsection, we examine a source of international law that is designed to providing such interpretation: "judicial decisions and the teachings of the most highly qualified publicists of the various nations."

3.4. SUBSIDIARY INTERPRETIVE SOURCES

The fourth source of international legal authority that the ICJ can apply is that comprised of "judicial decisions and the teachings of the most highly qualified publicists of the various nations."[90] The Court can use judicial decisions and the teachings of international legal experts of the various nations as a subsidiary means for interpreting all of the earlier-mentioned

[87] *See, e.g.*, Geneva Convention Relative to the Protection of Civilian Persons in Time of War, Aug. 12, 1949, art. 33, 75 U.N.T.S. 287, 6 U.S.T. 3516, T.I.A.S. No. 3365 (entered into force Oct. 21, 1950) (prohibiting reprisals against protected persons and property) [hereinafter *Fourth Geneva Convention*].

[88] Matter of Von Leeb and Others (*German High Command Trial*), 15 I.L.R. 376 (1949), 11 Trials of War Criminals (1950) (prohibiting *tu quoque* defense).

[89] *See* Case Concerning Barcelona Traction, Light and Power, Ltd. (Belgium v. Spain), (1970) I.C.J. 3 at ¶ 33 (norms *erga omnes*).

[90] As in the case of the "general principles of law recognized by nations," "judicial decisions and the teachings of the most highly qualified publicists of the various nations" are not necessarily state-centered in that some judges may sit on international courts and some publicists may not be state actors.

positive rules of international law. Much of the law of nations has developed through a process of interpretation by judges (both international and national) and international legal experts.[91] Most importantly, judicial decisions can provide greater definition to vague treaty guarantees, customary international legal norms, and general principles by applying these rules to concrete cases in which particular parties in specific situations provide competing notions of rule interpretation that serve to refine the issues for the court to articulate an international rule with sufficient specificity.

This source of international legal authority is only subsidiary. How authoritative such materials are depends on a number of factors, including consistency and coherence of reasoning. Some materials will be wanting in this regard, and these materials sometimes will be considered but justifiably rejected as poor interpretive authorities.

Accordingly in the case of judicial opinions, international courts generally are not bound by the doctrine of *stare decisis*[92] even though such courts as a matter of practice do cite case precedents in cases between different states-parties.[93] As noted earlier, the ICJ can apply "judicial decisions . . . as a subsidiary means for the determination of rules of law";[94] and the decisions from the European Court of Human Rights, Inter-American Court of Human Rights, and the U.S. Supreme Court are replete with citations to their own and other tribunals' precedents. Such precedents include judicially made rules, even if such rules (*e.g.*, the European Court

[91] Before the twentieth century, the law of nations primarily was "ascertained by consulting the works of jurists, writing professedly on public law; . . . or by judicial decisions recognising [*sic*] and enforcing that law." United States v. Smith, 18 U.S. (5 Wheat.) 153, 160–61 (1820).

[92] *See, e.g., I.C.J. Statute*, art. 59 ("The decision of the [ICJ] has no binding force except between the parties and in respect of that particular case."); T. C. HARTLEY, THE FOUNDATIONS OF EUROPEAN COMMUNITY LAW 75 (4th ed., Oxford University Press, 1998) (European Court of Justice does not follow *stare decisis* doctrine).

[93] Courts cite case precedents often as a shortcut for establishing a norm's international legal status. *See, e.g.*, United States v. Smith, 5 U.S. (5 Wheat.) 153, 160 (1820) (law of nations primarily ascertained "by judicial decisions recognizing and enforcing that law"); Commonwealth v. Kosloff, 5 Serg. & Rawle 545 Pa. (1816) ("The law of nations is sought for . . . in the decisions of Judges.")

[94] *I.C.J. Statute*, art. 38 (1) (d).

of Human Rights' "evolutive technique" principle[95] and the U.S. Supreme Court's "evolving standards" principle[96]) allow for the rejection of their own precedents.[97]

The *stare decisis* doctrine has begun to acquire explicit acceptance in the international legal system as evidenced by two recent treaties. The *Agreement Establishing the Caribbean Court of Justice* states that "[j]udgments of the Court shall be legally binding precedents for parties in proceedings before the Court . . . ." [98] Although the states-parties to this treaty have common law systems that adhere to the *stare decisis* principle,[99] the trend has continued even in the European Union whose member-states most often do not have common law systems, suggesting that this acceptance of the *stare decisis* doctrine is not exceptional. The Preamble to the *Charter of Fundamental Rights of the European Union* [*European Charter*], which is incorporated into the *Treaty Establishing a Constitution for Europe* [*European Constitution*], states the following:

> This Charter reaffirms, with due regard for the powers and tasks of the Community and the Union and the principle of subsidiarity, the rights as they result, in particular, from the constitutional traditions and international obligations common to the Member States, the Treaty on European Union, the Community Treaties, the European Convention for the Protection of Human Rights and Fundamental Freedoms, the Social Charters adopted by the Community and by the Council of Europe and

95 *See, e.g.*, Bankovic and Others v. Belgium and Others, Application No. 52207/99 (2001) (discussing evolutive technique for interpreting *ECHR*).

96 *See, e.g.*, Trop v. Dulles, 356 U.S. 86, 101 (1958) (Eighth Amendment "must draw its meaning from the evolving standards of decency.").

97 *See, e.g.*, Cossey v. United Kingdom, 13 Eur. H.R. Rep. 622, ¶ 35 (1990) (departure from earlier decisions justified if Court finds earlier interpretation erroneous or other "cogent reason" including the need to "ensure that the interpretation of the [*ECHR*] reflects societal change and remains in line with present day conditions.").

98 *CCJ Agreement*, art. 22.

99 The *CCJ Agreement*'s adoption of the *stare decisis* doctrine is not limited to the exercise of the Caribbean Court of Justice's appellate jurisdiction but also applies to its international jurisdiction.

> the *case-law* of the Court of Justice of the European Communities and of the European Court of Human Rights.[100]

The *European Charter* explicitly makes the case law of the European Court of Justice and the European Court of Human Rights binding on all European Union members regardless of whether they were parties to the case from which the case law emanated.

Judicial interpretation also can include advisory opinions. Many international tribunals issue advisory opinions or general comments. States often request an international tribunal to issue an advisory opinion, but states are not bound to these opinions in the same sense if they were parties to a dispute before the tribunal. Nevertheless, in providing an authoritative interpretation of international law that is binding on all states-parties to the treaty from which the tribunal receives its jurisdiction, it can be said that such advisory opinions carry more positive legal authority than case law because case law consists only of *ad hoc* commands to specific parties in specific situations.

Viewed from a natural law perspective, both judges and international legal experts exercising their natural reason often formulate rules that they consider necessary for the consistent and coherent operation of the law of nations. Accordingly, like general principles recognized by civilized nations, this fourth source of international legal authority also arguably sounds in natural law. Indeed, by listing the available international legal authorities in a manner that moves from positive law sources to ones sounding in natural law, Article 38 cracks the door to a room populated by a potentially enormous number of norms to be used by the ICJ. And, as we shall see later, this door is swung wide open when the ICJ exercises its *ex aequo et bono* jurisdiction.

In conclusion, it is important to note that Article 38 of the *I.C.J. Statute* does not represent a complete list of international law sources. For example, treaties sometimes create lawmaking institutions whose laws are considered international law, too. European Union directives and U.S. federal

[100] Treaty Establishing a Constitution for Europe, Dec. 16, 2004, II-pmbl., ¶ 5, 47 Official Journal of the European Union (C 310) (emphasis provided) [hereinafter *European Constitution*].

statutory law are examples. Also, although norms *erga omnes*[101] and *jus cogens* norms[102] reflect "general principles of law recognized by civilized nations,"[103] they are not explicitly mentioned even though such norms bind all nations.[104]

[101] *See, e.g.*, Case concerning the Barcelona Traction, Light and Power Company, Limited (Belgium v. Spain), [1970] I.C.J. 3, 32 (discussing norms *erga omnes*); Interpretation of the American Declaration on the Rights and Duties of Man within the Framework of Article 64 of the American Convention on Human Rights (1989), Advisory Opinion OC-10/89, Inter-Am. Ct. H.R. (Ser. A) No. 10 (discussing norms *erga omnes*).

[102] *See, e.g., Vienna Convention* art. 53 (*Jus cogens* "is a norm accepted and recognized by the international community of States as a whole as a norm from which no derogation is permitted and which can be modified only by a subsequent norm of general international law having the same character."); *Vienna Convention-SIO*, art. 53 (same); *Western Sahara*, Advisory Opinion, [1975] I.C.J. 12 (*jus cogens*); Prosecutor v. Kunaraç, Kovaç and Vukoviç (2001), Case Nos. IT-96–23-T, IT-96–23/1-T, ICTY-Tr. Chamber, at ¶ 466 (*jus cogens*); Prosecutor v. Furundija, Case No. IT-95–17/1-T, ICTY-Tr. Chamber, at ¶ 155 (*jus cogens*) (1998); Prosecutor v. Delaciç *et al.*, Case No. IT-96–21-T, ICTY-Tr. Chamber, at ¶ 454 (1998) (*jus cogens*); Aloeboetoe *et al.* v. Suriname, Inter-Am. Ct. H.R. (Ser. C) No. 15, at ¶ 57 (1993) (*jus cogens*); Domingues v. United States, Report No. 62/02, Case 12.285, Inter-Am. Comm. H.R., at § 49 (*jus cogens*) (2002). Victims of the Tugboat "13 de Marzo" v. Cuba, Inter-Am. Comm. H.R. No. 47/96, Annual Report of the Inter-American Commission on Human Rights: 1996, OEA/Ser.L/V/II.95/doc.7 127 at ¶ 79 (1997) (*jus cogens*); Coard v. United States, Inter-Am. Comm. H.R. No. 109/99 (1999); Pinkerton and Roach v. United States, Inter-Am. Comm. H.R., No. 3/87, Annual Report of the Inter-American Commission on Human Rights: 1986–87, OEA/Ser.L/V/II.71/doc.9 147 (1987) (regional *jus cogens*); Al-Adsani v. United Kingdom, Appl. No. 35763/97, Eur. Ct. H.R. at ¶ 61 (2001); Ringeisen v. Austria, Appl. No. 2614/65, 13 Eur. Ct. H.R. (Ser. A) (1971) (separate opinion by Verdross J.) (*jus cogens*); Committee of United States Citizens Living in Nicaragua v. Reagan, 859 F.2d 929 (D.C. Cir. 1988) (*jus cogens*); Siderman de Blake v. Argentina, 965 F.2d 699, 714 (9th Cir. 1992) (*jus cogens*); Hawkins v. Comparet-Cassani, 33 F. Supp. 2d 1244, 1255 (C.D. Cal. 1999) (*jus cogens*).

[103] *I.C.J. Statute*, art. 38. Norms *erga omnes* and *jus cogens* norms belong to what Vattel called the "voluntary law of nations," which is made by the presumed consent of all nations. Vattel, Law of Nations, *Preliminaries*, *supra* note 1 at § 27.

[104] Ware v. Hylton, 3 U.S. (3 Dall.) 199, 227 (1796) (Chase, C.J.) ("The law of nations may be considered of three kinds, to wit, general, conventional, or customary. The first is universal, or established by the general consent of mankind, and binds all nations.").

4

The Natural Law of Nations

International tribunals sometimes also have a natural law of nations jurisdiction. For example, the ICJ has jurisdiction to decide cases *ex aequo et bono* ("according to what is just and good") if the parties agree.[1] And, most recently, the *Agreement Establishing the Caribbean Court of Justice* also explicitly has allowed the Caribbean Court to decide cases *ex aequo et bono* if the parties so agree.[2]

. Modern jurists generally attempt to avoid basing their decisions on natural law, and modern international jurists avoid basing their decisions on the necessary law of nations. Natural law approaches to jurisprudence generally are not in vogue. Most modern jurisprudence has replaced the *deus ex machina* of natural law with human choice.[3] However, even some positive international law (such as treaties outlawing the slave trade and governing the conduct of warfare) explicitly recognizes natural law norms. For example, a 1786 U.S.-Prussia treaty explicitly recognized that prisoners of war were protected by "the law of nature or nations."[4] Other times, treaties use phrases such as "principles of natural justice,"

[1] *I.C.J. Statute*, art. 38 (2) ("This provision shall not prejudice the power of the Court to decide a case *ex aequo et bono*, if the parties agree thereto."). However, the ICJ as of the date of writing has not had an opportunity to exercise its *ex aequo et bono* jurisdiction.

[2] *CCJ Agreement*, art. 17 (3) (Caribbean Court of Justice has jurisdiction "to decide a dispute *ex aequo et bono* if the parties so agree.").

[3] *Cf.* Sosa v. Alvarez-Machain, 542 U.S. 692, 124 S. Ct. 2739, 2764, 159 L. Ed. 2d 718 ("[W]e now tend to understand common law not as a discoverable reflection of universal reason but, in a positivistic way, as a product of human choice.").

[4] Treaty of Amity and Commerce Between His Majesty the King of Prussia, and the United States of America, Sept. 10, 1785, art. 24, *available at* http://usa.usembassy.de/etexts/ga1–860606.htm (last visited Nov. 22, 2006) (entered into force May 17, 1786).

"principles of Justice," "principles of humanity," and/or "dictates of public conscience," to signify the natural law of nations status of the norms to which these phrases are attached. For example, Great Britain and France in the *Treaty of Paris* (1814) explicitly recognized that the slave trade violated "principles of natural justice."[5] The United States and Great Britain explicitly recognized in the *Treaty of Ghent* (1814) that the slave trade violated "principles of humanity and Justice."[6] This treaty language was not rhetorical flourish. States were making explicit recognitions in positive law that certain practices violated what they considered to be the necessary law of nations. Subsequently, other states joined with Great Britain, France, and the United States in recognizing the necessary law of nations status of the slave trade's prohibition.[7] Such state recognition of necessary law of nations norms in the positive law of nations has continued. For example, states-parties to the *Hague Conventions* (1907) and the *Geneva Convention-Protocol I* (1977) explicitly guarantee the observance of the "laws [or principles] of humanity" and "the dictates of public conscience."[8]

[5] Treaty of Paris (Great Britain-France), May 30, 1814, additional article, 1 British and Foreign State Papers (London: James Ridgway and Sons, 1812/14).

[6] Treaty of Ghent, Dec. 28, 1814, art. 10 (entered into force Feb. 17, 1815), *available at* http://www.yale.edu/lawweb/avalon/diplomacy/britian/ghent.htm (last visited Oct. 5, 2003).

[7] *See, e.g.*, Great Britain-Portugal Treaty, done in London July 28, 1817, pmbl., *available at* http://www.pdavis.nl/Treaty_Portugal.htm (last visited May 22, 2005) ("IN the Name of the Most Holy and Undivided Trinity: His Royal Highness the Prince Regent of Portugal having, by the Tenth Article of the Treaty of Alliance concluded at Rio de Janeiro on the 19th February 1810, declared His Determination to cooperate with His Britannic Majesty in the Cause of Humanity and Justice, by adopting the most efficacious Means for bringing about a gradual Abolition of the Slave Trade; and His Royal Highness, in pursuance of His said Declaration, and desiring to effectuate, in concert with His Britannic Majesty and the other Powers of Europe who have been induced to assist in this benevolent Object, an immediate Abolition of the said Traffic . . .").

[8] Hague Convention (IV) Respecting the Laws and Customs of War on Land, with Annex of Regulations, Oct. 18, 1907, pmbl., T.S. No. 539, 1 Bevans 631, 36 Stat. 2277 (entered into force Jan. 26, 1910) [hereinafter *Hague Convention (IV)*] ("Until a more complete code of the laws of war has been issued, the High Contracting Parties deem it expedient to declare that, in cases not included in the Regulations adopted by them, the inhabitants and the belligerents remain under the protection and the rule of the principles of the law of nations, as they result from the usages established among civilized peoples, from the *laws of humanity*, and the *dictates of the public conscience*." [emphases provided]); Protocol Additional to the Geneva Conventions of 12 August 1949, and Relating to the

Also, many international courts have an equitable jurisdiction that sounds in natural law in fashioning remedies to ensure that a harmed party is returned to the *status quo ante*. The general principle governing the reach of such jurisdiction is the international legal principle of *restitutio in integrum*.[9] However, not all international tribunals consider themselves to exercise full equitable jurisdiction. For example, the European Court of Human Rights has held that the *ECHR* sometimes does not allow it to provide injunctive remedies[10] – unless the injunctive relief is urgently needed to stop the *ECHR* violation.[11] However, it must be noted that the Court's position is somewhat puzzling because the *ECHR* states that the Court is authorized to "afford just satisfaction," and satisfaction includes injunctive remedies.[12]

Allowing international tribunals to decide disputes *ex aequo et bono* often is prompted by the states-parties' desire to prevent war.[13] In some disputes, there may be no positive law (*e.g.*, treaty law, customary international law, or general principles of law recognized by civilized nations) for international tribunals to apply and, therefore, also no judicial decisions

Protection of Victims of International Armed Conflicts (Protocol I), Dec. 8, 1977, art. 1(2), 1125 U.N.T.S. 3, 16 I.L.M. 1391, (entered into force Dec. 7, 1978) [hereinafter *Geneva Convention-Protocol I*] ("In cases not covered by this Protocol or by other international agreements, civilians and combatants remain under the protection and authority of the principles of international law derived from established custom, from the *principles of humanity and from dictates of public conscience*." [emphases provided]).

9 *See, e.g.*, Chorzow Factory Case, 1928 P.C.I.J. (ser. A) No. 17, at 47 (13 Sept.) (recognizing *restitutio in integrum* principle).

10 McGoff v. Sweden, 83 Eur. Ct. H.R. (ser. A) at § 31 (1984).

11 *See, e.g.*, Assanidze v. Georgia, Appl. No. 71503/01, Eur. Ct. H.R., §§ 202–203, 208 (2004) (ordering state-respondent to release applicant from detention).

12 *ECHR*, art. 50.

13 *See, e.g.*, Treaty of the Delawares, Sept. 17, 1778, art. IV, 7 Stat. 13, *in* 2 Indian Affairs: Laws and Treaties, (Charles J. Kappler, ed., 1904), *available at* http://www.yale.edu/lawweb/avalon/ntreaty/del1778.htm (last visited Aug. 8, 2005) ("For the better security of the peace and friendship now entered into by the contracting parties, against all infractions of the same by the citizens of either party, to the prejudice of the other, neither party shall proceed to the infliction of punishments on the citizens of the other, otherwise than by securing the offender or offenders by imprisonment, or any other competent means, till a fair and impartial trial can be had by judges or juries of both parties, as near as can be to the laws, customs and usages of the contracting parties and natural justice.").

or publicist teachings interpreting this law. Early international tribunals tasked under a treaty to resolve interstate complaints most often did not cite law in their decisions. Their opinions only contained a recitation of the claims of the states-parties and a decision as to the outcome. For example, a federal court established under the Articles of Confederation and the tribunal established under the *Treaty of Ghent* never discussed any positive law in reaching their decisions.[14] Indeed, in *Pennsylvania v. Connecticut*, the federal court stated that they intended "to govern themselves by the principles of law, *so far as they ought to apply* in the present case,"[15] which suggests that they were also to work natural justice. Subsequently, the federal court issued its two-sentence long decision in favor of Pennsylvania.[16] Although the federal court's summary decision in *Pennsylvania v. Connecticut* undercut the court's credibility by not providing any normative reasons and arguably would violate present positive international law for not providing reasons,[17] the court was exercising its jurisdiction lawfully when it resolved the conflict according to what they conceived as natural justice.

This equitable jurisdiction also appears to allow parties to ignore their positive international legal obligations and rights between them (with the exception of *jus cogens* norms) because – at least in the case of the ICJ – the ICJ's equitable jurisdiction is not "prejudiced" by the sources of positive law it is to apply.[18] However, again, the ICJ's decision is only binding on the parties.[19] The parties' international legal obligations in respect to other states (and their peoples) remain binding. Furthermore, the parties' international human rights and humanitarian obligations remain binding because such obligations transcend the interstate dimension

[14] *See* Pennsylvania v. Connecticut, 24 Journals of the Continental Congress 6–32 (1912) (1782 dispute over Wyoming Valley adjudicated by federal court established under the Articles); *see also* Declarations and Decisions of the Commissioners under the Fourth, Sixth, and Seventh Articles of the Treaty of Ghent, *available at* http://www.lexum.umontreal.ca/ca_us/en/cus.1814.01.en.html (last visited Aug. 8, 2005).

[15] 24 Journals of the Continental Congress 23 (1912) (emphasis provided).

[16] *Ibid.* at 31.

[17] *Cf.* Van de Hurk v. The Netherlands, Eur. Ct. H.R. (ser. A) at § 61 (1994) (national courts must give reasons for their judgments).

[18] *I.C.J. Statute*, art. 38 (2).

[19] *Id.* at art. 59.

of international law.[20] The parties might allow the ICJ to decide a case *ex aequo et bono* because the application of their mutual arbitrary law of nations obligations may lead to politically controversial, absurd, and/or unjust results. For example, judges often have jurisdiction to equitably waive procedural law establishing time limits on filing or amending pleadings or requiring the exhaustion of domestic remedies.[21] Also, states-parties to a dispute may not wish to negotiate a settlement but instead want to have an international tribunal decide the case *ex aequo et bono* in order to acquire "judicial cover" over a controversial political issue.[22]

* * * * *

In the Part III, this book will integrate the previous discussion of international law into U.S. law.

[20] *Cf.* UN Human Rights Committee, General Comment No. 24, U.N. Doc. HRI/GEN/1/Rev.3 at ¶ 8 (1997) ("Although treaties that are mere exchanges of obligations between States allow them to reserve *inter se* applications of rules of general international law, it is otherwise in human rights treaties, which are for the benefit of persons within their jurisdiction . . ."); *Vienna Convention*, art. 60 (5) (termination or suspension of humanitarian treaty not justified by breach).

[21] *See, e.g.*, Federal Rules of Civil Procedure, Rule 15 (d) ("Upon motion of a party the court may, upon reasonable notice and *upon such terms as are just*, permit the party to serve a supplemental pleading setting forth transactions or occurrences or events which have happened since the date of the pleading sought to be supplemented." [emphasis provided]).

[22] *Cf.* Mark A. Graber, "The Non-Majoritarian Difficulty: Legislative Deference to the Judiciary," *in* STUDIES IN AMERICAN POLITICAL DEVELOPMENT 7, 35 (1993) (discussing propensity of elected politicians to delegate controversial issues to judiciary when issues put pressure on partisan coalitions).

PART THREE

UNITED STATES LAW AS INTERNATIONAL LAW

In Part III, this book will internationalize U.S. law. As demonstrated in Part I, the U.S. federal court system is an international tribunal system with interstate and national dimensions. In Part II, this book provided a transitional discussion of international law in general in order to provide a template against which to analyze U.S. law. In Part III, this book will demonstrate that U.S. federal law is international law with interstate and national dimensions. Like other international tribunals, U.S. federal tribunals exercise jurisdiction over positive international law claims and sometimes even natural law of nations claims. In exercising such jurisdictions, both international and U.S. federal tribunals have developed a number of interpretive principles. In the following chapters, we will examine these how these jurisdictions and principles overlap and differ.

The U.S. federal courts exercise both federal law claims and party-based jurisdictions. The judicial power of the federal courts is set out in Article III of the Constitution, which states in relevant part:

> The judicial Power shall extend to all Cases, in Law and Equity, arising under this Constitution, the Laws of the United States, and Treaties made, or which shall be made, under their Authority; – to all Cases affecting Ambassadors, other public Ministers and Consuls; – to all Cases of admiralty and maritime Jurisdiction; – to Controversies to which the United States shall be a Party; – to Controversies between two or more States; – between a State and Citizens of another State;[[1]] – between Citizens of different States, – between Citizens of the same State claiming Lands under

[1] This clause was amended by the Eleventh Amendment. U.S. CONST. amend. XI ("The Judicial power of the United States shall not be construed to extend to any suit in law or

Grants of different States, and between a State, or the Citizens thereof, and foreign States, Citizens or Subjects.[2]

equity, commenced or prosecuted against one of the United States by Citizens of another State, or by Citizens or Subjects of any Foreign State.").

[2] *Id.* at art. III, § 2, cl. 1.

Article III makes mention of both "cases" and "controversies" that indicates that the two are different. The U.S. Supreme Court in *Aetna Life Ins. Co. v. Haworth* held that "[t]he two terms may be used interchangeably, inasmuch as a 'controversy,' if distinguishable from a 'case' at all, is so only because it is a less comprehensive word and includes only suits of a civil nature." 300 U.S. 227, 239 (1937). Bouvier's Dictionary (1856) also defined "controversy" as a "dispute arising between two or more persons. It differs from case, which includes all suits criminal as well as civil; whereas controversy is a civil and not a criminal proceeding." John Bouvier, A Law Dictionary adapted to the Constitution and the Laws of the United States of America and of the Several States of the American Union (6th ed. 1856) (citing 2 Dall. R. 419, 431, 432; 1 Tuck. Bl. Com. App. 420, 421; Story, Const. 1668.). In *Wisconsin v. Pelican Ins. Co.*, the Supreme Court held that for purposes of original jurisdiction over controversies between a state and citizens of another state, such cases are confined to civil suits. 127 U.S. 265 (1888). Interestingly enough, the Court partly relied upon the international legal rules that prohibit states from executing the penal laws of foreign states. *Id.* at 289–300.

5

Article III, International Legal Interpretation

Article III states that the federal courts have law claims jurisdiction over

> All Cases, in Law and Equity, arising under this Constitution, the Laws of the United States, and Treaties made, or which shall be made, under their Authority.[1]

Recall that the word "federal" comes from the word "*foedus*," which is a treaty. Accordingly, "federal" law is intrinsically "treaty" law. Article III empowers federal courts to adjudicate cases by applying and interpreting three sources of international law: (i) the Constitution, which is a treaty; (ii) treaties to which the United States are parties;[2] and (iii) federal statutory law implementing the Constitution, other U.S. treaties, and the law of nations.

The Supreme Court has original jurisdiction in Article III, international law claims cases "affecting Ambassadors, other public Ministers and Consuls, and those in which a State shall be a Party."[3] And Congress has vested

[1] U.S. CONST. art. III.

[2] Note that this clause of Article III refers to the United States in the plural.

[3] *Id.* at art. III, § 2, cl. 3. The Supreme Court arguably also has original jurisdiction in Article III, international law claims jurisdiction for all other cases. *See* Laurence Claus, *The One Court that Congress Cannot Take Away: Singularity, Supremacy, and Article III*, San Diego Legal Papers No. 07–71, *available at* http://papers.ssrn.com/sol3/papers.cfm?abstract_id=935368 (last visited Nov. 21, 2006) (arguing that U.S. Supreme Court retains original jurisdiction when Congress fails to create inferior federal courts with federal question jurisdiction or makes exceptions to the Court's appellate jurisdiction); Akhil Reed Amar, *A Neo-Federalist View of Article III: Separating the Two Tiers of Federal Jurisdiction*, 65 B.U.L. REV. 205 (1985) (arguing that inclusion of "all" cases

original jurisdiction of Article III, international law claim cases in the federal district courts for both criminal[4] and civil matters.[5]

5.1. U.S. CONSTITUTION: THE INTERNATIONAL LEGAL CONSTRUCTIONIST APPROACH

The International Legal Constructionist (ILC) approach to constitutional interpretation requires that the Constitution's text be construed in conformity with the United States' international legal obligations because the Constitution is a treaty that *per* the conventional law of nations must be construed in conformity with the states-parties' other international legal obligations. As the International Court of Justice (ICJ)[6] and the Inter-American Court of Human Rights[7] have opined, the *Vienna Convention on the Law of Treaties*[8] explicitly says, and the Inter-American Commission on Human Rights[9] and U.S. Supreme Court[10] has held,

of admiralty and maritime jurisdiction in Article III indicates that Supreme Court shares concurrent original jurisdiction with lower federal courts).

[4] 18 U.S.C. § 3231 ("The district courts of the United States shall have original jurisdiction, exclusive of the courts of the States, of all offenses against the laws of the United States.").

[5] 28 U.S.C. §1331 ("The district courts shall have original jurisdiction of all civil actions arising under the Constitution, laws, or treaties of the United States.").

[6] *See* Legal Consequences for States of the Continued Presence of South Africa in Namibia (South West Africa) notwithstanding Security Council Resolution 276 (1970), Advisory Opinion, 1971 I.C.J. 16, 31 (1971) ("an international instrument has to be interpreted and applied within the framework of the entire [international] legal system prevailing at the time of the interpretation").

[7] *See* Interpretation of the American Declaration of the Rights and Duties of Man within the Framework of Article 64 of the American Convention on Human Rights, Advisory Opinion OC-10/89, Inter-Am. Ct. H.R. Ser. A, No. 10, at ¶ 37 (1989) (quoting language from the Namibia advisory opinion).

[8] *See Vienna Convention*, art. 31 (3)(c) (treaty must be interpreted in light of "any rules of international law applicable in the relations between the parties"); *see also* Vienna Convention on the Law of Treaties Between States and International Organizations or Between International Organizations, Mar. 21, 1986, art. 31 (3) (c), U.N. Doc. A/CONF.129/15, 25 I.L.M. 543 (treaty between intergovernmental organization and state must be interpreted in light of "any relevant rules of international law applicable in the relations between the parties").

[9] *See* Coard v. United States, Inter-Am. Cm. H.R., No. 109/99 at ¶ 40 (1999), *available at* http://www.cidh.oas.org/annualrep/99eng/Merits/UnitedStates10.951.htm (last visited Feb. 15, 2003) (quoting language in the Namibia advisory opinion).

[10] *Cf.* Geofroy v. Riggs, 133 U.S. 258, 271 (1890) (meaning of treaty language "to be taken in their ordinary meaning, as understood in the public law of nations").

treaties are to be construed in conformity with present international legal obligations binding on their states-parties.

Aside from these positive legal justifications, there are two policy reasons why treaties must be construed in conformity with the other international legal obligations states-parties. First, to violate such international legal norms is to violate the fundamental principle of *pacta sunt servanda* ("promises are to be observed") that establishes the foundation of most of international law – whether treaty or customary international law. A state is not credible and reliable when it promises to abide by a certain treaty norm or accepts a customary international legal norm, then later promise to abide by or accept a conflicting norm. Second, violating an international legal norm could result in the unraveling of the international legal order through a "domino-effect" of state withdrawals from the conventional or customary international legal obligations with the violating states. The only exception to this general rule according to international law is when the norm is of a human rights or humanitarian nature because such norms transcend the interstate dimensions of international law.[11] A state's violation of international human rights or humanitarian law is an insufficient reason for another state to terminate its own compliance with this law.

The ILC approach also accommodates and complements the core principles of three other major theories of constitutional interpretation: (i) Textualism, (ii) Originalism, and (iii) the Living Constitution approach. Textualism is a formalist interpretive approach that examines the ordinary meaning of the Constitution's text and generally is opposed to using extratextual authorities for interpreting the Constitution,[12] especially if such authorities provide an evolving meaning of constitutional text.[13]

[11] *See* UN Human Rights Committee, General Comment No. 24, U.N. Doc. HRI/GEN/1/Rev.3 at ¶ 8 (1997) ("Although treaties that are mere exchanges of obligations between States allow them to reserve *inter se* applications of rules of general international law, it is otherwise in human rights treaties, which are for the benefit of persons within their jurisdiction . . . ."); *Vienna Convention*, art. 60 (5) (termination or suspension of humanitarian treaty not justified by breach).

[12] *Cf., e.g.*, K-Mart v. Cartier, 486 U.S. 281, 319 (1988) (Scalia, J., concurring in part and dissenting in part) (providing Textualist approach to federal statutory interpretation).

[13] *See, e.g.*, Antonin Scalia, "A Theory of Constitutional Interpretation," remarks delivered at The Catholic University of America, Washington, D.C., Oct. 18, 1996, *available at*

The ILC approach is truly "textualist" in two senses of the word. First, ILC is textualist in that it relies on what the Constitution's text expressly *states*. The ILC claim that the Constitution is a treaty is based on the text of Article VII indicating that the Constitution is a treaty "between the States so ratifying the Same."[14] Furthermore, ILC maintains that the Constitution as a treaty must be interpreted – to use the words of the *Vienna Convention* – "in accordance with the ordinary meaning" to be given to the terms of the Constitution in their context and "in the light of its object and purpose" as reflected in its Preamble.[15] Textualism also maintains that the ordinary meaning of the Constitution's text should be the governing meaning. Second, the ILC approach is textualist in that it relies on what the Constitution as a text *is* – a treaty. Insofar as ILC is textualist in this latter sense of the word, it goes beyond what conventional Textualism has claimed and completes it.

An Originalist approach to constitutional interpretation uses the public understanding of the Constitution's meaning around the time of its ratification in order to interpret the Constitution's text. This original public understanding of the Constitution is garnered from extratextual authorities, such as the proceedings of the Continental Congress, Constitutional Convention, and state constitutional conventions; writings by the Founding Fathers (including the Federalist and sometimes Anti-Federalist Papers); speeches, resolutions, and laws from the early Congress; statements by the early Executive Branch; and early judicial opinions.[16] Much of the original public understanding of the Framers is located in the proceedings of the Constitutional Convention – what international law calls the "*travaux préparatoires*." International law allows the *travaux préparatoires* and the circumstances of the treaty's conclusion to be used (i) as supplementary means of *confirming* the meaning of a treaty when the treaty already has been interpreted "in good faith in accordance with the ordinary meaning to be given to the terms of the treaty in their context and in light of its object and purpose,"

http://courttv.com/legaldocs/rights/scalia.html (last visited Feb. 15, 2003) (criticizing evolving standards interpretive approach).

[14] U.S. Const. art. VII.

[15] *Vienna Convention*, art. 31 (1).

[16] *See* Keith Whittington, Constitutional Interpretation: Textual Meaning, Original Intent, and Judicial Review (2001) (discussing Originalist theories).

and in conformity with other subsequent treaties or treaty practice, and other binding international law;[17] and (ii) as a means of determining the meaning of the treaty when the application of the aforementioned rules still leaves the treaty's "meaning ambiguous or obscure . . . or . . . leads to result which is manifestly absurd or unreasonable."[18]

The ILC approach accommodates Originalism because ILC's claim that the Constitution is a treaty that must be construed in conformity with the United States' international legal obligations is confirmed by the original understanding of the Constitution as indicated by statements of both its Framers and detractors, including James Madison, Alexander Hamilton, John Jay, and Rufus King. As already pointed out in the Introduction, the Framers justified the Constitution's adoption of the nine-state ratification rule for establishing the Constitution on the basis of international law. To this extent, the Framers recognized that the Constitution as a treaty was governed by international law. The Framers also stated that the Constitution could not be construed to violate the United States' international legal obligations, and to ensure that the Constitution was governed by international law, they wrote international legal rules into its text.[19] The ILC approach relies on the original public understanding of the Framers to confirm what the text of the Constitution indicates, namely, that the Constitution is a treaty that incorporates international law. Furthermore, the ILC approach complements Originalism by providing a rule based on law (*viz.*, the law of nations) that allows the original public understanding of the Constitution to be used for constitutional interpretation that is otherwise absent in Originalism because Originalism does not offer any textual or independent legal authority for justifying the use of the original public understanding for construing the Constitution.

The Living Constitution Theory of constitutional interpretation considers the meaning of the Constitution to be evolving[20] because, as the U.S. Supreme Court said in *McCulloch v. Maryland*, "we must never forget,

[17] *Vienna Convention*, art. 31.

[18] *Id.* at art. 32.

[19] *See generally* Francisco Forrest Martin, *Our Constitution as Federal Treaty: A New Theory of United States Constitutional Construction Based on an Originalist Understanding for Addressing a New World*, 31 Hastings Const. L. Quart. 269 (2004).

[20] *See, e.g.*, Trop v. Dulles, 356 U.S. 86, 101 (1958) (Eighth Amendment "must draw its meaning from the evolving standards of decency.").

that it is a constitution we are expounding."[21] The Living Constitution approach generally is associated with the loose-constructionist schools of legal realism (and its subgenre of Critical Legal Studies), and moralist or naturalist theories,[22] although some adherents increasingly identify themselves with the Originalist camp.[23] The ILC approach also accommodates the core meaning of the Living Constitution approach by requiring constitutional text to be construed in conformity with the United States' customary international legal obligations, "any subsequent agreement" between the parties regarding the interpretation or the application of U.S. treaties, and/or "any subsequent practice" in the application of U.S. treaties which establishes the agreement of the parties regarding the interpretation of these treaties.[24] As customs, treaties, and treaty practices evolve, so must the meaning of the Constitution change when its text is construed with these new international legal developments. Indeed, as readers will learn later, federal judicial power often includes the constitutional duty to decide cases according to naturalist or moralist principles.[25]

In conclusion, ILC is based in part on Textualist, Originalist, and Living Constitution interpretive approaches. However, it is important to note that ILC departs from these conventional theories when they fail to accept the Constitution's status as a treaty and its consequent legal implications as a treaty. Nevertheless, the ILC approach provides two important advantages. First, unlike the use of other extraconstitutional authorities, the use of international law for construing the Constitution is mandatory because the law of treaties requires the Constitution as a treaty be construed in conformity with such law. Other extraconstitutional authorities do not have a constitutional textual basis for requiring their use in

[21] 17 U.S. (4 Wheat.) 316, 407 (1819).

[22] *See, e.g.*, BRUCE ACKERMAN, WE THE PEOPLE: FOUNDATIONS (1991) (arguing that three great transformative movements of constitutional law and politics (called "constitutional moments") were characterized by legal creativity bordering on illegality but were authentic response to political crises and eventually legitimized by American people); RONALD DWORKIN, FREEDOM'S LAW: THE MORAL READING OF THE AMERICAN CONSTITUTION (1996) (arguing for moral reading of Constitution and criticizing strict historical reading of Constitution); SANFORD V. LEVINSON, CONSTITUTIONAL FAITH (1988) (arguing for critical legal studies interpretation of Constitution).

[23] *See, e.g.*, BRUCE ACKERMAN, WE THE PEOPLE: FOUNDATIONS (1991).

[24] *Vienna Convention*, art. 31 (3).

[25] *See* Subsection 6.5.

construing the Constitution, and the Originalist and Living Constitution approaches often employ such other extraconstitutional authorities. Second, in the case of those international legal obligations that are evolving, the use of such evolving international law for construing the Constitution ensures that the Constitution's meaning is evolving to meet new global challenges.

There is an elegant economy about ILC. It simply maintains that the Constitution is a treaty that *per* the law of nations requires the Constitution to be construed in conformity with the United States' international legal obligations. In doing so, ILC can accommodate the core principles of other major theories of constitutional interpretation somewhat peculiar to the United States. At the same time, the ILC approach ensures that U.S. constitutional interpretation is not disengaged from the community of nations of which the United States is a member.

5.2. TREATIES AND THEIR LIBERALIZATION AND LIMITATIONS

It is hardly controversial that treaties represent international law. The Supremacy Clause of the Constitution also makes U.S. treaties national law, and Article III gives federal courts the authority to exercise jurisdiction over U.S. treaty claims. There are major two rules governing treaty interpretation: the *Lynham* Liberal Construction Rule and the Non–Self-Execution Doctrine.

The *Lynham* Liberal Construction Rule

In *Hauenstein v. Lynham*, the U.S. Supreme Court held that "[w]here a treaty admits of two constructions, one restrictive as to the rights, that may be claimed under it, and the other liberal, the latter is to be preferred. ... Such is the settled rule in this court."[26] Furthermore, the construction

[26] 100 U.S. 483, 487 (1879); *see also* Jordan v. Tashiro, 278 U.S. 123, 127 (1928) ("where a treaty fairly admits of two constructions, one restricting the rights that may be claimed under it and the other enlarging them, the more liberal construction is to be preferred"); Tucker v. Alexandroff, 183 U.S. 424, 437 (1902) ("As treaties are solemn engagements entered into between independent nations for the common advancement of their interests and the interests of civilization, and as their main object is, not only to avoid war and secure

must the most liberal.[27] This rule shall be called the "*Lynham* Liberal Construction Rule." The Supreme Court has justified this settled rule on the basis that it is necessary "as to carry out the apparent intention of the parties to secure equality and reciprocity between them."[28] It is important to note that this liberal construction rule does not apply only to interstate cases but also to cases in which the parties are not states but nationals of different state-parties to the treaty being construed or in which one party is a state-party and the other party is a national of another state-party.[29] Congruent with the *Lynham* Liberal Construction Rule, the Supreme Court has applied the strict scrutiny test[30] to state alienage discrimination, effectively providing a liberal construction to the constitutional rights of aliens by requiring that the interference with an alien's constitutional rights must be narrowly tailored to pass constitutional muster.

However, it is less clear whether the liberal construction rule would apply to cases between nationals of the same state-party or between a state-party and its own citizens because the rule's rationale is based on securing equality and reciprocity between states-parties, and there is no need in such cases to secure equality and reciprocity between states-parties. There is no state-party or its citizens challenging another state-party's or its citizens' construction of their treaty obligations. Absent an interstate complaint procedure provided by a treaty by which a foreign

a lasting and perpetual peace, but to promote a friendly feeling between the people of the two countries, they should be interpreted in that broad and liberal spirit which is calculated to make for the existence of a perpetual amity, so far as it can be done without the sacrifice of individual rights or those principles of personal liberty which lie at the foundation of our jurisprudence."); Geofroy v. Riggs, 133 U.S. at 271 ("It is a general principle of construction with respect to treaties that they shall be liberally construed so as to carry out the apparent intention of the parties to secure equality and reciprocity between them.").

27 Shanks v. Dupont, 28 U.S. (3 Pet.) 242, 249 (1830) ("If the treaty admits of two interpretations, and one is limited, and the other liberal; one which will further, and the other exclude private rights; why should not the most liberal expositions be adopted?").

28 Geofroy v. Riggs, 133 U.S. at 271.

29 *See, e.g., id.* (applying liberal construction rule to case involving inheritance rights of state-party's national protected by treaty).

30 *See, e.g.* Graham v. Richardson, 403 U.S. 365 (1971).The strict scrutiny test requires that a law or state activity serve a compelling state interest and that the law or activity must be narrowly tailored in achieving such an interest.

state-party could intercede on behalf of another state-party's nationals,[31] there arguably is no reason that another state-party could have any standing to challenge the state-party's treatment of its own nationals.

In such noninterstate cases, an exception to the *Lynham* Liberal Construction Rule would appear to be present. Indeed, in the context of international human rights legal protections, the UN Human Rights Committee has noted that interstate reciprocity has no place.[32] Furthermore, sometimes human rights treaties provide greater protection to a state-party's own citizens. For example, the *ICCPR* and *ACHR* only guarantee the right to participate in government to a state-party's citizens.[33] Of course, difference in treatment based on citizenship in the case of the right to government participation is reasonable given the duties attendant to citizenship/nationality.[34]

Nevertheless, it is somewhat odd that a state's own citizens acquire less international legal protection in cases not implicating interstate relations than aliens under the *Lynham* Liberal Construction Rule in cases implicating such relations. Does not the state owe its own citizens at least the same legal protection as it affords aliens?

At least in the international human rights area, such disparate treatment is mooted by the fact that many human rights treaties do guarantee states-parties the right to intercede on behalf of another state-party's nationals through interstate complaint procedures.[35] Indeed, the United States has explicitly accepted the competence of the UN Human Rights

[31] *See, e.g.*, *ICCPR*, art. 41 (providing interstate complaint procedure); *ACHR*, art. 45 (same).

[32] *See supra* Chapter 2, note 19.

[33] *See, e.g.*, *ICCPR*, art. 25 (guaranteeing right to take part in conduct of public affairs only to citizens); *ACHR*, art. 23 (same).

[34] And, some international human rights courts sometimes have strictly construed their constituent human rights treaties in cases in which a national is challenging his/her own state's actions. For example, the European Court of Human Rights has strictly construed the right to freedom of expression guaranteed by the *ECHR* in cases concerning public criticism of judges. *See, e.g.*, Prager & Oberschlick v. Austria, 313 Eur. Ct. H.R. (ser. A) (1995); Barfod v Denmark, 149 Eur. Ct. H.R. (ser. A) (1989). However, such a strict construction of the right to freedom of expression did not turn on the issue of the complainant's nationality. The strict construction arguably applied regardless of the applicant's nationality/citizenship.

[35] *See, e.g.*, *ICCPR*, art. 41 (providing for interstate complaint procedure); *ECHR*, art. 24 (same); *ACHR*, art. 45 (same); *see also* Ireland v. United Kingdom, 25 Eur. Ct. H.R. (ser. A) at § 239 (1978) (Ireland allowed to intercede on behalf of British nationals).

Committee to consider complaints against the United States submitted by other states-parties to the *ICCPR*.[36] Therefore, interstate reciprocity dynamic justifying the use of the *Lynham* Liberal Construction Rule would be present, and the Rule's use would be appropriate in treaty construction.

Furthermore, the Fourteenth Amendment's Privileges and Immunities Clause includes privileges and immunities guaranteed by treaty,[37] and both the Fifth and Fourteenth Amendment guarantees equal protection of the laws,[38] which includes U.S. treaties because treaties are part of the supreme law of the land under the Supremacy Clause. Therefore, both the federal and state governments constitutionally cannot provide greater legal protection to aliens than its own nationals.[39]

However, there are three kinds of cases in which it would be improper to apply the Rule. First, if a state-party has not provided a liberal construction of its treaty obligation, then another state's court should not construe its treaty obligation liberally in regard to the state-party in order to ensure interstate reciprocity and to not encourage the state-party's unjust enrichment at the expense of the other state-party.

Second, the Rule is inapplicable to crimes because crimes are to be construed narrowly. Both international criminal and U.S. constitutional law require a strict construction of crimes. For example, the *ICC Statute* establishes the following:

> The definition of a crime shall be strictly construed and shall not be extended by analogy. In case of ambiguity, the definition shall be interpreted in favour of the person being investigated, prosecuted or convicted.[40]

As the U.S. Supreme Court has noted:

[36] U.S. Reservations, Declarations, and Understandings to the International Covenant on Civil and Political Rights, at § III (3), 138 Cong. Rec. S4783–4 (daily ed., April 2, 1992).

[37] Slaughter-House Cases, 83 U.S. (16 Wall.) 36, 79 (1873) (Fourteenth Amendment's privileges and immunities include "all rights secured to our citizens by treaties with foreign nations").

[38] U.S. Const. amend. XIV, § 1; Hampton v. Wong, 426 U.S. 88 (1976) (federal alienage discrimination violative of Fifth Amendment guarantee prohibiting denial of liberty without due process of law).

[39] *Cf.* Erie Railroad Co. v. Tompkins, 304 U.S. 64, 74–75 (1938) (equal protection of the law "rendered impossible" when noncitizen given privilege of selecting court over citizen).

[40] *ICC Statute* art. 22 (2).

> The rule that penal laws are to be construed strictly is perhaps not much less old than construction itself. It is founded on the tenderness of the law for the rights of individuals, and on the plain principle that the power of punishment is vested in the legislative, not in the judicial, department. It is the legislature, not the Court, which is to define a crime, and ordain its punishment. [41]

This is consistent with the Supreme Court's later holding in *Tucker v. Alexandroff*, in which the Court held that there is an exception to the liberal construction rule for treaties when a liberal construction would "sacrifice . . . individual rights or those principles of personal liberty which lie at the foundation of our jurisprudence."[42] This raises the third exception: the Lynham Liberal Construction Rule cannot be applied in cases in which individual rights and/or liberties are violated.

In conclusion, with the exceptions of cases in which crimes are being construed and in which a treaty partner has not liberally construed a treaty, federal courts must provide the most liberal construction of U.S. treaties for both aliens and U.S. citizens/nationals under the *Lynham* Liberal Construction Rule.[43]

[41] Yates v. United States, 354 U.S. 298, 305 (1957) (*citing* United States v. Wiltberger, 5 Wheat. 76, 95–96 (1820) (Marshall, C.J.)).

[42] 183 U.S. 424, 437.

[43] The question of whether a strict construction of an international legal obligation will result in war arguably may be a political question whose answer may be best left to the political branches that have access to better information than the federal courts regarding how a treaty-partner would react to a strict interpretation of a treaty, thereby obviating the need for a federal court to consider whether to apply the *Lyham* Liberal Construction Rule. However, in foreign relations cases addressing the political question doctrine, the Supreme Court in *Baker v. Carr* has observed that "if there has been no conclusive 'governmental action' [by the political branches] then a court can construe a treaty and may find it provides the answer." 369 U.S. 186, 212 (1962). In a case in which the United States has construed its treaty obligation strictly resulting in a suit by a party urging the treaty's liberal interpretation, there has been no "conclusive 'governmental action'" by the political branches because there has been no congressional declaration of war or presidential recognition of belligerency – actions that would be considered by the Court in *Baker v. Carr* to be conclusive in such a case. *See id.* at 212–14. If there were such a declaration or recognition, then the issue of the treaty's interpretation would be moot because there already exists a state of war and the war-avoidance rationale of the *Lynham* Liberal Construction Rule would be eliminated. The most that can be said is that in the absence of war, the president's opinion as to the proper interpretation of the treaty should be given "great weight," but such an interpretive opinion could call for either a

However, the federal courts have come to embrace a distinction in treaties that sometimes has served to undermine the United States' compliance with its treaty obligations: the Non–Self Execution Doctrine.

The Limits of the Non-Self–Execution Doctrine

The Non–Self-Execution Doctrine maintains that a legislative body must enact legislation to give domestic implementation to a treaty and/or that an executive organ must perform some act to give domestic effect to a treaty. The Doctrine is a domestic doctrine; it is not an international legal doctrine. International tribunals are not encumbered by the fact that a state-party to a treaty has failed to perform its treaty obligations by, for example, not enacting legislation giving domestic effect to the treaty. International tribunals only view such inaction as the state-party's failure to comply with its treaty obligation, and such tribunals generally[44] have the authority to order relief that will bring the state-party into compliance under the *restitutio in integrum* principle. Under the Constitution, it is the

liberal or strict construction. *See, e.g.*, Kolovrat v. Oregon, 366 U.S. 187, 194 (1961) ("While courts interpret treaties for themselves, the meaning given them by the departments of the government particularly charged with their negotiation and enforcement is given great weight."). For the president's opinion to be competent, it must take into account whether the treaty partner(s) has interpreted the treaty liberally. *See Vienna Convention*, 31 (3) (c) (treaty to be interpreted in light of "any subsequent practice in the application of the treaty which establishes the agreement of the parties regarding its interpretation").

Moreover, the *Lynham* Liberal Construction Rule also was designed to ensure that treaty partners observe reciprocity, and such reciprocity is essential during a state of war to ensure that the conduct of war does not create unnecessary harm. Some treaties remain in force between even hostile states. *See, e.g., Fourth Geneva Convention*, art. 2 (Convention applies to all cases of war). The severance of diplomatic relations resulting from a state of war between such parties sometimes is a legally insufficient basis for terminating a treaty. *Vienna Convention*, art. 63. If the United States' treaty partner with whom the United States is at war has not materially breached or has not construed the treaty strictly, then the federal courts must construe the treaty liberally. As the U.S. Supreme Court recently reaffirmed, "[i]f treaties are to be given effect as federal law under our legal system, determining their meaning as a matter of federal law 'is emphatically the province and duty of the judicial department.'" Sanchez-Llamadas v. Oregon, No. 04–10566, 548 U.S. –, 19 (2006) (slip opinion) (citing *Marbury v. Madison*).

[44] The European Court of Human Rights generally has construed its remedial authority to include only declaratory and damages relief – not injunctive relief. As noted in Chapter 4 (*see* text accompanying notes 9 and 10), this construction is inconsistent with the *resititutio in integrum* principle.

same case for U.S. federal courts insofar as the Non–Self-Execution Doctrine is applied to the states of the United States because the Supremacy Clause requires state judges to give effect to treaties.

However, an international tribunal cannot order another branch of its intergovernmental organization to comply with their constituent treaty obligations unless the treaty allows it. For example, the *UN Charter* allows only states to be parties to cases before the ICJ,[45] and the UN Security Council is not a state; therefore, the ICJ cannot order the Security Council to perform some act. Nevertheless, the *UN Charter* still requires the UN Security Council to ensure that the ICJ's orders are observed in cases properly before the Court.[46] The situation is different for other international courts. For example, the *EU Treaty* gives the ECJ jurisdiction over cases in which the European Parliament and European Council are parties.[47]

Most importantly, Article III of the U.S. Constitution gives the federal courts jurisdiction over cases in which the United States is a party.[48] Therefore, the federal courts can order the political branches to perform some act when they are proper parties to a case before it. When the United States ratifies a treaty, the treaty is part of the "supreme Law of the Land" – language that indicates that it has not only international legal effect but also domestic legal effect because of the language's territorial reference.

However, Mr. Chief Justice John Marshall in 1829 articulated the Non–Self-Execution Doctrine in *Foster v. Neilson*.[49] Marshall stated that those treaties addressed "to the political, not the judicial department" are non–self-executing.[50] Therefore, "the legislature must execute the contract (*i.e.*, the treaty) before [the treaty] can become a rule for the Court."[51] Subsequently, the president and/or Senate sometimes have declared that

[45] *See UN Charter*, arts. 4 (1) ("Membership in the United Nations is open to . . . states") and 93 (1) ("All Members of the United Nations are ipso facto parties to the Statute of the International Court of Justice."). The Security Council can only request advisory opinions from the ICJ. *Id.* at art. 96 (1) (Security Council may request ICJ for advisory opinions).

[46] *See UN Charter*, art. 24 (1) ("In order to ensure prompt and effective action by the United Nations, its Members confer on the Security Council primary responsibility for the maintenance of international peace and security, and agree that in carrying out its duties under this responsibility the Security Council acts on their behalf.").

[47] *EU Treaty*, art. 230.

[48] U.S. Const.art. III, § 2, cl. 1.

[49] 27 U.S. (2 Pet.) 253 (1829).

[50] *Id.* at 314.

[51] *Id.*

implementing legislation is required to give a treaty domestic effect. Examples include human rights treaties[52] whose major object and purpose is to provide domestic protection.[53]

It is important to note that the Constitution does not make a distinction between self-executing and non–self-executing treaties. Specifically, Article III extends the federal courts' judicial power to U.S. treaties apparently regardless of whether these treaties purportedly are non–self-executing. The Non–Self-Execution Doctrine appears to have been borrowed from the British constitutional concept of Parliamentary Supremacy in that a non–self-execution doctrine requires that Parliament legislate before treaty obligations can be performed domestically.[54] Otherwise, British treaties – which can be made only by the Crown – could have domestic legal effects that conflict with acts of Parliament, thereby destroying Parliamentary Supremacy.

In contrast, the Supremacy Clause explicitly gives U.S. treaties domestic application by making them part of the supreme law of the land, and Article III explicitly enables federal courts to exercise jurisdiction over all cases arising from U.S. treaties. Unlike British constitutional law in

[52] *See, e.g.*, Multilateral Treaties Deposited with the Secretary General: Status as at 31 Dec. 1992, at 132, U.N. Doc. ST/LEG/SER.E/11 (1993) (U.S. deposit of declaration that Articles 1–27 of the *International Covenant on Civil and Political Rights* are non–self-executing); Multilateral Treaties Deposited with the Secretary General: Status as at 31 Dec. 1994, at 185, U.N. Doc. ST/LEG/SER.E/13 (1995) (U.S. deposit of declaration that *Convention Against Torture and Other Cruel, Inhuman or Degrading Treatment or Punishment* is non–self-executing).

[53] *See, e.g.*, *ICCPR*, art. 2 (1) ("Each State Party to the present Covenant undertakes to respect and to ensure to all individuals within its territory and subject to its jurisdiction the rights recognized in the present Covenant . . . . "); Convention Against Torture and Other Cruel, Inhuman or Degrading Treatment or Punishment, Dec. 10, 1984, art. 2 (1), 39 UN GAOR, Supp. (No. 51), UN Doc. A/39/51, at 197 (1984) (entered into force June 26, 1987) [hereinafter *CAT*] ("Each State Party shall take effective legislative, administrative, judicial or other measures to prevent acts of torture in any territory under its jurisdiction.").

[54] The Non-Self-Execution Doctrine appeared to not extend to British treaties of peace and alliance:

> It is also the king's prerogative to make treaties, leagues and alliances with foreign states and princes. . . . Whatever contracts he therefore engages in, no other power in the kingdom can legally delay, resist, or annul.

William Blackstone, 1 Commentaries on the Laws of England 257 (1769) [hereinafter Blackstone's Commentaries].

which a democratically unaccountable Crown could make treaties, U.S. constitutional law only allowed treaties to be made by a democratically accountable president with the consent of a democratically accountable Senate. In a similar mannter that the Parliamentary Supremacy Principle and the concept of non–self-execution ensured that British national sovereignty and accountability to the British nation was maintained in regard to treaty-making, the U.S. Constitution ensured American national sovereignty and accountability to the American nation by allowing U.S. treaties to be made only by the president with consent from the Senate.

Insofar as the United States rejected the Parliamentary Supremacy Principle and the Non–Self-Execution Doctrine prevents courts enforcing treaties without implementing legislation, this Doctrine relies on an inapplicable British constitutional principle. Article III gives the federal courts the power to decide *all* cases arising under treaties – whether arguably self-executing or non–self-executing[55] – and the Supremacy Clause requires that state judges enforce U.S. treaties, thereby obviating the arguable need for the treaty to be self-executing.[56]

Nevertheless, since *Foster v. Neilson*, federal courts have interpreted *some* treaty obligations to be non–self-executing.[57] Whether a particular treaty requires action from the political branches should turn on whether its particular provisions require such action. In this regard, we have to distinguish between treaty duties that require its states-parties to refrain from the performance of an overt act and those treaty duties that require the performance of an overt act.

In the case of a treaty duty requiring its states-parties to refrain from performing an overt act, it still may be necessary to define the treaty duty because its language is vague. Certainly, Congress has the Article I authority "[t]o define and punish ... Offences against the Law of Nations," which would include treaty offenses. However, this constitutional authority is not exclusive to Congress. Article III judicial power extends to U.S.

[55] U.S. Const. art. III, § 2, cl. 1 ("The judicial Power shall extend to all Cases, in Law and Equity, arising under ... Treaties ....").

[56] *Id.* at art. VI (Supremacy Clause).

[57] Federal courts also have extended the Non–Self-Execution Doctrine to include some customary international legal norms. *See, e.g.*, Sosa v. Alvarez-Machain, 542 U.S. 692, 124 S. Ct. 2739, 2768, 159 L. Ed. 2d 718 (2004) (indicating need for federal legislation to give customary international legal norms domestic effect) (dictum).

treaties, and such judicial power includes interpreting treaties to provide them with the necessary definition. Furthermore, the United States' treaty partners also have the international legal authority to define the treaty's language through "subsequent agreements between the parties" and "subsequent practices in the application of the treaty which establishes the agreement of the parties regarding [the treaty's] interpretation.[58] For example, in the context of human rights treaties, many of their substantive rights guarantees require their states-parties to refrain from performing overt acts, and these guarantees require definition. However, like many similar human rights guarantees in the Bill of Rights, such rights are still considered to be self-executing insofar as the federal courts have the constitutional authority to enforce them. Although Congress may enact legislation giving further definition to such international legal norms under its constitutional authority to define offences against the law of nations,[59] the federal courts also have a say – indeed, often the final say – on their definition.[60]

However, in the case of a treaty duty requiring its states-parties to perform an overt act, the situation is more complex. At the outset is must be noted that if Congress or the president fails to perform an overt act giving domestic effect to the treaty's obligations, then there should be a factual

[58] *See Vienna Convention*, art. 31 (2) & (3); *see also* Nielsen v. Johnson, 279 U.S. 47, 52 (1929) ("When [a treaty's] meaning is uncertain, recourse may be had to the negotiations and diplomatic correspondence of the contracting parties relating to the subject matter and to their own practical construction of it.").

[59] U.S. Const. art. I, § 8, cl. 10.

[60] *Cf.* Boerne v. Flores, 521 U.S. 507 (1997) (Supreme Court – not Congress – determines final meaning of federal law); Fourteen Diamond Rings v. United States, 183 U.S. 176, 180 (1901):

> We need not consider the force and effect of a resolution of this sort. . . . It is enough that this was a joint resolution; that it was adopted by the Senate by a vote of 26 to 22, not two thirds of a quorum; and that it is absolutely without legal significance on the question before us. The meaning of the treaty cannot be controlled by subsequent explanations of some of those who may have voted to ratify it. What view the House might have taken as to the intention of the Senate in ratifying the treaty we are not informed, nor is it material; and if any implication from the action referred to could properly be indulged, it would seem to be that two thirds of a quorum of the Senate did not consent to the ratification on the grounds indicated.

See supra Subsection 1.1 (discussing final and conclusive judicial review authority of U.S. Supreme Court); *see also infra* Subsection 6.4 (same).

presumption that no such action is needed;[61] otherwise, the members of Congress and the president have failed to comply with their constitutional duties respectively under Article VI "to support the Constitution"[62] by enacting legislation necessary for implementing treaties and under Article II to "faithfully execute the Office of the President."[63] Furthermore, if Congress is presumed to legislate in conformity with the United States' international legal obligations *per* the *Charming Betsy* Rule, at the very least it also should be presumed to have complied with its constitutional obligations to make the necessary legislation implementing the United States' treaty obligations. Otherwise, the United States will be unjustly enriched at the expense of its treaty partners when its treaty partners observe treaties having reasonably expected that the political branches of the United States would enact any necessary legislation to implement the treaty.

An example of a non–self–executing treaty provision is a provision that requires states-parties to perform the overt act of setting penalties for violations of a treaty's provisions that the treaty requires but failed to explicitly set.[64] For example, the *Fourth Geneva Convention* only required that "[t]he High Contracting Parties undertake to enact any legislation necessary to provide effective penal provisions for persons committing, or ordering to be committed, any of the grave breaches of the present Convention."[65] Although somewhat belatedly,[66] Congress consequently enacted the "War Crimes Act of 1996" that implemented this provision

[61] Restatement (Third) of Foreign Relations Law of the United States § 111, n.5 (1987) ("[I]f the Executive Branch has not requested implementing legislation and Congress has not enacted such legislation, there is a strong presumption that the treaty has been considered self-executing by the political branches, and should be considered self-executing by the courts.").

[62] U.S. Const. art. VI, cl. 3 ("The Senators and Representatives before mentioned . . . and all executive and judicial Officers . . . of the United States . . . shall be bound by Oath or Affirmation, to support this Constitution . . . . ").

[63] *Id.* at art. II, § 1, cl. 8.

[64] *See* U.S. Const. art, I, § 8, cl. 10 (Congress has power to punish offences against the law of nations).

[65] Geneva Convention Relative to the Protection of Civilian Persons in Time of War, Aug. 12, 1949, art. 146, 75 U.N.T.S. 287, 6 U.S.T. 3516, T.I.A.S. No. 3365 (entered into force Oct. 21, 1950) [hereinafter *Fourth Geneva Convention*].

[66] The United States became a party to the *Fourth Geneva Convention* in 1955 – over forty years earlier than the War Crimes Act of 1996. However, Congress earlier had implemented

of the *Fourth Geneva Convention* by setting fines, imprisonment, and/or the death penalty.[67]

Unfortunately, Congress and/or the president sometimes fail to comply with their constitutional duties. What is a federal court to do? If the treaty requires the United States to make laws giving domestic effect to the treaty, the court still could not order Congress to make a federal statute because that would be an encroachment on Congress' (and sometimes the president's) exclusive legislative power in violation of the separation of powers principle. If the treaty requires the United States, for example, to undertake diplomatic measures, the court could not order the president to do so because diplomatic missions are exclusively within the power of the Executive Branch.

However, a federal court under the *restitutio in integrum* principle can order injunctive relief on behalf of a prevailing party with proper standing that requires performance of the overt act by the executive branch. Such injunctive relief is not making law because the injunctive relief only applies to the party. Such relief is a proper exercise of the federal judiciary's equitable jurisdiction. However, a federal court cannot order non-parties to perform some act.

If a political branch has failed to comply with its constitutional duty to execute a treaty in regard to non-parties, this fact is not a dispositive issue preventing a federal court from exercising its jurisdiction in equity or at law on behalf of parties to a case. It is merely a political fact that a political branch has failed to fulfill its constitutional duty. Courts are not required to not enforce a treaty because a political branch has violated its constitutional duty. Federal courts constitutionally still must enforce the treaty.

However, it is essential to note the difference between a treaty provision that does not say exactly what is required and a provision that allows a variety of compliance measures. An example of the latter case is when the *ICCPR* allows each state-party "to take the necessary steps, in accordance with its constitutional processes and with the provisions of the [*ICCPR*], to adopt such legislative *or other* measures as may be

many other *Fourth Geneva Convention's* provisions in the Uniform Code of Military Justice, codified at 10 U.S.C. ch. 47.

67 18 U.S.C. § 2441(a).

necessary to give effect to the rights recognized in the [*ICCPR*]."[68] International law sometimes allows states to decide exactly how they go about complying with their international legal obligations within a certain margin.[69] However, this does not mean that states-parties are allowed to not undertake *any* measures. Moreover, such measures must be available, effective, and sufficient.[70] When the United States or one of its member-states either fails to undertake *any* compliance measure or undertakes a compliance measure that is *not effective*, then it is the duty of the federal court exercising its equitable jurisdiction to order such measures that are necessary for bringing the United States or its member-state into compliance insofar as the parties to the case are concerned. For example, when proper equitable relief is unavailable in the case of the Executive Branch's failure to execute a treaty on behalf of a party to a case before the court, the court still can order declaratory relief and monetary damages. And, even though Congress ultimately must make the funding available for satisfaction of the damages award through appropriations legislation, the court's damages order still is a proper exercise of its jurisdiction at law. After all, federal courts often award money damages that eventually must come out of the U.S. treasury, and such damages awards are considered constitutional. Even when a state is allowed a great degree of deference in how it goes about remedying its violation of its international legal obligations, it still must remedy the violation.[71]

The Non–Self-Execution Doctrine has become controversial. In the area of human rights, the United States ratified the *ICCPR* and deposited a declaration stating that the substantive human rights guarantees contained in Articles 1–27 of the *ICCPR* were non–self-executing.[72] The United States also deposited a similar declaration,when it ratified the *Conven-*

[68] *ICCPR*, art. 2 (2) (emphasis provided).

[69] *See, e.g.*, Anguelova v. Bulgaria, Application No. 38361/97, Eur. Ct. H.R. at § 161 (2002) (states allowed "some discretion" as to how they provide remedy to individuals for international law violations).

[70] *See, e.g.*, De la Grange v. Italy, 293-B Eur. Ct. H.R. (ser. A) (1994).

[71] *See, e.g.*, Assanidze v. Georgia, Appl. No. 71503/01, Eur. Ct. H.R., §§ 202–203, 208 (2004) (ordering state-respondent to release applicant from detention because release was urgently needed to stop right to liberty violation).

[72] Multilateral Treaties Deposited with the Secretary General: Status as at 31 Dec. 1992, at 132, U.N. Doc. ST/LEG/SER.E/11 (1993).

tion Against Torture.[73] The constitutionality and international legality of such non–self-execution declarations have been the subject of much academic discussion, and it is not even clear what exactly the Bush administration and the Senate meant by "non–self-executing" in relation to the *ICCPR* and *CAT*.[74] Some federal and state courts often have provided the most sweeping definition to the term by holding that the declaration effectively guts the treaty by denying any enforcement of the treaty's human rights by the courts.[75] The treaty's human rights obligations do not in any way bind the states or the federal government. This is particularly striking in the case of state courts holding that the *ICCPR* does not bind the states because the Supremacy Clause expressly requires that state court judges are "bound" to apply this "supreme Law."[76] For example, the Nevada Supreme Court in *Domingues v. Nevada* held that the *ICCPR*'s prohibition of juvenile executions did not bind the State of Nevada because the Senate had declared that provision of the treaty to be non–self-executing.[77] Although a treaty may allow states to exercise a certain margin of appreciation in how they go about complying with their treaty obligations,[78] it is a wholly different matter to say that a court cannot give the treaty's obligations any legal effect whatsoever without implementing legislation. To implement this latter claim effectively voids

[73] Multilateral Treaties Deposited with the Secretary General: Status as at 31 Dec. 1994, at 185, U.N. Doc. ST/LEG/SER.E/13 (1995).

[74] *See, e.g.*, David Sloss *The Domestication of International Human Rights: Non–Self-Executing Declarations and Human Rights Treaties*, 24 Yale J. Int'l L. 129, 153 (1999) ("The Bush Administration presented different explanations at different times, shifting back and forth between the Foster concept and the 'private cause of action concept.'"), Michael J. Glennon, *The Constitutional Power of the United States Senate to Condition Its Consent to Treaties*, 67 Chi-Kent L. Rev. 533 (1991); Jordan J. Paust, *Self-Executing Treaties*, 82 Am. J. Int'l L. 760 (1988).

[75] *See, e.g.*, Igartua de la Rosa v. United States, 32 F.3d 8, 10 n.1 (declaring rights provisions in *ICCPR* non-self-executing); Ralk v. Lincoln Country, Georgia, 81 F. Supp. 2d 1372 (same); Heinrich v. Sweet, 49 F. Supp. 2d 27, 44 (same); White v. Paulsen, 997 F. Supp. 1380 (same); In the Matter of the Extradition of Cheung, 968 F. Supp. 791, 803 n.17 (same).

[76] U.S. Const. art. VI.

[77] Domingues v. State, 114 Nev.783, 917 P.2d 1279 (1998).

[78] *See, e.g.*, Handyside v. United Kingdom, 24 Eur. Ct. H.R. (ser. A) (1976) (allowing state-party to *ECHR* to exercise a margin of appreciation in protecting morals of children).

the legal nature of the treaty in violation of international law[79] and the U.S. Constitution.[80]

In the situation of the Non–Self-Execution Doctrine's application to the federal government, federal courts have held some treaties to be self-executing.[81] Even those constitutional scholars who have set forth the extremist argument that most treaties should be presumed to require implementing legislation have not dared venture to argue that all treaties have no legally binding authority under the U.S. constitutional scheme.[82] After all, the Supremacy Clause clearly eliminates that possibility by making treaties part of the supreme *law* of the land.

The controversy over the constitutionality of such non–self-execution declarations already appears to have adversely affected Supreme Court jurisprudence. In *Lawrence v. Texas*,[83] the Supreme Court appeared to want to avoid the controversy by not citing the UN Human Rights Committee's decision in *Toonen v. Australia*,[84] which held that the right to privacy guaranteed by the *ICCPR* extended to the protection of homosexual conduct. By not citing *Toonen* – a case particularly on point – the Court appeared to want to avoid addressing the issue of whether the *ICCPR* is indeed non–self-executing as the president and Senate declared. However, whether the *ICCPR* is self-executing or not is not relevant because the Texas antisodomy statute at issue in *Lawrence* did not implicate the separation of powers principle that undergirds the Non–Self-Execution Doctrine in that no action was required from a political branch of the federal government. The Supremacy Clause disposes the issue by

79 *Vienna Convention*, art. 27 ("A party may not invoke the provisions of its internal law as justification for its failure to perform a treaty.").

80 U.S. CONST. art. VI (treaties are part of the supreme law of the land).

81 *See, e.g.*, United States v. Percheman, 32 U.S. (7 Pet.) 51 (1833) (holding that treaty earlier found to be non–self-executing in *Foster v. Neilson* was self-executing according to Spanish version).

82 *See, e.g.*, John C. Yoo, *Globalism and the Constitution: Treaties, Non–Self-Execution, and the Original Understanding*, 99 COLUM. L. REV. 1955 (1999) ("original understanding does not definitively show that all treaties must be non–self-executing").

83 539 U.S. 558 (2003).

84 Communication No. 488/1992, UN Hum. Rts. Ctte., U.N. Doc. CCPR/C/50/D/488 (1994) (right to privacy includes right to engage in homosexual conduct under *ICCPR*).

explicitly requiring Texas state court to comply with the United States' treaty obligations.

Instead, the Court cited several European Court of Human Rights decisions that interpreted the *European Convention of Human Rights*' guarantee of the right to privacy to include the protection of homosexual conduct.[85] In doing so, the Court effectively opted to employ a treaty to which the United States is not a party in construing our Constitution. This move unnecessarily strengthened the hand of those who see some judges as improperly using purportedly "foreign law" in construing the Constitution.[86] This issue avoidance now has resulted with the Supreme Court continuing to affirm the non–self-execution declaration without any critical analysis.[87]

However, the constitutional controversy over such non–self-execution declarations and the Non–Self-Execution Doctrine itself sometimes can be circumvented by employing the ILC approach. The solution to ensure that treaty provisions are given domestic effect is to construe similar provisions of the Constitution in conformity with these treaty provisions. For example, the human rights guaranteed by the first eight amendments are self-executing.[88] Indeed, the Supreme Court already has noted that the privileges and immunities guarantee of the Fourteenth Amendment include those guaranteed by treaty.[89] Therefore, construing these constitutionally guaranteed human rights in conformity with the United States' human rights treaty obligations gives effect to this international human

[85] *See* Lawrence v. Texas, 539 U.S. 558, 573 (citing *Dudgeon v. United Kingdom, Modinos v. Cyprus*, and *Norris v. Ireland*).

[86] Supreme Court justices (whether supportive or non-supportive of the use of international law) also often use refer to international law merely as "world opinion" or "foreign law" in an apparent attempt distance themselves from a constitutional construction with international law that is mandatory. *See, e.g.*, Roper v. Simmons, No. 03–633, – U.S. – (2005) (Kennedy, J.,) (referring to international law as "world opinion"); *id.* at – (Scalia, J. dissenting) (referring to international law as "foreign law").

[87] Sosa v. Alvarez-Machain, 542 U.S. 692, 124 S. Ct. 2739, 2767, 159 L. Ed. 2d 718 ("[A]lthough the [*ICCPR*] does bind the United States as a matter of international law, the United States ratified the Covenant on the express understanding that it was not self-executing and so did not itself create obligations enforceable in the federal courts.") (dictum).

[88] *See* City of Bourne v. Flores, 521 U.S. 507, 524 ("first eight Amendments to the Constitution set forth self executing prohibitions on governmental action").

[89] Slaughter-House Cases, 83 U.S. (16 Wall.) 36, 79 (1873).

rights law. Even those human rights treaties prohibiting the commission of overt acts that the United States has declared to be non–self-executing can be used as evidence of the United States' explicit acceptance of customary international law norms codified in such treaties. Such customary international law can be used to construe the human rights guarantees in the Constitution because the Constitution as a treaty must be construed in conformity with customary international law according to the conventional law of nations.[90]

Furthermore, in cases where the Constitution's language is silent on other human rights (such as privacy and the right to travel), the Ninth Amendment[91] can be construed in conformity with international human rights law that *does* explicitly guarantee such rights.[92] Such an international legal construction is essential for recognizing human rights that are not explicitly mentioned in the Constitution and, as a result, are

[90] *See Vienna Convention*, art. 31(3)(c) (treaty must be interpreted in light of "any rules of international law applicable in the relations between the parties"); *Vienna Convention-SIO*, art. 31(3)(c) (treaty between intergovernmental organization and state must be interpreted in light of "any relevant rules of international law applicable in the relations between the parties"); Geofroy v. Riggs, 133 U.S. 258, 271 (1890) (meaning of treaty language "to be taken in their ordinary meaning, as understood in the public law of nations"); Legal Consequences for States of the Continued Presence of South Africa in Namibia (South West Africa) notwithstanding Security Council Resolution 276 (1970), Advisory Opinion, 1971 I.C.J. 16, 31 (1971) ("an international instrument must be interpreted and applied within the overall framework of the [international] juridical system in force at the time of the interpretation"); Interpretation of the American Declaration of the Rights and Duties of Man within the Framework of Article 64 of the American Convention on Human Rights, Advisory Opinion OC-10/89, Inter-Am. Ct. H.R. Ser. A, No. 10, at ¶ 37 (1989) (same); Coard v. United States, Inter-Am. Cm. H.R., No. 109/99 at ¶ 40 (1999), *available at* http://www.cidh.oas.org/annualrep/99eng/Merits/UnitedStates10.951.htm (last visited Feb. 15, 2003) (same).

[91] U.S. CONST. amend. XIV ("The enumeration in the Constitution, of certain rights, shall not be construed to deny or disparage others retained by the people."). Ninth Amendment rights are enforceable in federal and state courts. *See, e.g.*, Griswold v. Connecticut, 381 U.S. 479 (1965) (right to privacy enforceable in federal court); In re Sherol, 581 P.2d 884 (Okla. 1978) (Ninth Amendment right to respect for family integrity enforceable in state court); Voichahoske v. City of Grand Island, 194 Neb. 175 (1975) (Ninth Amendment right to marry enforceable in state court).

[92] *See, e.g.*, *ICCPR*, arts. 12 (right to privacy) and 13 (right to travel); *see also* FRANCISCO FORREST MARTIN, CHALLENGING HUMAN RIGHTS VIOLATIONS: USING INTERNATIONAL LAW IN U.S. COURTS 64–65 (2001) [hereinafter, MARTIN, CHALLENGING]; Jordan J. Paust, *Human Rights and the Ninth Amendment: A New Form of Guarantee*, 60 CORNELL L. REV. 231 (1975).

sometimes not protected.[93] Accordingly, one can make an end-run around the issue of non–self-execution by using the ILC approach because the issue of requiring implementing legislation is made moot.[94]

5.3. FEDERAL STATUTES: IMPLEMENTING THE CONSTITUTION AND OTHER TREATIES

Federal statutes represent a species of international law by being treaty-implementing law made by an intergovernmental organization. Congress (with sometimes the President) as an intergovernmental organization makes law that implements the Constitution or other U.S. treaties. Because Article III expressly mentions "the laws of the United States," federal statutory law is an Article III, international legal authority. There are two rules that are important to federal statutory interpretation that impact the constitutional interpretation of federal judicial power: the *Charming Betsy* Rule and the Last-in-Time Rule.

[93] *See, e.g.*, Bowers v. Hardwick, 478 U.S. 186 (1986) (no privacy right to engage in homosexual conduct under the Fourth and Fifth Amendments), *rev'd* in Lawrence v. Texas, 539 U.S. 558.

[94] In civil cases against federal defendants accused of constitutional violations as construed by the United States' international legal obligations *per* the ILC Rule, plaintiffs can use a *Bivens/Bolling* action for seeking damages and/or injunctive relief. *See* Bivens v. Six Unknown Named Agents, 402 U.S. 388 (1971) (recognizing private cause of action for Fourth Amendment violations); Bolling v. Sharpe, 347 U.S. 497 (1954) (recognizing private right to injunctive relief for Fifth Amendment violations).

In civil cases against state defendants accused of constitutional violations as construed by the United States' international legal obligations *per* the ILC approach, plaintiffs can use 42 U.S.C. § 1983. 42 U.S.C. § 1983 states:

> Every person who, under color of any statute, ordinance, regulation, custom, or usage, of any State or Territory or the District of Columbia, subjects, or causes to be subjected, any citizen of the United States or other person within the jurisdiction thereof to the deprivation of any rights, privileges, or immunities secured by the Constitution and laws, shall be liable to the party injured in an action at law, suit in equity, or other proper proceeding for redress, except that in any action brought against a judicial officer for an act or omission taken in such officer's judicial capacity, injunctive relief shall not be granted unless a declaratory decree was violated or declaratory relief was unavailable. For the purposes of this section, any Act of Congress applicable exclusively to the District of Columbia shall be considered to be a statute of the District of Columbia.

The *Charming Betsy* Rule

It is a settled rule of federal statutory interpretation that "an act of Congress ought never to be construed to violate the law of nations if any other possible construction remains."[95] This rule generally is known as the *Charming Betsy* Rule, named after the 1804 U.S. Supreme Court case whose opinion was authored by Mr. Chief Justice John Marshall.[96] It is an important interpretive rule that ensures federal statutory law does not violate the United States' international legal obligations.

The U.S. Supreme Court effectively appears to have been the first international tribunal to articulate a rule that an act of a constituent organ of a treaty implementing that treaty must be construed to avoid conflicts with the organ's other international legal obligations. Many years later, the International Court of Justice in its 1970 *Namibia Advisory Opinion* would opine that "an *international instrument* must be interpreted . . . within the overall framework of the [international] juridical system."[97] The Court's use of the phrase "international instrument" includes legal instruments other than treaties, such as treaty implementing legislation.

It is a mistake to interpret the *Charming Betsy* Rule to imply that if it is *unavoidable* to construe a federal statute to *not* violate the law of nations, then the federal statute constitutionally can violate all such norms. Some jurists may be led to believe that such an interpretive implication is correct on the basis that the Rule is based on British common law. British common law held that statutes in abrogation of the common law (which was considered to have fully adopted the law of nations[98]) were to be

95 Murray v. Schooner Charming Betsy, 6 U.S. (2 Cranch.) 64, 118; Weinberger v. Rossi, 456 U.S. 25 (1982) (federal statutes must be construed in conformity with the United States' treaty obligations).

96 However, the Supreme Court in an earlier case had used another formulation of the Rule. *See* Talbot v. Seeman, 5 U.S. (1 Cranch) 1, 43 (1801) (*per* Marshall, C.J.) ("the laws of the United States ought not, if it be avoidable, so to be construed as to infract the common principles and usages of nations").

97 Legal Consequences for States of the Continued Presence of South Africa in Namibia (South West Africa) notwithstanding Security Council Resolution 276 (1970), Advisory Opinion, 1971 I.C.J. 16, 31 (1971) (emphasis provided).

98 *See, e.g.*, 4 BLACKSTONE'S COMMENTARIES 67 (law of nations in England "adopted in its full extent by the common law").

construed strictly;[99] if a statute did conflict with common law, the statute trumped the common law because Parliament was the supreme lawmaker. However, this interpretive position relies on incorporating the notion of Parliamentary Supremacy in lawmaking into the U.S. constitutional law, and the U.S. Constitution rejected the notion of Parliamentary Supremacy by not making Congress the supreme law making body.[100]

An international legal construction of the Rule provides the proper interpretive implication of the Rule by taking into account the whole meaning of the law of nations. The law of nations has two parts. The first part is the positive law of nations, which consists of the voluntary, customary, and conventional law of nations.[101] The second part is the necessary law of nations (*i.e.*, the natural law of nations).[102] A state can impose its own notion of the necessary law of nations only on itself. A state cannot impose its own notion of the necessary law of nations on other states[103] in the same sense that it cannot impose its own legislation on other states.[104] Therefore, the *Charming Betsy* Rule must be construed to imply only that federal statutes constitutionally can sometimes violate another state's understanding of the necessary law of nations.

99 *See, e.g.*, Donaldson v. Becket, 4 Burr. 2408, 98 Eng. Rep. 257 (H.L. 1774) (copyright statute strictly construed to not abrogate common law).

100 *See infra* discussion on Last-in-Time Rule.

101 Emmerich de Vattel, The Law of Nations or Principles of the Law of Nature Applied to the Conduct and Affairs of Nations and Sovereign, *Preliminaries*, § 27 (1758) [hereinafter, Vattel, Law of Nations].

102 *See, e.g., ibid., Preliminaries*, at § 7; J.J. Burlamaqui, 1 The Principles of Natural Law, pt. II, ch. VI, § IX (1748) (one kind of law of nations is "universal, necessary, and self-obligatory . . . [and] differs in nothing from the law of nature, and is consequently immutable") [hereinafter Burlamaqui, Principles].

103 *See, e.g.*, Vattel, Law of Nations, *supra* note 101 at *Preliminaries*, § 28 ("as the Necessary law is always obligatory on the conscience, a nation ought never to lose sight of it in deliberating on the line of conduct she is to pursue in order to fulfil her duty; but when there is question of examining what she may demand of other states, she must consult the Voluntary law, whose maxims are devoted to the safety and advantage of the universal society of mankind.").

104 *See* Joseph Story, Commentaries on the Conflict of Laws19, 21–22 (2d ed. 1841) ("no state or nation can, by its laws, directly affect, or bind property out of its own territory, or persons not resident therein"); Ulrich Huber, De Conflictu Legum *in* E. Lorenzen, Selected Articles on the Conflict of Laws 136 (1947) ("Every state's laws apply within the state's territory, but not beyond.").

This distinction between the positive law of nations and the necessary law of nations comes out more clearly in two subsequent Supreme Court opinions also authored by John Marshall. In *The Antelope*, Marshall recognized that the slave trade violated the necessary law of nations, but that the slave trade did not violate the positive law of nations for some states because some states had accepted a rule permitting the practice.

> That [the slave trade] is contrary to the law of nature will scarcely be denied. . . . But from the earliest times war has existed, and war confers rights in which all have acquiesced. Among the most enlightened nations of antiquity, one of these was, that the victor might enslave the vanquished. This, which was the usage of all, could not be pronounced repugnant to the law of nations, which is certainly to be tried by the test of general usage. That which has received the assent of all, must be the law of all.
>
> * * * * *
>
> Throughout Christendom, this harsh rule has been exploded, and war is no longer considered as giving a right to enslave captives. But this triumph of humanity has not been universal. The parties to the modern law of nations do not propagate their principles by force; and Africa has not yet adopted them. Throughout the whole extent of that immense continent, so far as we know its history, it is still the law of nations that prisoners are slaves. Can those who have themselves renounced this law, be permitted to participate in its effects by purchasing the beings who are its victims?
>
> Whatever might be the answer of a moralist to this question, a jurist must search for its legal solution, in those principles of action which are sanctioned by the usages, the national acts, and the general assent, of that portion of the world of which he considers himself as a part, and to whose law the appeal is made. If we resort to this standard as the test of international law, the question, as has already been observed, is decided in favour of the legality of the trade. Both Europe and America embarked in it; and for nearly two centuries, it was carried on without opposition, and without censure. A jurist could not say, that a practice thus supported was illegal, and that those engaged in it might be punished, either personally, or by deprivation of property.
>
> In this commerce, thus sanctioned by universal assent, every nation has an equal right to engage. How is this right to be lost? Each may renounce it for its own people; but can this renunciation affect others?

> No principle of general law is more universally acknowledged, than the perfect equality of nations. Russia and Geneva have equal rights. It results from this equality, that no one can rightfully impose a rule on another. Each legislates for itself, but its legislation can operate on itself alone. A right, then, which is vested in all by the consent of all, can be devested only be consent; and this trade, in which all have participated, must remain lawful to those who cannot be induced to relinquish it. As no nation can prescribe a rule for others, none can make a law of nations; and this traffic remains lawful to those whose governments have not forbidden it.
>
> If it is consistent with the law of nations, it cannot in itself be piracy. It can be made so only by statute; and the obligation of the statute cannot transcend the legislative power of the state which may enact it.[105]

In *The Schooner Exchange v. McFaddon*, the Supreme Court held that states could not violate the conventional law of nations:

> In almost every instance, the treaties between civilized nations contain a stipulation to this effect in favor of vessels driven in by stress of weather or other urgent necessity. In such cases the sovereign is bound by compact to authorize foreign vessels to enter his ports. The treaty binds him to allow vessels in distress to find refuge and asylum in his ports, and *this is a license which he is not at liberty to retract.*"[106]

Accordingly, if another state's legislation instantiated a rule that it considered to reflect the necessary law of nations and this rule clearly conflicted with a U.S. federal statute, then the federal statute could violate this arguable necessary law of nations rule without violating the rest of the law of nations. If the *Charming Betsy* Rule were to be interpreted to allow federal statutes to violate all law of nations norms, then Marshall's subsequent opinions violated his own *Charming Betsy* Rule. The proper implication to draw from the *Charming Betsy* Rule is the recognition of an international legal principle itself, namely, that unless a domestic law reflects a positive law of nations obligation on other states, a state cannot impose its domestic law on these states.

[105] 23 U.S. 66, 20–21 (1825).

[106] *See* The Schooner Exchange v. McFaddon, 11 U.S. (7 Cranch) 116, 141 (1812) (emphasis provided).

Unfortunately, this incorrect interpretive implication of the *Charming Betsy* Rule may have laid the conceptual groundwork for another federal statutory interpretation rule that has seriously undermined international legal accountability for the United States: the Last-in-Time Rule.

The International Illegitimacy of the Last-in-Time Rule

Probably the most fundamental tenet of international law is *pacta sunt servanda* ("promises are to be kept"), that is, treaties are to be observed.[107] Treaties must be observed notwithstanding a state-party's domestic law to the contrary.[108] However, the U.S. Supreme Court in 1870 began to hold that a federal statute could violate a U.S. treaty if the statute was enacted after the treaty's ratification.[109] This is known as the "Last-in-Time" Rule. The Rule also states that a federal statute is trumped by a later ratified treaty. Both statements of the Rule are premised on the claim that federal statutes and treaties have equal legal authority because the Constitution's Supremacy Clause makes both federal statutes and U.S. treaties part of "the supreme Law of the Land."[110] Of course, this claim conveniently ignores the fact that the Supremacy Clause also makes the Constitution part of the supreme law of the land, and yet the Constitution clearly can trump federal statutes.

Nonetheless, the Rule continues to be considered well-settled law, as evidenced by the Supreme Court's 1998 ruling in *Breard v. Greene*[111] in which the Court denied petitioner's request for a writ of habeas corpus in part on the basis that the Antiterrorism and Effective Death Penalty Act (AEDPA)[112] superseded the earlier ratified the *Vienna Convention on Consular Relations* that guaranteed foreign nationals the right to consular assistance when they are arrested.[113]

I submit that the Last-in-Time Rule is an unconstitutional and immoral judge-made rule on a number of grounds. First, the text of the Supremacy

107 *See, e.g., Vienna Convention*, art. 26 ("Every treaty in force is binding upon the parties to it and must be performed by them in good faith.").

108 *See, e.g., id.* at art. 27 ("A party may not invoke the provisions of its internal law as justification for its failure to perform a treaty.").

109 The Cherokee Tobacco, 78 U.S. (11 Wall.) 616 (1870) (Last-in-Time Rule).

110 U.S. Const. art. VI.

111 523 U.S. 371 (1998).

112 28 U.S. C. A. §§ 2254(a)-(e)(2) (Supp. 1998).

113 Apr. 24, 1963, [1970] 21 U. S. T. 77, T.I.A.S. No. 6820.

Clause indicates that treaties have greater authority than federal statutory law. Treaties are made "under the authority of the United States,"[114] and such authority precedes the establishment of our constitutional government as the text of the Supremacy Clause indicates by recognizing the continuing supreme legal authority of treaties made under the Articles of Confederation. The United States legally could dissolve the Constitution (as it did earlier with the Articles of Confederation[115]) and establish a new form of government. If it did so, treaties would continue to bind the United States (as they do under the Constitution). The treaty-making authority comes from the United States like the Constitution.

By contrast, federal statutes are only made in "pursuance" of the Constitution.[116] Articles III and VI do not say that federal statutes are made under the authority of the United States. The authority of federal statutes is based solely on the Constitution, and federal statutes only implement the Constitution. If the United States dissolved the Constitution and established a new constitution, federal statutes enacted in pursuance of the old Constitution would no longer be valid (unless the new constitution provided so).

Furthermore, if Congress enacts a federal statute on subject-matter that exceeds the powers explicitly delegated to the political branches[117] or enacts a federal statute that violates substantive provisions of the

[114] U.S. CONST. art. VI, § 2.

[115] However, unanimous state consent would be required this time. Nonunanimity was legally sufficient for ratifying the Constitution because state violations of the Articles and the failure of the states to use federal courts for resolving allegations of state Articles violations enabled the United States to adopt a nine-state rule for ratifying the Constitution. *See* Francisco Forrest Martin, *Our Constitution as Federal Treaty: A New Theory of United States Constitutional Construction Based on an Originalist Understanding for Addressing a New World*, 31 HASTINGS CONST. L. QUART. 269, 283–91 (2004). Furthermore, a constitutional amendment probably would be insufficient because all states are parties to the Constitution, and the ratification of only three-fourths of the states is required for an amendment to go into force. U.S. CONST. art. V. Therefore, unanimous state consent would be required in order to dissolve the Constitution.

[116] U.S. CONST. art. VI, § 2 ("This Constitution, and the Law of the United States which shall be made in Pursuance thereof; . . . shall be the supreme Law of the Land").

[117] *See, e.g.*, Clinton v. City of New York, 524 U.S. 417 (1998) (federal statute allowing line-item veto held unconstitutional because veto exceeds political branches' constitutional powers).

Constitution,[118] such federal statutes are constitutionally void. By contrast, treaties constitutionally can govern matters not explicitly addressed in the Constitution because there is no subject-matter limitation on the treaty-making authority of the president and Senate in the Constitution. For example, Congress could not enact a law that violates a treaty guaranteeing the right to explore Mars for scientific purposes because Congress has no apparent enumerated power to prohibit scientific exploration in outer space. In such a case, the treaty has greater constitutional authority than a federal statute.

The only constitutional limitation on the treaty power, as the U.S. Supreme Court in *Reid v. Covert* held,[119] is that treaties cannot violate the Constitution.[120] Indeed, this holding is consistent with international law. The *Vienna Convention on the Law of Treaties* allows a state to nullify a treaty if the treaty manifestly violates a fundamental rule of its internal law, such as its constitution.[121]

Therefore, if treaties have greater constitutional authority then federal statutes, then the Last-in-Time Rule's assumption that federal statutes have equal constitutional authority with treaties, is false.

A second problem with the Last-in-Time Rules is that early U.S. Supreme Court precedent also indicated that treaties could not be violated. In *The Schooner Exchange v. McFaddon*, the Court in 1812 noted that treaties could not be violated.

> In almost every instance, the treaties between civilized nations contain a stipulation to this effect in favor of vessels driven in by stress of weather or other urgent necessity. In such cases, the sovereign is bound by compact to authorize foreign vessels to enter his ports. The treaty binds him to allow

118 *See, e.g.*, Marbury v. Madison, 5 U.S. (1 Cranch.) 137 (1803) (federal statute in violation of Constitution is void).

119 Reid v. Covert, 354 U.S. 1, 15–19 (1957).

120 Interestingly enough, however, no U.S. court has ever found any treaty unconstitutional.

121 *See Vienna Convention*, art. 46 (1) ("A state may not invoke the fact that its consent to be bound by a treaty has been expressed in violation of a provision of its internal law regarding competence to conclude treaties as invalidating its consent unless that violation was manifest and concerned a rule of its internal law of fundamental importance."); *Vienna Convention-SIO*, art. 46.

vessels in distress to find refuge and asylum in his ports, and *this is a license which he is not at liberty to retract.*"[122]

Fifty-two years later, the Supreme Court failed to address this earlier rule and effectively reversed itself by recognizing the Last-in-Time Rule. In doing so, the Court legitimized a continuing legacy of racial discrimination against Native-Americans and aliens[123] that later culminated in the Court's *Plessy v. Ferguson* decision against African Americans.[124] For example, in the *Chinese Exclusion Cases*, the Supreme Court, in allowing Congress to break a U.S.-China treaty guaranteeing Chinese immigration to the United States, approvingly stated that the presence of Chinese laborers had a baneful effect upon the material interests of the state, and upon public morals; that their immigration was in numbers approaching the character of an Oriental invasion, and was a menace to our civilization.[125]

Seven years later, the Court would extend its racism to African Americans in *Plessy v. Ferguson* by facetiously asserting that "[l]aws permitting, and even requiring, [the separation of Whites and Negroes], in places where they are liable to be brought into contact, do not necessarily imply the inferiority of either race to the other . . ."[126] What is duplicitous about the Supreme Court's rulings in the *Chinese Exclusion Cases* and *Plessy* is that the Court in the former case criticized Chinese non-citizens for not assimilating with Americans whereas the Court in the latter case prevented African American citizens from assimilating with their fellow Americans.

Indeed, this discrimination against not only African Americans but also Native Americans and aliens runs afoul of the constitutional guarantee of equal protection of the laws. Although the Fourteenth Amendment's

[122] *See* The Schooner Exchange v. McFaddon, 11 U.S. (7 Cranch) 116, 141 (emphasis provided).

[123] *See, e.g.*, The Cherokee Tobacco, 78 U.S. (11 Wall.) 616 (1870) (breaking treaty with Cherokee nation by charging tax on tobacco); Head Money Cases, 112 U.S. 580 (1884) (breaking friendship treaties by charging head tax on entering aliens); Chae Chan Ping v. United States ("*Chinese Exclusion Cases*"), 130 U.S. 581 (1889) (breaking treaty with China by excluding Chinese immigrants); Thomas v. Gay, 169 U.S. 264 (1898) (breaking treaty with Cherokee nation by denying self-government); Stephens v. Cherokee Nation, 174 U.S. 445 (1899) (breaking treaty with Cherokee nation by taking land).

[124] 163 U.S. 537 (1896).

[125] 130 U.S. 581, 595.

[126] 163 U.S. 537, 544.

equal protection guarantee only applies, strictly speaking, to the states,[127] the Supreme Court later has interpreted the Fifth Amendment's substantive due process protections to include the right to equal protection of the laws – especially in regard to aliens.[128] Such an interpretation of the Fifth Amendment also is consonant with earlier Supreme Court precedent that held that the United States' treaty obligations should be construed liberally in order to avoid conflicts with our treaty-partners whose nationals could otherwise be the subject of harmful alienage discrimination.[129] Accordingly, any federal statute that discriminates against aliens by voiding previous treaty obligations protecting them should be subjected to strict scrutiny, at the very least.[130]

A third problem with the Last-in-Time Rule is that it unnecessarily overreaches to flatly assert that the Congress constitutionally could void treaties anytime that it wished by later enacting legislation. International law itself allows states to void, suspend, or withdraw from treaty obligations on a number of grounds. For example, material breach by a treaty partner and fraud are lawful grounds for abrogating a treaty; a fundamental change of circumstances is a lawful ground for withdrawing from a treaty; and treaty suspension or withdrawal may be allowed by the treaty itself.[131]

Although states have inherent sovereignty (that sometimes includes a right to expel[132] or prevent entry of aliens as was the case with the *Chinese Exclusion Cases*[133]), this sovereignty is limited by the sovereign's own capacity to impose self-limits by entering into treaties. Sovereignty

[127] *See* U.S. CONST. amend. XIV, § 1 ("No State shall . . . deny to any person within its jurisdiction the equal protection of the laws.").

[128] *See* Hampton v. Wong, 426 U.S. 88 (1976) (federal alienage discrimination violative of Fifth Amendment guarantee prohibiting denial of liberty without due process of law).

[129] *See* Geofroy v. Riggs, 133 U.S. 258, 271 (1890) ("It is a general principle of construction with respect to treaties that they shall be liberally construed so as to carry out the apparent intention of the parties to secure equality and reciprocity between them.").

[130] *Cf.* Bernal v. Fainter, 467 U.S. 216 (1984) (strict scrutiny test applied to state discrimination on basis of alienage).

[131] *See, e.g.*, VATTEL, 2 LAW OF NATIONS, *supra* note 101, at § 202 (treaty breach); *id.* at § 296 (change of circumstances); *Vienna Convention*, arts. 54 (termination or withdrawal allowed by treaty); 60 (breach), and 62 (fundamental change of circumstances).

[132] Harisiades v. Shaughnessy, 342 U.S. 580, 587–88 (1952).

[133] 130 U.S. 581, 595.

is not a trump card for getting out of one's legal obligations when s/he has the predilection to do so.

A fourth reason for rejecting the Last-in-Time Rule is that when the U.S. government violates its treaty obligations, its treaty partners under the conventional law of nations can lawfully abrogate their international legal obligations with the American people (with the exception of humanitarian or human rights norms). Such action by the U.S. government would violate the social contract established by the American people by eliminating the recognition of rights enjoyed by the American people, and we should recall that violations of international law by the British Parliament constituted one of the justifications for breaking our ties with Great Britain mentioned in the Declaration of Independence.[134]

The fifth reason is that the need for the Last-in-Time Rule sometimes is justified on a false notion of Congressional Supremacy. The Constitution does not explicitly incorporate the Last-in-Time Rule; therefore, one must attempt to provide a justification of it on the basis of some general constitutional principle extrapolated from the text of the Constitution. The obvious choice is a principle of Congressional Supremacy in lawmaking extrapolated from Article I that states "[a]ll legislative Powers . . . shall be vested in [the] Congress . . ." The notion of Congressional Supremacy in lawmaking appears to be derived from the British principle of Parliamentary Supremacy, and the British Parliamentary Supremacy Principle requires the use of a last-in-time rule that always allows Parliament to reverse its own supreme laws.

As we saw earlier,[135] the notion of Congressional Supremacy has unconstitutionally undermined the domestic effect of U.S. treaties through an application of the Non–Self-Execution Doctrine. Indeed, the Last-in-Time Rule intrinsically is related to the Non–Self-Execution Doctrine because if Congress has the Article I authority to make a federal statute implementing a treaty, it also would appear that it also has the authority to make a subsequent federal statute violating the treaty. The notion of

[134] *See* DECLARATION OF INDEPENDENCE at ¶ 3 (dissolution of social contract with Great Britain justified on bases of Britain's "cutting off our Trade with all parts of the world . . . [and the] . . . plunder[ing of] our seas."). The law of nations guarantees freedom of trade and the seas. *See, e.g.*, HUGO GROTIUS, OF THE FREEDOM OF THE SEAS ch. 12 (1609).

[135] *See supra* Subsection 5.2.

Congressional Supremacy in conjunction with the Non–Self-Execution Doctrine has been used to justify the Last-in-Time Rule on the basis that because some treaty provisions require implementing legislation, treaties cannot have greater legal authority than federal statutes.[136] However, this conclusion is invalid. Just because a legal instrument requires another kind of legal instrument for the first instrument's implementation does not entail that the second instrument has equal legal authority – much less greater authority. For example, the Constitution sometimes requires

[136] *See, e.g.*, Vasan Kesavan, *Three Tiers of Federal Law*, 100 Nw. U. L. Rev. 1479 (2006) (arguing for federal statutes' superiority to most treaties). Kesavan's argument is based on (i) the fact that the laws of the United States textually precede treaties in the Supremacy Clause and (ii) an interpretation of the Founders' understanding of U.S. treaty-making based on the British treaty-making model. Although Kesavan's textual argument is appealing at first glance, the argument fails when one examines other parts of the Constitution. For example, it is difficult to see how Congress' power to borrow money is greater than its power to declare war just because the power to borrow textually precedes the power to declare war in Article I – especially given Kesavan's own recognition of the importance of war and peace in both the U.S. and British treaty-making models. *Ibid.* at 1616. A more plausible explanation for placing treaties after laws of the United States in the text of the Supremacy Clause is that not all treaties mentioned in the Supremacy Clause were made "in Pursuance [of the Constitution]" unlike all federal statutes. Some U.S. treaties were made before the Constitution's entrance into force. The textual placement of treaties after federal statutes can best be explained as an exercise in semantic conciseness.

As for Kesavan's interpretation of the Founders' understanding, Kesavan mistakenly concludes from some of the Founders' analogizing of the U.S. treaty-making model to the British non–self-execution model that non–self-execution logically entails the legal superiority of federal statutes to treaties in most cases. Although some of the Founders' certainly did believe in the superiority of federal statutes to treaties, it is not the case with other Founders when both are analogizing the U.S. model to the British model. As discussed later, Hamilton, Jay, and Davie certainly did not believe that federal statutes were legally superior to treaties. Indeed, when some members of the Pennsylvania convention proposed an amendment that explicitly would have made those U.S. treaties, which "were opposed to the existing laws of the United States," invalid in the absence of Congress repealing those laws, the amendment was not approved, and all of the amendment's supporters subsequently voted against ratification of the Constitution.

The best conclusion to be drawn from Founders' statements (and a conclusion that appears to be consistent with Kesavan's own research) is that there was a division of opinion as to the relative authority of federal statutes and treaties. In light of the division, it probably is best not to place too much reliance on the original public understanding. This approach would be consistent with the international law governing treaty interpretation which allows the *travaux préparatoires* and the circumstances of the treaty's conclusion to be used only as supplementary means of *confirming* the meaning of a treaty. *See Vienna Convention*, art. 31.

Congress to make statutes in order to implement the Constitution, but this necessity does not make federal statutes equal to the Constitution in terms of legal authority. The Constitution has greater legal authority than federal statutes. Furthermore, just because a legal instrument may require another kind of legal instrument to repeal or alter an earlier legal instrument of the same kind does not entail that the legal instruments of the second kind are equal to the first in terms of legal authority. For example, a new federal statute sometimes requires the president to issue a new executive order altering or repealing an old executive order, but this necessity does not make such executive orders equal to federal statutes in terms of legal authority. Federal statutes have greater legal authority than executive orders.

A comparison of purported Congressional Supremacy with Parliamentary Supremacy highlights how the Last-in-Time Rule's application to treaties is based on the false premise of Congressional Supremacy. Insofar as the American Last-in-Time Rule is premised on the basis of its need to ensure Congressional Supremacy, the premise for this justification is false. The United States rejected the British constitutional principle of Parliamentary Supremacy by declaring its independence from Great Britain and forming governments under the Articles of Confederation and the Constitution that did not make their respective Congresses supreme. The American Last-in-Time Rule itself makes Congressional Supremacy impossible by allowing the president (with the consent of the Senate) to make a treaty that supersedes an earlier congressionally enacted federal statute. If there is no valid constitutional principle upon which to justify the Last-in-Time Rule, the Rule is the mere product of judges exercising a political predilection in favor of Congress.[137]

[137] Furthermore, the American Last-in-Time Rule is a corruption of the British last-in-time rule because treaties under British constitutional law never have domestic legal effect (without acts of Parliament giving them such effect). This is not the case with U.S. constitutional law in which treaties often do have domestic legal effect without the need for implementing legislation. The British last-in-time rule only applies to acts of Parliament, whereas the American Last-in-Time Rule applies to both statutes and treaties.

On the other hand, one may argue that the American Last-in-Time Rule is just an *adaptation* – not a corrupted version – of the British rule to the peculiar American constitutional scheme purportedly making treaties equal to statutes, which British constitutional law does not. If Parliament in the future were to enact legislation stating that all treaties have equal legal status to acts of Parliament and subsequently enacts a statute violating

This grafting of the notion of Parliamentary Supremacy onto the U.S. constitutional plan for treaty-making unfortunately led some members of the Constitutional Convention and state constitutional conventions to argue that U.S. treaties should not have greater constitutional authority than federal statutes. For example, John Francis Mercer and George Mason during the Constitutional Convention believed that treaties should not be "final so as to alter the laws of the land" or "repeal" federal statutes unless such treaties had been ratified by legislative authority [because] this was the case of Treaties in Great Britain," and they contended that "the Senate ought not to have the power of treaties."[138] However, the Constitution finally did include the Senate in the treaty-making process, and Mercer and Mason subsequently did not vote for the adoption of the Constitution, thereby undercutting the authority of their statements at the Constitutional Convention. Most importantly, Mercer and Mason incorrectly imposed the notion of legislative supremacy and its consequent demand for implementing legislation onto the U.S. constitutional treaty-making process.[139]

Other Framers did not agree with Mercer and Mason. Alexander Hamilton stated that it was "understood by all" during the Constitutional Convention that the Constitution's treaty power was "competent to . . . controul and bind the legislative power of Congress" and that "no objection was made to the idea of its controuling *future* exercises of the legislative power."[140] John Jay gave one reason why federal statutes could not supersede the United States' treaty obligations:

one of these treaties, this statute would be constitutional under the British last-in-time rule only because of the Parliamentary Supremacy Principle. Hence, a last-in-time rule would be applicable. However, if Congress were to enact a statute inconsistent with an earlier ratified U.S. treaty, the application of a last-in-time rule to supersede the treaty could not be based on a rule of congressional supremacy because the president still later could make a treaty superseding this statute. Again, there is no Congressional supremacy on which to base the Last-in-Time Rule's application to treaties.

138 2 THE RECORDS OF THE FEDERAL CONVENTION OF 1787 297–98 (Max Farrand ed. 1937) [hereinafter FARRAND'S RECORDS].

139 Unfortunately, this incorrect imposition has continued. *See, e.g.*, AKHIL REED AMAR, AMERICA'S CONSTITUTION: A BIOGRAPHY 305–307 (2005) (incorrectly arguing for Last-in-Time Rule on basis of Mercer and Mason's statements relying on legislative supremacy).

140 Alexander Hamilton, *The Defence No. 38* (1795), in 20 THE PAPERS OF ALEXANDER HAMILTON 22, 25 n.* (Harold C. Syrett ed. 1974) (emphasis provided).

> They who make laws may, without doubt, amend or repeal them; and it will not be disputed that they who make treaties may alter or cancel them; but still let us not forget that treaties are made, not by only one of the contracting parties, but by both; and consequently, that as the consent of both was essential to their formation at first, so must it ever afterwards be to alter or cancel them. The proposed Constitution, therefore, has not in the least extended the obligation of treaties. They are just as binding, and just as far beyond the lawful reach of legislative acts now, as they will be at any future period, or under any form of government.[141]

William Davie elaborated further and stated that treaties were supreme over federal statutes:

> [A]lthough treaties are mere conventional acts between the contracting parties, yet, by the law of nations, they are the supreme law of the land to their respective citizens or subjects. All civilized nations have concurred in considering them as paramount to an ordinary act of legislation.[142]

In 1791, James Wilson argued that the reason why a nation could not violate its treaties with other nations was because such a violation was a disservice to the nation's own members:

> When men have formed themselves into a state or nation, they may reciprocally enter into particular engagements, and, in this manner, contract new obligations in favour of the members of the community; but they cannot, by this union, discharge themselves from any duties which they previously owed to those, who form no part of the union. They continue under all the obligations required by the universal society of the human race – the great society of nations. The law of that great and universal society requires, that each nation should contribute to the perfection and happiness of the others. It is, therefore, a duty which every nation owes to itself, to acquire those qualifications, which will fit and enable it to discharge those duties which it owes to others.[143]

Jay's, Davie's, and Wilson's explanations undercut an otherwise compelling claim in support of the Last-in-Time Rule: U.S. treaties should

[141] THE FEDERALIST NO. 64 (Jay) at ¶ 12 (1788).

[142] 4 THE DEBATES IN THE SEVERAL STATE CONVENTIONS ON THE ADOPTION OF THE FEDERAL CONSTITUTION 119 (Jonathan Elliot ed. 1968) [hereinafter ELLIOT'S DEBATES].

[143] JAMES WILSON, LECTURES ON LAW, Of the Law of Nations, ¶ 32 (1791).

not be able to bind future generations of Americans who had no say in their adoption. This claim ignores the fact that these treaties also bind the future generations of foreign nations that are also state-parties to these treaties. Moreover, future generations of Americans often also have been the recipients of benefits produced by the observance of these treaties by foreign nations. Just because a treaty may become considered later by Congress to not be beneficial to the American people is an insufficient reason for no longer observing the treaty. The American people owe their treaty-partner for the benefits that they received earlier. Indeed, if we constitutionally could ignore our *treaty* obligations, we could ignore our *constitutional* obligations because our generation did not participate in the ratifications of the Constitution.

During the Jay Treaty controversy five years later, U.S. Supreme Court Chief Justice Oliver Ellsworth wrote that "a Treaty cannot be repealed or annulled by Statute because it is a compact with a foreign power, and one party to a compact cannot dissolve it without the consent of the other."[144] However, also during the Jay Treaty controversy, Treasury Secretary Oliver Wolcott opined that Congress lawfully could enact a law to "repeal" an earlier treaty, but it is important to note that Wolcott used the example of a congressional declaration of war "repealing" an earlier treaty.[145] Wolcott was effectively correct. As noted earlier, under the law of nations, a state lawfully could "terminate" or "suspend" (not "repeal") a treaty on the grounds that another state had violated either its treaty or customary international legal obligations with the first state. Violations of treaty or customary international legal obligations could be sufficient grounds in the nineteenth century under the law of nations for waging war.[146] James

[144] William Casto, *Two Advisory Opinions*, 6 GREENBAG 414 (2003) (letter dated Mar. 13, 1796, to John Trumbull); *see* ANNALS OF CONGRESS 479, 4th Cong. 2nd Sess. (Mar. 1796) (Roger Griswold: treaty superior to congressional act and, consequently, treaty provision cannot be repealed by mere congressional act).

[145] OLIVER WOLCOTT, 1 MEMOIRS OF THE ADMINISTRATIONS OF WASHINGTON AND JOHN ADAMS 1796 (1846).

[146] *See* CHRISTIAN WOLFF, THE LAW OF NATIONS § 572 (1750) ("If in a doubtful case one nation is not willing to accept a conference for an amicable adjustment or compromise, or to accept a submission to an arbiter, the one making the offer has the right of war against the one unwilling to accept, by which the former is driven to a settlement by force of arms."); VATTEL, THE LAW OF NATIONS, *supra* note 101 at *Preliminaries*, § 28, n.1, ¶ 8 (Citing Vattel, Chitty notes: "If the perfect general rights or law of nations be violated, then it appears to

Madison during the Jay Treaty controversy staked out a middle ground. He argued that federal statutes could not violate treaties, but he also argued that treaties could not violate federal statutes.[147] This position, of course, creates a dilemma when federal statutes do violate treaties or *vice versa.*

However, Thomas Jefferson later wrote that legislative acts constitutionally could violate treaties: "Treaties being declared, equally with the laws of the United States, to be the supreme law of the land, it is understood that an act of the legislature alone can declare them infringed and rescinded."[148] However, Jefferson contradicted himself because he had indicated that the Constitution was a treaty and that federal legislation lawfully could not violate it.[149]

be conceded, that such violation may be the actual and avowed ground of a just war; and it is even laid down that it is the duty of every nation to chastise the nation guilty of the aggression."); *see also* 3 ELLIOT'S DEBATES, *supra* note 142 at 342 (William Grayson: "by the law of nations, if a negotiator makes a treaty, in consequence of a power received from a sovereign authority, non-compliance with his stipulations is a just cause of war.").

Present international law does not allow the violation of any treaty to be a just cause for war. *See Vienna Convention,* art. 60 (2) (listing acts that state-parties may undertake in case of material breach of multilateral treaty by other state-party).

Although the rights to self-defense and the recommencement of hostilities for serious violations of a peace treaty have been maintained under international law, treaty violations must be resolved by pacific means under present international law. *See, e.g., UN Charter,* arts. 2 (3) ("All Members shall settle their international disputes by peaceful means . . . ") and 51 ("Nothing in the present Charter shall impair the inherent right of individual or collective self-defense if an armed attack occurs against a Member of the United Nations . . . "); General Treaty for the Renunciation of War (Kellogg-Briand Pact), Aug. 27, 1928, art. II, 46 Stat. 2343, 94 L.N.T.S. 57 (entered into force July 24, 1929) ("The High Contracting Parties agree that the settlement or solution of all disputes or conflicts of whatever nature or of whatever origin they may be, which may arise among them, shall never be sought except by pacific means."); Hague Convention (IV) Respecting the Laws and Customs of War on Land, Oct. 18, 1907, art. 40, T.S. 539, 1 Bevans 631 (entered into force Jan. 26, 1910) ("Any serious violation of the armistice by one of the parties gives the other party the right of denouncing it, and even, in cases of urgency, of recommencing hostilities immediately.").

147 ANNALS OF CONGRESS 479, 4th Cong. 2nd Sess. (Mar. 1796).

148 THOMAS JEFFERSON, A MANUAL OF PARLIAMENTARY PRACTICE: FOR THE USE OF THE SENATE OF THE UNITED STATES § L LII (1812).

149 Letter from Thomas Jefferson to Edward Everett (Apr. 8, 1826), *reprinted in* THE POLITICAL WRITINGS OF THOMAS JEFFERSON 151 (E. Dumbauld ed. 1955) (Constitution is a compact between independent nations); Kentucky Resolution at ¶ 1 (1799) (drafted by Jefferson), *available at* http://www.yale.edu/lawweb/avalon/kenres.htm (last visited Oct. 5, 2003) (stating that federal Alien and Sedition Acts were unconstitutional). In this regard, it is

When the United States in its early years did stop complying with its treaty obligations, it did so because its treaty partner had breached the treaty or the treaty itself allowed termination, and treaty breach by one of its parties or unilateral withdrawal *per* a treaty's provisions is sufficient ground to void a treaty under the law of nations.[150] For example, President Polk in 1846 requested that Congress approve his authority to withdraw from the *Oregon Territory Treaty* (1827) with Great Britain and notify the British government of the United States' withdrawal *per* the Treaty's terms. Congress did so in its Joint Resolution of April 27, 1846.[151]

Most importantly, the sixth reason for rejecting the Last-in-Time Rule is that fundamental morality dictates that we keep our promises. We teach our children that they should keep their promises unless the promise itself is wrong or circumstances have changed that would lead to greater harms. It is the same with treaties in which our elected representatives enter into agreements with other peoples (*i.e.*, nations) on our behalf and with our constructive consent. This is a lesson that the Supreme Court has not learned. Our national honor demands that we comply with our agreements with other nations.

Although we have examined textual, historical, jurisprudential, political, and moral reasons for rejecting the Last-in-Time Rule, there is a more direct route for such a rejection by means of construing the Constitution in conformity with the United States' international legal obligations. *Per* the ILC approach, Congress' constitutional authority under Article I, § 8 to enact legislation must be construed in conformity with international law, and international law prohibits states from failing to perform their treaty obligations.[152] If such an approach is taken, the Last-in-Time Rule's application to earlier ratified treaties is no longer constitutional.

important to note that Jefferson was not a Framer. He was in France during the drafting and ratification of the Constitution.

150 *See, e.g.*, An Act to Declare the Treaties Heretofore Concluded with France, no Longer Obligatory on the United States, 1 Stat. 578 (1798) (repeated treaty violations by France and French failure to compensate for violations justifies U.S. voiding of treaties); VATTEL, 2 LAW OF NATIONS, *supra* note 101 at § 202 (breach); *Vienna Convention*, arts. 42 (2) (withdrawal according to treaty provisions) and 60 (breach).

151 9 Stat. 109–110 (1846).

152 *Vienna Convention*, art. 27 ("A party may not invoke the provisions of its internal law as justification for its failure to perform a treaty . . . ").

6

Extra–Article III, International Legal Interpretation

Article III states in relevant part:

> The judicial Power shall extend to . . . – to all Cases affecting Ambassadors, other public Ministers and Consuls; – to all Cases of admiralty and maritime Jurisdiction; – to Controversies to which the United States shall be a Party; – to Controversies between two or more States; – between a State and Citizens of another State;[[1]] – between Citizens of different States, – between Citizens of the same State claiming Lands under Grants of different States, and between a State, or the Citizens thereof, and foreign States, Citizens or Subjects.[2]

These jurisdictions often are "non-federal law claims" jurisdictions, and Article III does not require a party to plead a federal law claim for the federal courts to exercise jurisdiction. Article III's party-based, admiralty, and maritime jurisdictions implicate international and interstate relations – areas in which international law clearly is material to their proper operation and organization. To understand these jurisdictions, one must construe them in light of the Preamble's object and purpose to ensure "domestic Tranquility."[3] Recall that in *Chisholm v. Georgia*, Justices Wilson and Cushing used the Constitution's object and purpose "to ensure domestic Tranquility" for ensuring that interstate armed conflicts do not

[1] This clause was amended by the Eleventh Amendment. U.S. CONST. amend. XI XI ("The Judicial power of the United States shall not be construed to extend to any suit in law or equity, commenced or prosecuted against one of the United States by Citizens of another State, or by Citizens or Subjects of any Foreign State.").

[2] *Id.* at art. III, § 2, cl. 1.

[3] *Id.* at pmbl.

result from interstate disputes.[4] Disputes can arise between states (or their citizens), between the states (or their citizens) of the United States and foreign states (or their nationals), or between the United States and foreign states resulting in interstate or international armed conflicts.

Although the Constitution recognizes the potential problem of interstate or international conflicts and provides a partial solution by giving the federal courts the above jurisdictions to resolve these conflicts, Article III does not explicitly state *which* authorities the federal courts should use in resolving these disputes. The Supreme Court exercising its original jurisdiction arguably could apply any relevant authorities, whereas the lower federal courts are subject to those limitations that Congress places on them when it vests jurisdiction because the lower federal courts are created by Congress – not Article III *per se* as in the case of the Supreme Court. Furthermore, the law and equity classes of cases, which are mentioned in the federal law claims jurisdiction clauses, are not mentioned in these other jurisdictional clauses. Congress pursuant to its authority to make all laws necessary and proper "for carrying into Execution the foregoing [judicial] Power[]" arguably could allow the federal courts to apply any principle – be it legal, political, or aesthetic – to adjudicate disputes. The very idea of federal courts having limited jurisdiction as to rules of decision would appear to be false.

However, only when one construes these jurisdictional provisions in conformity with the United States' international legal obligations is the idea of limited jurisdiction recovered. Although international law sometimes allows international tribunals to have an expansive jurisdiction because the *Non Liquet* Prohibition Principle requires international tribunals to settle international disputes, international tribunal jurisdiction is limited by international law. The same applies to the U.S. Supreme Court (and lower federal courts). Accordingly, federal courts sometimes have the constitutional authority to decide disputes by *directly* applying extra-Article III international legal norms (as distinguished from using such sources to *construe* federal law).

As seen earlier in the *I.C.J. Statute*'s failure to list expressly all sources of international law, Article III also does not list explicitly all the sources

[4] *See supra* discussion in Subsection 1.1 accompanying notes 47–51.

of international law. For example, Article III does not expressly mention the customary law of nations, executive agreements with foreign states, signed but not ratified treaties, interstate and foreign compacts, general principles of law recognized by civilized nations, and subsidiary interpretive sources (including "judicial decisions and the teachings of the most highly qualified publicists of the various nations").

Although Article I mentions Congress' authority to define offenses against the law of nations, which would include these other sources, Article III does not. Nevertheless, federal courts can use these extra–Article III international legal authorities to construe federal law because the Constitution, treaties, and federal statutory law are all species of conventional international law that in turn can be construed in conformity with the rest of these law of nations norms. Indeed, federal courts already have used many of these kinds of norms in construing federal law. For example, the U.S. Supreme Court has construed federal law in conformity with treaties to which the United States was only a signatory,[5] with the "teachings of the most highly qualified publicists,"[6] and with UN General Assembly resolutions that reflect the United States' customary international legal obligations.[7] Furthermore, the Supreme Court's use of such extra–Article III international legal authorities in constitutional construction has not been limited to international affairs but also has extended to purely domestic affairs.[8]

Finally, it must be noted that federal courts cannot use these kinds of law sources if they violate federal law because constitutional provisions (including the federal court jurisdiction provisions) must be

[5] *See, e.g.*, Thompson v. Oklahoma, 487 U.S. 815, n. 34 (1988) (citing *ICCPR* – to which the United States in 1988 was only a signatory – for construing Eighth Amendment's prohibition of cruel and unusual punishment in prohibiting execution of persons under the age of sixteen committing capital crimes).

[6] *See, e.g.*, U.S. Steel Corp. v. Multistate Tax Comm'n, 434 U.S. 452, 462 n. 12 (1978) (using Vattel's Law of Nations to construe Art. I Interstate Compact Clause).

[7] Kennedy v. Mendoza-Martinez, 372 U.S. 144, 161 n. 16 (1963) (citing Universal Declaration of Human Rights for construing Fifth and Sixth Amendment in citizenship revocation case); *see* Filártiga v. Peña-Irala, 630 F.2d 876, 882 (2d Cir. 1980) (Universal Declaration of Human Rights reflects customary international law).

[8] *See, e.g.*, U.S. Steel Corp. v. Multistate Tax Comm'n, 434 U.S. 452, 462 n. 12 (using Vattel's Law of Nations in interstate compact case).

construed consistently with each other.[9] Furthermore, other normative principles (such as purely political or aesthetic principles) or laws (such as purely foreign law or state law) have no place in the international law corpus – unless international law itself allows their use.[10] If international law itself does not allow the use of such normative principles and laws, the federal courts cannot use such normative principles and laws. Accordingly, the idea of the federal courts' limited jurisdiction is maintained.

In conclusion, the aforementioned extra–Article III international legal authorities can be used to construe federal law. In the next subsections, we will examine how federal courts can directly apply such extra–Article III international legal authorities when exercising Article III party-based and admiralty and maritime jurisdictions.

Party-Based Jurisdictions

What is particularly striking about Article III is its primary focus on diversity jurisdiction. Whereas inferior federal courts were not given general federal claims jurisdiction until 1875,[11] the first Judiciary Act of 1789 vested the inferior federal courts with diversity jurisdiction.[12] Diversity jurisdiction clearly is a species of interstate or international jurisdiction because the opposing parties are either states (foreign or U.S.) and/or

[9] *See* Billings v. United States, 232 U.S. 261, 282 (1914) ("It is also settled beyond dispute that the Constitution is not self-destructive."); *cf. Vienna Convention*, art. 31 (treaty to be interpreted in light of its object and purpose).

[10] For example, a treaty may require a state-party's court to use foreign law in adjudicating prize cases or in providing evidence of customary international law. *See, e.g.*, Treaty of Amity and Commerce Between His Majesty the King of Prussia, and the United States of America, Sept. 10, 1785, art. 21, *available at* http://usa.usembassy.de/etexts/ga1–860606.htm (last visited Nov. 22, 2006) (entered into force May 17, 1786) ("The vessels of war, public & private, of the two parties, shall be reciprocally admitted with their prizes into the respective ports of each: but the said prizes shall not be discharged nor sold there, until their legality shall have been decided according to the laws & regulations of the states to which the captor belongs, but by the judicatures of the place into which the prize shall have been conducted."). Another example is that federal statutes (which reflect a species of international law) may require state law "be regarded as rules of decision, in trials at common law, in the courts of the United States, in cases where they apply." Judiciary Act of 1789, Sept. 24, 1789, 1 Stat. 73, § 34.

[11] Act of March 3, 1875, 18 Stat. 470, *now codified at* 28 U.S.C. § 1331.

[12] Judiciary Act of 1789, Sept. 24, 1789, § 11, 1 Stat. 73. Diversity jurisdiction is now codified at 28 U.S.C. § 1332(a), which states in relevant part:

citizens (or subjects) of other states. Federal court jurisdiction in diversity cases is designed to settle interstate and international disputes that otherwise could result in armed conflict. In cases in which a party is a state of the United States, the Supreme Court can exercise original jurisdiction; therefore, the Supreme Court also can directly apply extra–Article III international legal authorities because Congress cannot create exceptions to the Court's jurisdiction and, hence cannot limit its adjudicative method. Furthermore, it would be constitutionally acceptable for Congress to allow or require the inferior federal courts to use such extra–Article III international legal authorities when it vests jurisdiction in such courts.

Although the U.S. Supreme Court in *Erie Railroad Co. v. Tompkins* held that federal courts can no longer be in the business of making federal common law in diversity cases,[13] the Supreme Court has recognized that federal courts retain constitutional authority to apply common law in certain cases.[14] Among these cases are those involving international law, such as admiralty/maritime and torts committed in violation of international law. In Subsection 6.3, we will examine other limitations on *Erie*'s sweeping holding.

The other party-based jurisdiction is one in which the United States is a party. Jurisdiction over such cases can be characterized as interstate because the United States is a hybrid interstate/national organization.[15] And, again, in cases in which a party is a state of the United States, the Supreme Court can exercise original jurisdiction; therefore, the Supreme Court also can directly apply extra–Article III international legal

(a) The district courts shall have original jurisdiction of all civil actions where the matter in controversy exceeds the sum or value of $75,000, exclusive of interest and costs, and is between –

1. citizens of different States;
2. citizens of a State and citizens or subjects of a foreign state;
3. citizens of different States and in which citizens or subjects of a foreign state are additional parties . . .

[13] 304 U.S. 64 (1938).

[14] *See* Sosa v. Alvarez-Machain, 542 U.S. 692, 124 S. Ct. at 2764, 159 L. Ed. 2d at 9H (federal courts retain jurisdiction for common law claims notwithstanding *Erie Railroad Co. v. Tompkins*).

[15] James Brown Scott, The United States of America: A Study in International Organization (1920) (arguing that United States is an intergovernmental organization).

authorities because Congress cannot create exceptions to the Court's jurisdiction and, hence, cannot limit its adjudicative method. Furthermore, it would be constitutionally acceptable for Congress to allow or require the inferior federal courts to use such extra–Article III international legal authorities when it vests jurisdiction in such courts.

The other party-based jurisdiction based on cases affecting "Ambassadors, other public Ministers and Consuls" also clearly implicates international legal relations. In such cases, the United States' treaty obligations could govern the case, thereby allowing the Supreme Court (which exercises original jurisdiction in such cases) to exercise its federal law claims jurisdiction. However, because the Supreme Court has original jurisdiction in such controversies, it also can directly apply extra–Article III international legal authorities because Congress cannot create exceptions to the Court's jurisdiction and, hence, cannot limit its adjudicative method.

Furthermore, even lower federal courts (whose jurisdictions are limited by Congress) in some cases could directly apply extra–Article III international legal sources in federal law claims cases. Some federal statutes explicitly incorporate international law without limiting such international law to the United States' treaty obligations.[16] For example, if an alien sued a foreign consul[17] under the Alien Tort Statute,[18] it is quite possible that the international law governing their relations does not bind

[16] *See, e.g.*, 18 U.S.C. § 1116 ("Whoever kills or attempts to kill a[n] . . . internationally protected person shall be punished . . . 'Internationally protected person' means – . . . any other representative, officer, employee, or agent of . . . a foreign government . . . who at the time and place concerned is entitled pursuant to *international law* to special protection against attack upon his person . . ." [emphases provided]).

[17] Consular officials can be sued in certain cases under international law. *See, e.g.*, Vienna Convention on Consular Relations, Apr. 23, 1963, art. 43, 596 U.N.T.S. 261 (entered into force Mar. 19, 1967) ("1. Consular officers and consular employees shall not be amenable to the jurisdiction of the judicial or administrative authorities of the receiving State in respect of acts performed in the exercise of consular functions. 2. The provisions of paragraph 1 of this Article shall not, however, apply in respect of a civil action either: (a) arising out of a contract concluded by a consular officer or a consular employee in which he did not contract expressly or impliedly as an agent of the sending State; or (b) by a third party for damage arising from an accident in the receiving State caused by a vehicle, vessel or aircraft."); *see also* Bors v. Preston, 111 U.S. 252 (1884) (suit allowed against consul of Norway and Sweden for unlawful conversion of merchandise for his own use).

[18] 28 U.S.C. § 1350 (district courts have jurisdiction over torts committed against aliens in violation of the law of nations).

the United States. Nevertheless, the federal district courts constitutionally could apply this international law.[19]

The Supreme Court's original jurisdiction extends to some civil and criminal cases. In civil cases, foreign state representatives, foreign states, foreign nationals, states,[20] U.S. nationals, and the United States could be parties. Foreign state representatives can sue and be sued in federal[21] (and state[22]) courts. In most cases, the Court would apply federal or state law, including the United States' international legal obligations. However, this would not preclude the Supreme Court from applying extra–Article III international legal authorities.

In criminal cases over which the Supreme Court exercises original jurisdiction, foreign nationals and U.S. nationals could be defendants. (Some foreign state representatives could not because they are immunized under international law.[23]) Although in most cases, the Supreme Court also would be exercising its federal law jurisdiction, it is possible that there would be no federal statute criminalizing the defendant's action. Indeed, it may not be necessary to have a federal criminal statute authorizing prosecution if the law of nations allows prosecution. However, as the U.S. Supreme Court recently noted in *Hamdan v. Rumsfeld*, "[w]hen . . . neither the elements of the offense nor the range of

[19] As Chitty put it:

> Controversies are decided by the Courts and Laws of the Country where they are tried. But the rights of the parties sometimes depend on the laws of another country. These are then looked into, not as law to the Court, but to ascertain the rights of the parties.

Chitty, *A Running Commentary on Vattel's Law of Nations, Consisting of Short Notes and Parallel Remarks: Intended for the Use of the Class of National Law at William and Mary College, in* EMMERICH DE VATTEL, 2 THE LAW OF NATIONS OR PRINCIPLES OF THE LAW OF NATURE APPLIED TO THE CONDUCT AND AFFAIRS OF NATIONS AND SOVEREIGN (1758) [hereinafter, VATTEL, LAW OF NATIONS].

[20] States could be parties subject to the Eleventh Amendment's prohibition of suits against states.

[21] Bors v. Preston, 111 U.S. 252.

[22] Ohio ex rel. Popovici v. Agler, 280 U.S. 379, 383, 384 (1930), *now precluded by* 28 U.S.C. § 1351.

[23] *See* Case concerning the Arrest Warrant of 11 April 2000 (Democratic Republic of the Congo v. Belgium), General List No. 121 (2002), *available at* http://www.icjcij.org/icjwww/idocket/iCOBE/icobejudgment/icobe_ijudgment_20020214.PDF (last visited Sept. 24, 2002) (issuance of arrest warrant by third-party state for foreign minister held violative of consular and diplomatic immunity).

permissible punishments is defined by statute or treaty, the precedent [in the law of nations] must be plain and unambiguous." Vague international crimes cannot pass constitutional muster.[24] Therefore, the Supreme Court exercising its original jurisdiction in a criminal case sometimes could use extra–Article III international legal authorities in the absence of a federal statute.

Admiralty and Maritime Jurisdictions

Admiralty law is a subset of the law of nations (now known as "the law of the sea"); therefore, admiralty jurisdiction is a law of nations jurisdiction. Even maritime jurisdiction implicates interstate or international affairs because rivers often flow into the high seas, or cross or define state borders. Therefore, admiralty and maritime courts apply the international law governing the high seas. Such international law can include *jus in bello* ("laws of war") when admiralty courts sit as prize courts. The Articles Congress earlier had established prize courts during the Revolutionary War that were governed by international law,[25] and the Constitution Congress has vested original jurisdiction over admiralty/maritime cases in the federal district courts.[26]

The judicial power extends to *all* admiralty cases, leading Professor Amar to conclude that the Supreme Court exercises concurrent original jurisdiction in such cases with lower federal courts.[27] Therefore, even in the absence of federal law, the Supreme Court could directly apply extra–Article III international legal authorities in admiralty/maritime cases. For example, the Supreme Court has applied regional European customary

[24] *See* Connally v. General Constr. Co., 269 U.S. 385 (1926).

[25] *See, e.g.*, 19 Journals of the Continental Congress 315 (1912) (prize courts governed by law of nations).

[26] 28 U.S.C. § 1333:

> The district courts shall have original jurisdiction, exclusive of the courts of the States, of: (1) Any civil case of admiralty or maritime jurisdiction, saving to suitors in all cases all other remedies to which they are otherwise entitled. (2) Any prize brought into the United States and all proceedings for the condemnation of property taken as prize.

[27] Akhil Reed Amar, *A Neo-Federalist View of Article III: Separating the Two Tiers of Federal Jurisdiction*, 65 B.U.L. Rev. 205 (1985).

international law in admiralty cases.[28] As Mr. Chief Justice John Marshall put it:

> A case in admiralty does not, in fact, arise under the Constitution or laws of the United States. These cases are as old as navigation itself; and the law, admiralty and maritime, as it has existed for ages, is applied by our Courts to the cases as they arise.[29]

Let us now turn to the different types of extra–Article III international law sources that can be applied in party-based and admiralty/maritime cases.

6.1. SPONSIONS AS SPECIES OF TREATIES: SIGNED TREATIES, EXECUTIVE AGREEMENTS, AND INTERSTATE AND FOREIGN COMPACTS

One group of extra–Article III international legal authorities are what international law calls "sponsions." These include treaties that the United States has signed but not ratified, executive agreements, compacts between states of the United States, and compacts between a state of the United States and a foreign state. As Hugo Grotius stated, "[a] sponsion is made when those who do not have from the supreme authority a commission for such an act[,] promise something which essentially affects that authority."[30]

There are many treaties that the United States has signed – but not ratified. Such treaties *per se* do not constitute federal law because either the Senate has not given its consent and/or the president has not ratified the treaty by, for example, exchanging the instruments of ratification with the parties to the treaty or depositing the instrument of ratification with the UN Secretary General. Nevertheless, the conventional law of nations requires the United States "to refrain from acts which would defeat the object and purpose of [the] treaty when . . . it has signed the

[28] *See, e.g.*, The Antelope, 23 U.S. 66, 121 (1825) (applying European customary international law).

[29] American Insurance Co. v. 356 Bales of Cotton, 26 U.S. 511, 545–46 (1828).

[30] Hugo Grotius, 2 The Laws of Nature and Nature's God, chap. 15, § III (1).

treaty,"[31] and the United States has recognized such an obligation.[32] Insofar as such treaties are mere sponsions, they still create some international legal obligations for the United States under the law of treaties until the United States has "made its intention clear not to become a party to the treaty."[33] When a signed treaty is eventually approved by the Senate and its instrument of ratification deposited by the president, the treaty represents the United States' conventional obligations.

In the case of executive agreements, these sponsions sometimes create conventional obligations under international law when approved by the proper constitutional authority. For example, those executive agreements made by the president under the authority of a federal statute or treaty are sponsions that acquire conventional obligations. Under the *Vienna Convention on the Law of Treaties*, heads of states (such as the president) are considered to have sufficient authority to enter into treaties.[34] Furthermore, such executive agreements are considered constitutional because the president is exercising his/her constitutional duty to "take Care that the Laws be faithfully executed,"[35] and such executive agreements merely are implementing federal law – the exercise of which the president constitutionally can undertake.

However, some sponsions do not create treaty obligations because they have not been approved by the proper constitutional authorities. For example, Maj. Gen William T. Sherman of the U.S. Army and Gen. Joseph E. Johnston of the Confederate States Army in North Carolina made a sponsion during the Civil War that would have brought a cessation to hostilities. The sponsion stated the following: "Not being fully empowered by our respective principals to fulfill these terms, we individually and officially pledge ourselves to promptly obtain the necessary authority . . .[36] Subsequently, President Jefferson Davis approved the sponsion, but President Andrew Johnson did not after President Abraham

[31] *Vienna Convention*, art. 18.

[32] *See, e.g.*, James P. Rubin, Dept. of State Daily Press Briefing, Nov. 5, 1999 ("[A]s a signatory, there is an understanding in the international community that if you're a signatory, and you intend to seek ratification later, that you not take steps to defeat the object and purpose of a treaty. That is the legal term of art.").

[33] *Vienna Convention*, art. 18 (a).

[34] *Vienna Convention*, art. 7 (2) (a).

[35] U.S. Const. art. II, § 3.

[36] Sherman-Johnston Agreement of April 18th, 1865 (not entered into force).

Lincoln's assassination. Therefore, the sponsion did not create conventional obligations for the United States because the sponsion required the approval of President Johnson (and the Senate). If President Johnson had approved the sponsion and the Senate had not, the sponsion still would not have created conventional obligations.[37] Early federal court decisions and views of the U.S. State Department confirmed that such an executive agreement could be considered by the United States to not form a conventional obligation because they were improperly concluded by the president's failure to get the Senate's concurrence.[38] Most important, the *Vienna Convention on the Law of Treaties* also supports this view:

> A State may not invoke the fact that its consent to be bound by a treaty has been expressed in violation of a provision of its internal law regarding competence to conclude treaties as invalidating its consent *unless that violation was manifest and concerned a rule of its internal law of fundamental importance.*[39]

However, an executive agreement does not require senatorial concurrence when the agreement governs an area over which the president exercises exclusive authority. For example, the U.S. Supreme Court held in *United States v. Belmont* that the president as the "sole organ" in international relations for the United States did not need the concurrence of the Senate to enter into an international agreement. Those Supreme Court cases recognizing such presidential authority addressed foreign state recognition,[40] and the president has exclusive authority in

[37] Assuming *arguendo* that the Provisional Constitution of the Confederate States of America was legal, President Davis also would have needed to get the concurrence of the Confederate Senate for the sponsion to have the effect of a treaty. *See* Provisional Constitution of the Confederate States of America, May 21, 1861, art. II, § 2 (president "shall have power, by and with the advice and consent of the Senate, to make treaties; provided two-thirds of the Senators present concur").

[38] *See, e.g.*, United States v. One Bag of Paradise Feathers, 256 F. 301, 306 (2d Cir. 1919); G. Hackworth, 5 Digest of International Law 426 (1944) (Dept. of State considers executive agreements to not have effect of treaties because Senate's consent not obtained).

[39] *Vienna Convention*, art. 46 (1) (emphasis provided). The *Vienna Convention* goes on to define a manifest violation as one that "would be objectively evident to any State conducting itself in the matter in accordance with normal practice and in good faith." *Id.* at art. 46 (2).

[40] *See* United States v. Belmont, 301 U.S. 324 (U.S.-U.S.S.R. executive agreement addressing recognition of Soviet Government); United States v. Pink, 315 U.S. 203 (1942) (same).

recognizing states through his/her Article III authority to receive ambassadors,[41] whereas the Constitution gives the Senate a joint role with the president in making peace treaties,[42] such as the *Sherman-Johnston Agreement* and the *Versailles Peace Treaty of 1919* ending World War I that was rejected by the Senate.[43]

In the case of interstate and state-foreign state compacts, such agreements are treaties under the conventional law of nations notwithstanding the Constitution's denotation of such agreements as "compacts" and not treaties. The *Vienna Convention on the Law of Treaties* defines a "treaty" as an "international agreement concluded between States in written form and governed by international law... *whatever its particular designation*." The U.S. Supreme Court confirmed this definition of treaty in *Hinderlider v. La Plata Co.* in which the Court stated that "[t]he Compact adapts to our Union of sovereign States the age-old treaty-making power of independent sovereign nations."[44] However, the Constitution sometimes requires states of the United States to acquire congressional approval for such compacts.[45] However, if the compact does not implicate federal concerns, congressional consent is not required.[46]

In all cases of sponsions that do not receive respectively the Senate's concurrence (*viz.*, signed treaties and executive agreements not governing areas under exclusive control of the president) or congressional approval (*viz.*, interstate and foreign state compacts) when such concurrence/approval is constitutionally required, Article III international law will trump these agreements because the Constitution established preexisting treaty (i.e., the constitutional) obligations for the states, and under the conventional law of nations, states cannot enter into

[41] U.S. Const. art. II, § 3.

[42] *See id.* at art II, § 2, cl. 2 (advice and consent of the Senate required to make treaties).

[43] *See id.* at art. I, § 8 (Congress has power "[t]o declare war G. . and make Rules concerning Captures on Land and Water; . . . [t]o . . . suppress Insurrections").

[44] 304 U.S. 92, 104 (1938).

[45] U.S. Const. art. I, § 10, cl. 3 ("No State shall, without the Consent of Congress, . . . enter into any Agreement or Compact with another State, or with a foreign Power. . . ."); *see, e.g.*, Public Law 85–145 (Joint Resolution consenting to agreement between New York and Canada providing for continued existence of Buffalo and Fort Erie Public Bridge Authority), 71 Stat. 367 (1957).

[46] U.S. Steel Corp. v. Multstate Tax Comm'n, 434 U.S. 452 (1978); Virginia v. Tennessee, 148 U.S. 503, 517–520 (1893).

treaties that violate their previous international legal obligations unless a new treaty (*i.e.*, a constitutional amendment) is made that governs all the states-parties to the former treaty (*i.e.*, the Constitution). However, in cases of executive agreements governing areas over which the president exercises exclusive authority (*e.g.*, the reception of foreign state ambassadors or public ministers, and the attendant recognition of these foreign states), Congress constitutionally cannot enact legislation limiting such authority – notwithstanding that they are not Article VI treaties and, hence, not part of the "supreme Law of the Land" – because Congress constitutionally cannot receive ambassadors and recognize foreign states.

In the next subsection, we examine customary international law.

6.2. CONSTITUTIONALLY CUSTOMIZING CUSTOMARY INTERNATIONAL LAW FOR THE UNITED STATES

An extra–Article III international legal source that has received much attention is customary international law. Neither Article III or the Supremacy Clause mentions the law of nations, including the customary law of nations. However, there was no need to mention this law. State courts – like the British courts – already could directly apply the customary law of nations because it was incorporated into the common law.[47] However, it was different with treaties. Given that British courts could not give domestic effect to treaties without implementing legislation from Parliament, the Supremacy Clause avoided such a scenario by ensuring that state judges could apply treaties (and other federal law) as the supreme law of the land.

Although Article III does not mention the customary law of nations, it probably is settled law that the customary law of nations (or customary international law) is federal law.[48] The U.S. Supreme Court appears to have vacillated between recognizing and not recognizing

[47] *See, e.g.*, Respublica v. de Longchamps, 1 U.S. (1 Dall.) 111, 120 (Pa. Oyer and Terminer, 1784) (applying law of nations); Nathan v. Commonwealth of Virginia, 1 U.S. (1 Dall.) 77, 78 (Common Pleas, Philadelphia County, 1781) (same); 4 BLACKSTONE'S COMMENTARIES ON THE LAWS OF ENGLAND 67 (1765–69) (law of nations in England "adopted in its full extent by the common law").

[48] *See* RESTATEMENT (THIRD) OF THE FOREIGN RELATIONS LAW OF THE UNITED STATES § 111 (1) & comment d (1987) (customary international law is federal law).

customary international law as federal law (except, of course, in cases in which the United States has persistently objected to the norm). In 1875, the Supreme Court in *York Life Ins. Co. v. Hendren* held that the "general laws of war" did not represent federal law.[49] Twenty-five years later in *The Paquete Habana*, the Court recognized customary international law as "part of our law."[50] This apparent vacillation by the Supreme Court may be attributed to customary international law not being mentioned in Article III. On the other hand, these two cases may be reconciled by distinguishing "federal law" from "our law." The Supreme Court's use of the phrase "federal law" suggests a reference to only those legal authorities contained in Article III; whereas "our law" refers to other legal authorities besides federal law that still is "U.S. law." For example, the state laws of the United States represent "U.S. law" when U.S. district courts apply such law in diverse civil cases.[51] Whatever is the case, a customary international legal norm represents "federal law" if the federal government has implicitly or expressly accepted the norm. However, for the sake of argument, this book will assume that the United States' customary international legal obligations are not federal law in the sense of being Article III, legal sources because Article III does not mention customary international law.

Furthermore, the First Congress bifurcated U.S. treaties and the law of nations – which includes customary international law – in the Alien Tort Statute suggesting that the two were different. The original Alien Tort Statute stated that federal district courts "shall also have cognizance, concurrent with the courts of the several States, or the circuit courts, as the case may be, of all causes where an alien sues for a tort only in violation of the law of nations or a treaty of the United States."[52] A reason for this bifurcation probably can be attributed to the fact that treaties dealt with particular obligations between states-parties that did not necessarily create general legal obligations for all states.[53] However, treaties

49 92 U.S. 286 (1875).

50 175 U.S. 677, 700 (1900).

51 28 U.S.C. § 1652 ("The laws of the several states . . . shall be regarded as rules of decision in civil actions in the courts of the United States, in cases where they apply.").

52 Act of Sept. 24, 1789, ch. 20, §9(b), 1 Stat. 79.

53 There may be another reason. Congress included the language "a treaty of the United States" in the ATS that at first glance would appear to be superfluous language given that U.S. treaties already were part of the law of nations. Act of Sept. 24, 1789, ch. 20, §9(b), 1 Stat. 79. However, this language is not superfluous in cases in which the plaintiff and

sometimes can reflect general customs among nations.[54] For example, the U.S. Supreme Court in 1825 held that evidence of an international legal custom could be found in treaties.[55] With the growing number of multilateral treaties in the twentieth century and the codification of cus-

defendant are nationals belonging to the same state-party to a foreign treaty that conflicts with a U.S. treaty or are nationals belonging to different states-parties to a foreign treaty that is subject to different interpretations by these states-parties. Congress appears to have included the disjunctive connective "or" to allow an alien plaintiff to sue for a tort committed in violation of a U.S. treaty alone – notwithstanding the existence of a foreign treaty (which also is part of the law of nations). The inclusion of the disjunctive connective serves to ensure that a U.S. federal court is not placed in either the dilemma of deciding whether a U.S. or foreign treaty controls the outcome or the dilemma of deciding which state interpretation of the foreign treaty controls the outcome. When there is a U.S. treaty that also governs the relations between an alien plaintiff and alien defendant, a U.S. federal court can rely solely on the U.S. treaty for deciding the case and can avoid giving what otherwise could appear to be preferential treatment of one state-party over another in arguable violation of the principle of state co-equality. Indeed, what is striking about the ATS' inclusion of the language "or a treaty of the United States" is how it allows a U.S. federal court to operate as an international court in much the same way that Article 103 of the *UN Charter* allows the ICJ to ignore a treaty conflicting with the *UN Charter* or a state interpretation of a treaty conflicting with the *UN Charter*. *See UN Charter*, art. 103 ("In the event of a conflict between the obligations of the Members of the United Nations under the present Charter and their obligations under any other international agreement, their obligations under the present Charter shall prevail.")

[54] *See* North Sea Continental Shelf Cases (Germany v. Denmark, Germany v. The Netherlands), 1969 I.C.J. 43 (treaty can generate customary international legal obligations even upon nonstate parties when treaty is widely adopted and representative of states whose interests are specially affected).

By definition, customary international legal norms emerge and crystallize in an evolutionary process as legally obligatory customs. *See* Ware v. Hylton, 3 U.S. (3 Dall.) 199 (1796) (distinguishing between ancient and modern law of nations); H. R. Rep. No. 102–367, pt. 1, p. 4 (1991) (norms "may ripen in the future into rules of customary international law").

[55] The Antelope 23 U.S. at 119 ("the law of nations, as fixed and evidenced by general, and ancient, and admitted practice, by treaties, and by the general tenor of the laws and ordinances, and the formal transactions of civilized states"); *cf.* Commonwealth v. Kosloff, 5 Serg. & Rawle 545 Pa. (1816) ("The law of nations is sought for in the usages of nations; in the opinions of approved authors; in treaties; and in the decisions of Judges."). Furthermore, the U.S. Supreme Court held that the law of nations primarily was ascertained not only "by the general usage and practice of nations but also "by consulting the works of jurists, writing professedly on public law; . . . or by judicial decisions recognizing and enforcing that law." United States v. Smith, 5 U.S. (5 Wheat.) at 160. These additional sources of evidence – jurists and judicial opinions – are confirmed by the Statute of the International Court of Justice's recognition that "judicial decisions

tomary international legal norms in many of these instruments, the bifurcation of the law of nations and treaties has become less pronounced.[56]

It is perhaps somewhat unfortunate that it continues to be the practice among jurists that treaty law often is wholly distinguished from customary law. Contributing to this dichotomization is that the Statute of the International Court of Justice separately lists "international conventions" (*i.e.*, treaties) and "international custom" as separate sources of law.[57]

Federal courts before and after the Constitution's ratification applied customary international law in prize, piracy, and other cases.[58] Unlike

and the teachings of the most highly qualified publicists of the various nations" provide a "subsidiary means for the determination of rules of law." *I.C.J. Statute*, art. 38 (1) (d).

56 As early as 1820, the U.S. Supreme Court in *United States v. Smith* held that the law of nations was established by the "common consent of nations" to a "public code." 5 U.S. (5 Wheat.) 153, 159 (1820). The Supreme Court's use of the phrase "public code" may have been prescient in that such public codes in the form of widely adopted multilateral treaties would provide in the future a good source of customary international law because these treaties often codify such norms. *See* ANTHONY D'AMATO, INTERNATIONAL LAW: PROCESS AND PROSPECT 123–47 (1987); CLIVE PARRY, THE SOURCE AND EVIDENCE OF INTERNATIONAL LAW 62–67 (1965); Richard R. Baxter, *Multilateral Treaties as Evidence of Customary International Law*, 41 BRIT. Y.B. INT'L L.275 (1965–66); *cf.* Vienna Convention, art. 38 ("Nothing . . . precludes a rule set forth in a treaty from becoming binding upon a third State as a customary rule of international law.").

57 *I.C.J. Statute*, art. 38.

58 For example, the Continental Congress ordered its army and naval forces as well as privateers to observe the laws of war in their conduct of war against Great Britain and authorized the capture and condemnation of ships belonging to U.S. citizens according to the law of nations. 21 JOURNALS OF THE CONTINENTAL CONGRESS 1154 (1912); 19 *ibid.* 361. Congress' prize courts were governed by the law of nations. *See* 19 *ibid.* 315 and 364 (privateers violating laws of nations subject to forfeiture of commission and "liable to an action for breach of the condition of [privateer's] bond, [and] responsible to the party grieved for damages sustained by such malversation"). The Constitutional Congress also applied the law of nations for governing the crime of piracy. *See* Act of Mar. 3, 1819, ch. 77, § 5, 3 Stat. 513–14 ("that if any person or persons whatsoever ever, shall, upon the high seas, commit the crime of piracy, as defined by the law of nations, and such offender or offenders shall be brought into, or found in the United States, every such offender or offenders shall, upon conviction thereof, &c., be punished with death."). The law of nations also created duties for private Americans *vis-à-vis* foreign nationals (such as ambassadors), and the United States was responsible for ensuring that private individuals observed this law of nations because, otherwise, the United States would acquire liability. *See* 1 Op. Att'y Gen. 57, 59 (1795) (foreign nationals have private cause of action against U.S. nationals for violation of law of nations or treaty under *Alien Tort*

some treaty guarantees, all customary international law is self-executing insofar as providing rules of decision, and the federal courts can enforce such law. Although Article I, § 8, cl. 10 states that Congress constitutionally can enact laws "[t]o define and punish . . . Offences against the Law of Nations" and customary international law is a subset of the law of nations, customary international legal rules do not require implementing legislation because the state already either has performed or not performed the overt act depending on whether the customary rule requires performance or non-performance, or not made a timely objection to the norm when it was emerging. Although Congress has the authority to clarify customary international legal rules, this authority does not preclude courts from also clarifying customary norms by using different sources of evidence for establishing the norm's customary international legal status. For example, the U.S. Supreme Court in *United States v. Smith* considered the crime of piracy to be sufficiently defined by extra-federal statutory sources to allow the federal statute defining piracy to refer only to the extant customary international law defining piracy for its definition.[59]

With the U.S. Supreme Court's recent decision in *Sosa v. Alvarez-Machain*,[60] it is clear that federal courts still can enforce the United States' customary international legal obligations – notwithstanding an unconventional and contrary position staked out by some academics over the last few years.[61] Although the *Sosa* Court held that courts cannot use vague customary international legal norms as rules of decision until such vague norms are given greater definition by Congress, the Court ironically used

Statute (1789), presently codified at 28 U.S.C. § 1350); Henfield's Case, 11 F. Cas. 1099, 1108 (C.C.D. Pa. 1793) (No. 6360) (Wilson, J.) (charge to grand jury) (stating if the nation refused to require its citizens to make reparation or to punish citizens for committing offenses against law of nations, the nation "renders itself in some measure an accomplice in the guilt, and becomes responsible for the injury").

59 18 U.S. (Wheat.) 153 (1820).

60 542 U.S. 692 (2004) (Alien Tort Statute provides federal court jurisdiction for torts committed in violation of the law of nations, including customary law of nations).

61 *See, e.g.*, Curtis A. Bradley & Jack L. Goldsmith, *Customary International Law as Federal Common Law: A Critique of the Modern Position*, 110 Harv. L. Rev. 815 (1997) (customary international law is unenforceable in U.S. courts) [hereinafter, Bradley & Goldsmith, *Federal Common Law*].

the standard set by *United States v. Smith* for measuring how much specificity was required of a customary international legal norm.[62]

The United States has undertaken a practice of declaring treaties non–self-executing,[63] thereby making the alternative use of customary international law often essential to any attempt at enforcing international law as U.S. law. For example, plaintiffs have avoided using the United States' human rights treaty obligations because the United States had declared many of the substantive rights provisions of these treaties as non–self-executing, and instead have used customary international law reflected by those or other treaties.[64] Consequently, the Persistent Objector Rule will become increasingly important for determining whether the United States is bound by newly emerging customary international legal norms.

However, important questions remain as to the extent of customary international law binding the federal and state governments. Are there any limits on federal statutory law and executive orders trumping the United States' customary international legal obligations? If not, the Persistent Objector Rule would not apply to the United States – at least insofar as persistency of objection is required. If there are limitations, how would the Persistent Objector Rule operate? Can states-parties to

[62] 542 U.S. at 732.

[63] *See, e.g.*, MULTILATERAL TREATIES DEPOSITED WITH THE SECRETARY GENERAL: STATUS AS AT 31 DEC. 1992, at 132, U.N. Doc. ST/LEG/SER.E/11 (1993) (U.S. deposit of declaration that Articles 1–27 of the *International Covenant on Civil and Political Rights* are non-self-executing); MULTILATERAL TREATIES DEPOSITED WITH THE SECRETARY GENERAL: STATUS AS AT 31 DEC. 1994, at 185, U.N. Doc. ST/LEG/SER.E/13 (1995) (U.S. deposit of declaration that *Convention Against Torture and Other Cruel, Inhuman or Degrading Treatment or Punishment* is non–self-executing).

[64] *See, e.g.*, Sosa v. Alvarez-Machain, 542 U.S. 692; 124 S. Ct. 2739, 2767; 159 L. Ed. 2d 718, 755 (2004):

> although the [*International Covenant on Civil and Political Rights*] does bind the United States as a matter of international law, the United States ratified the Covenant on the express understanding that it was not self-executing and so did not itself create obligations enforceable in the federal courts. []Accordingly, Alvarez cannot say that the [*Universal Declaration of Human Rights* and the *International Covenant on Civil and Political Rights*] themselves establish the relevant and applicable rule of international law. He instead attempts to show that prohibition of arbitrary arrest has attained the status of binding customary international law.

the Constitution be persistent objectors? Can the U.S. government as an intergovernmental organization – and not a state – be a persistent objector?

The following discussion will address these questions and argue for a formulation of the Persistent Objector Rule that conforms to the peculiar constraints of the Constitution as construed by international law. An international legal construction of the Constitution is necessary in a discussion of the Persistent Objector Rule because the Constitution does not mention a persistent objection rule that is so essential to the operation of the customary law of nations, which the Constitution does implicitly mention.[65] Therefore, those provisions of the Constitution that address the evidentiary sources of customary international legal norms (*e.g.*, treaties,[66] interstate and foreign compacts or agreements,[67] and the law of nations[68] generally) must be interpreted in the context of international law in order that one can discern whether federal or state governments have acceded to or rejected an emerging customary international legal norm reflected in these sources.

Indeed, the Constitution as a whole must be construed in light of international law in order that its constituent intergovernmental organization – that is, the federal government – has the lawful capacity to be a persistent objector to emerging global or extra-American regional customary international legal norms (*e.g.*, European customary international legal norms). Only by recognizing the Constitution as a treaty that must be

[65] *See* U.S. CONST. art. I, § 8, cl. 10 ("The Congress shall have Power . . . To define and punish . . . Offenses against the Law of Nations").

[66] *See id.* at art. I, § 10, cl. 1 ("No State shall enter into any Treaty, Alliance, or Confederation . . ."); art. II, § 2, cl. 2 (president "shall have Power, by and with the Advice and Consent of the Senate to make Treaties, provided two thirds of the Senators present concur"); art. III, § 2, cl. 1 ("The judicial Power shall extend to all Cases, in Law and Equity, arising under this Constitution, the Laws of the United States, and Treaties made, or which shall be made, under their Authority. . . ."); art. VI, § 2 ("This Constitution, and the Law of the United States which shall be made in Pursuance thereof, and all Treaties made, or which shall be made, under the Authority of the United States, shall be the supreme Law of the Land; and the Judges in every State shall be bound thereby, any Thing in the Constitution or Laws of any State to the Contrary notwithstanding.").

[67] *See id.* at art. I, § 10, cl. 3 ("No State shall, without the Consent of Congress, . . . enter into any Agreement or Compact with another State, or with a foreign Power . . .").

[68] *See id.* at art. I, § 8, cl. 10.

construed in conformity with international law can the U.S. federal government avail itself of the Persistent Objector Rule because only states can make persistent objections,[69] this authority being made available by virtue of states becoming parties to the Constitution and, thereby, relinquishing some of this authority to the federal government by means of the Supremacy Clause.[70] Generally speaking, nations *per se* and intergovernmental organizations would appear not to have the capacities to become persistent objectors because they are not states and one of the necessary conditions of customary international law is *state* practice. However, relying on the ICJ's decision in the *Genocide Reservations Case*, the International Law Association correctly has stated that "the practice of intergovernmental organizations in their own rights is a form of 'State practice'" that contributes to the formation of customary international law.[71] Such an intergovernmental organization is the United States, and the United States' capacity to contribute to the formation of customary international law is only made possible by providing an international

69 It is not clear whether nations *per se* can make persistent objections because peoples alone generally do not have the sufficient political organization to collectively express a persistent objection. This is not to say that nations, states, and their combinations in certain circumstances cannot be persistent objectors. *See, e.g.*, The Antelope, 23 U.S. at 121 (African nations had not assented to prohibition of slave trade as evidenced by participation in trade); Pinkerton and Roach v. United States, Inter-Am. Comm. H.R. No. 3/87, ANNUAL REPORT OF THE INTER-AMERICAN COMMISSION ON HUMAN RIGHTS: 1986–87, OEA/Ser.L/V/II.71/doc.9 147 (1987) (recognizing persistent objection of some states to emerging customary international legal norm prohibiting execution of persons committing capital crimes under the age of eighteen); Fisheries Case (U.K. v. Norway), 1951 I.C.J. at 131 (dictum) (United States maintaining objection to claim that highly migratory species of tuna were within coastal state jurisdiction beyond territorial sea while withdrawing United States' objection to states claiming territorial seas in excess of three nautical miles).

70 *See* U.S. CONST. art. VI, § 2 ("This Constitution, and the Law of the United States which shall be made in Pursuance thereof, and all Treaties made, or which shall be made, under the Authority of the United States, shall be the supreme Law of the Land; and the Judges in every State shall be bound thereby, any Thing in the Constitution or Laws of any State to the Contrary notwithstanding.").

71 International Legal Association Committee on Formation of Customary (General) International Law, *Final Report of the Committee: Statement of Principles Applicable to the Formation of General Customary International Law* 19, *available at* http://www.ila-hq.org/pdf/CustomaryLaw.pdf (last visited Jan. 26, 2006) (2000).

legal construction of the Constitution that discloses its nature as a treaty between states.[72]

There has been no case law or literature closely scrutinizing the constitutional capacity of the U.S. federal government to make a persistent objection. Legal literature and jurisprudence dealing with customary international law within a U.S. constitutional legal regime only has addressed (i) whether there *is* an extant specific customary international legal norm, (ii) whether the political branches can act at any time to preclude its domestic operation, and (iii) whether the U.S. courts have competence to give it effect.[73] However, the task of determining which

[72] Other exceptions may include foreign federal states.

[73] *See, e.g.*, Sosa v. Alvarez-Machain, 542 U.S. 692, 124 S. Ct. at 2765 and 2769, 159 L. Ed. 2d at 15A and 24A, (federal jurisdictional statute can supersede law of nations norm at any time; Alien Tort Statute provides federal court jurisdiction for torts committed in violation of the law of nations, but nonprolonged arbitrary detention does not violate extant customary international law); Macintosh v. United States, 283 U.S. 605, 622 (1931) (Congress under its war powers authority cannot violate customary international law) (dictum); Galo-Garcia v. Immigration & Naturalization Serv., 86 F.3d 916 (9th Cir. 1996) (federal statute supersedes customary international law); Committee of United States Citizens Living in Nicaragua v. Reagan, 859 F.2d 929 (D.C. Cir. 1988) (federal statute supersedes customary international law); United States v. Merkt, 794 F.2d 950 (5th Cir. 1986) (federal statute supersedes customary international law); Garcia-Mir v. Meese, 788 F.2d 1446 (11th Cir. 1986) (federal statutes and executive orders supersede customary international law); United States v. Howard-Arias, 679 F.2d 363 (4th Cir. 1982) (federal statute supersedes customary international law); Rodriguez-Fernandez v. Wilkinson, 654 F.2d 1382, 1385 (10th Cir. 1981) (noting fundamental international law principle against arbitrary detention), *aff'g*, 505 F. Supp. 787 (D. Kan. 1980) (indefinite detention of excludable alien violative of customary international law, which trumps executive order); Tag v. Rogers, 267 F.2d 664 (D.C. Cir. 1959) (federal statute supersedes customary international law); United States v. Buck, 690 F. Supp. 1291 (S.D.N.Y 1988) (customary international law trumps controlling executive acts) (dictum); The Schooner Jane, 37 Ct. cl. 24, 29 (1901); The Ship Rose, 36 Ct. cl. 290, 301 (1901) (customary international law trumps federal statute); The Schooner Nancy, 27 Ct. Cl. 99, 109 (1892); 11 Op. Att'y Gen. 297, 299–300 (1865) (Congress has no power to abrogate customary international law or to authorize its infraction as "it is binding on all branches of our government and citizens"); 9 Op. Att'y Gen. 356, 362–63 (1859) (public law of nations "must be paramount to local law in every question when local laws are in conflict" and "[w]hat you will do must of course depend upon the law of our own country, as controlled and modified by the law of nations"); Jordan Paust, *Rediscovering the Relationship Between Congressional Power and International Law: Exceptions to the Last in Time Rule and the Primacy of Custom*, 28 Va. J. Int'l L. 393 (1988); Bradley & Goldsmith, *Federal Common Law*, *supra* note 61 (some customary international law is unenforceable in U.S. courts).

departments of the federal government have a constitutional authority to make a persistent objection to an emerging customary international legal norm is essential to providing answers to these three questions because these questions are themselves premised on whether there is a customary international legal norm to which the United States is constitutionally obliged to observe. The issue of which branches of the federal government have the constitutional authority to make a persistent objection to an emerging customary international legal norm precedes these three questions. There also has been no law or literature addressing the legal capacity of the United States as an intergovernmental organization to make a persistent objection. The following discussion also will shed new light on some aspects of intergovernmental organizations' legal capacities to make persistent objections. Finally, there has been little case law and no literature analyzing the capacity of states-parties to the Constitution to be persistent objectors.[74] If the sovereignty of states is to be maintained, then an analysis of their constitutional capacity to become persistent objectors is essential insofar as their customary international legal relations with each other and foreign states are concerned.

[74] Although the previous legal literature and jurisprudence has addressed the Persistent Objector Rule from the viewpoint of general international law, the literature has not addressed how U.S. constitutional law accommodates the Rule and how persistent objections can be made by the federal and state governments. *See, e.g.*, FRANCISCO FORREST MARTIN, CHALLENGING HUMAN RIGHTS VIOLATIONS: USING INTERNATIONAL LAW IN U.S. COURTS 47–55 (2001) [hereinafter, MARTIN, CHALLENGING] (providing minimal discussion of Persistent Objector Rule within U.S. constitutional regime); KAROL WOLFKE, CUSTOM IN PRESENT INTERNATIONAL LAW 66 (2d rev. ed. 1993); ANTHONY D'AMATO, THE CONCEPT OF CUSTOM IN INTERNATIONAL LAW 98 (1971) (no example of state protest operating to prove illegality of protested act by other states) [hereinafter, D'AMATO, CUSTOM]; Curtis A. Bradley, *The Juvenile Death Penalty and International Law*, 52 DUKE L.J. 485 (2002); Jack L. Goldsmith and Eric A. Posner, *A Theory of Customary International Law*, 66 U. CHI. L. REV. 1113 (1999). Lynn Loschin, *The Persistent Objector and Customary Human Rights Law: A Proposed Analytical Framework*, 2 U.C. DAVIS J. INT'L L. & POLICY 147, 171 (1996); Jonathan I. Charney, *Universal International Law*, 87 AM. J. INT'L.L. 529, 540 (1993); J. Brock McClane, *How Late in the Emergence of a Norm of Customary International Law May a Persistent Objector Object?*, 13 ILSA J. INT'L L. 1, 6 (1989); David A. Colson, *How Persistent Must the Persistent Objector Be?*, 61 WASH. L. REV. 957, 957 (1986); Ted L. Stein, *The Approach of the Different Drummer: The Principle of the Persistent Objector in International Law*, 26 HARV. INT'L L.J. 457, 459 (1985); Prosper Weil, *Towards Relative Normativity in International Law?*, 77 AM. J. INT'L L. 413, 434 (1983).

6.2.1. The Persistent Objector Rule: Constitutional capacities and incapacities

Let us now examine the specific contours of the constitutional capacities – if any – of the different departments of the federal government and state governments to be persistent objectors. At the outset, it is important to note that this analysis will focus on how persistent objections can be made within the context of conventional customary international law because (i) the Constitution does not expressly mention the customary law of nations and (ii) most modern customary international law is formed through the treaty process.

Presidential Capacities

From the outset, it is perhaps important to note that the president *qua* head of state would appear to have the international legal authority to object to an emerging customary international legal norm because s/he represents the United States in its international relations. However, this does not address how presidential authority is limited or shared with the other branches of the federal and state governments in any way under our peculiar U.S. constitutional legal system.

Let us begin our inquiry with the text of the Constitution and the recognition that treaties can provide evidence of customary international law. Under Article II, the president has the "Power, by and with the Advice and Consent of the Senate, to make Treaties, provided two thirds of the Senators present concur . . ."[75] The U.S. Supreme Court has interpreted this provision to provide exclusive authority to the president to negotiate treaties[76] – although initially President George Washington did try unsuccessfully to use the Senate as counsel in his treaty negotiations.[77] Furthermore, the president appears to be under no constitutional obligation to submit treaties to the Senate for its advice and consent once the treaty has been signed, nor is the president under any constitutional

[75] U.S. CONST. art. II, § 2, cl. 2.

[76] *See* United States v. Curtiss-Wright Export Corp., 299 U.S. 304, 319 (1936) ("He [the president] alone negotiates. Into the field of negotiation, the Senate cannot intrude; and Congress itself is powerless to invade it.")

[77] *See* E. CORWIN, THE PRESIDENT – OFFICE AND POWERS 1787–1957 207–217 (4th ed., New York, 1957).

obligation to bring treaties into force for the United States by exchanging or depositing their instruments of ratification.[78]

If the president merely signs – but does not ratify – a treaty reflecting emerging customary international legal norms, the United States still has signaled its acceptance of these emerging customary international legal norms because signatory states may not defeat the object and purpose of the treaty, which happens also to reflect emerging customary norms.[79] Signatory states can take no positive action to undermine the object and purpose of the treaty whose norms are reflecting emerging customary international law. However, this does not mean that signatory states must take positive action. Furthermore, if positive action requires further action by another branch of the federal government that has sole constitutional authority to take such action, then the United States is not under an international legal obligation to undertake such action.[80] For example, the U.S. House of Representatives has exclusive constitutional authority for introducing appropriations bills, and international law does not specifically compel the House to introduce such bills.

The president's constitutional authority to make treaties suggests that the president constitutionally can signal the United States' objection to an emerging conventional customary international legal norm in two ways. First, the president can deposit a reservation to one of the norms in the treaty stating to the effect that the United States does not accept the emerging norm. Second, the president can explicitly express an objection to the emerging norm during the treaty's negotiations in a case in which the Senate later refuses to give its consent to the treaty. This latter route was employed by President Ronald Reagan when he expressed an objection to the claim that highly migratory species of tuna were within the coastal state jurisdiction beyond the territorial sea during the negotiation of the *UN Convention on the Law of the Sea*.[81] This objection was recognized in dicta by the International Court of Justice in the *Fisheries*

[78] *See* S. Crandall, Treaties, Their Making and Enforcement 53 (2d ed., Washington, 1916).

[79] *See Vienna Convention*, art. 18 ("A State is obliged to refrain from acts which would defeat the object and purpose of a treaty when: (a) it has signed the treaty . . . until it shall made its intention clear not to become a party to the treaty. . . .").

[80] *Cf. Vienna Convention*, art. 46.

[81] Dec. 10, 1982, UN Doc. A/Conf.62/122, 21 I.L.M. 1261.

Case analyzing the Persistent Objector Rule.[82] The ICJ further noted, however, that the president did not withdraw the United States' objection to the claim that highly migratory species of tuna were within the coastal state jurisdiction beyond the territorial sea.

The president also can express an objection in his other constitutional roles, such as commander-in-chief. For example, President Reagan sent U.S. naval vessels into the Black Sea to exercise its right of innocent passage in the Soviet Union's territorial waters and to maintain its objection to the Soviet Union's claim that customary international law allowed states to prohibit other states the right to exercise the right of innocent passage when the state makes notice of this prohibition.[83] Unlike the president's treaty-making authority, the president's power to make a persistent objection is not limited by the Senate when the president exercises his capacity as commander-in-chief. However, the president's commander-in-chief's authority is limited by Congress' authority to make laws governing "the land and naval Forces."[84]

The president as the head of the United States has the constitutional role of managing the United States' foreign affairs.[85] In this role, s/he often makes executive agreements with foreign states. Although the U.S. Supreme Court has treated some executive agreements as treaties, not all executive agreements have the force of treaties.[86] Nevertheless, such agreements could be used to signal a persistent objection to an emerging customary international legal norm.

However, the president may make a persistent objection when s/he is exercising only her/his limited constitutional duties. For example, the president (with Congress) has a constitutional role in making federal statutory law. Federal statutory law is evidence of an

82 Fisheries Case (U.K. v. Norway), 1951 I.C.J. at 131 (President Reagan maintaining objection to claim that highly migratory species of tuna were within the coastal state jurisdiction beyond the territorial sea while withdrawing United States' objection to states claiming territorial seas in excess of three nautical miles).

83 For an account of the United States' Black Sea practices, see W.E. Butler, *Innocent Passage and the 1982 Convention: The Influence of Soviet Law and Policy*, 81 Am. J. Int'l L. 343–46 (1987).

84 U.S. Const. art. I, § 8.

85 United States v. Belmont, 301 U.S. 324.

86 *See supra* text accompanying notes 36–45.

American federal[87] customary international law in a similar way that UN General Assembly resolutions can be evidence of global customary international law[88] because federal statutes and General Assembly resolutions both implement widely adopted treaties that respectively represent regional and global customary international legal norms themselves. Insofar as the president can veto a bill that has passed the House of Representatives and the Senate,[89] the president constitutionally can express an objection to this emerging American, federal customary international law. Indeed, to exercise his/her veto in a sufficiently constitutional manner, the president must return the bill "with his Objections"[90] that effectively operate as an express objection to the emerging American, federal customary international law reflected in the congressional bill submitted to him/her. However, pocket vetoes cannot be evidence of objections because they are not *express* objections as are regular vetoes.

Senatorial Capacities

For treaties to become federal law, the consent of two-thirds of the Senate is required by Article II of the Constitution. Although the president is under no constitutional obligation to bring treaties into force for the United States by exchanging or depositing their instruments of ratification, once the president has submitted the treaty to the Senate for its consent, the Senate acquires constitutional authority to signal the United States' objection to emerging customary international legal norm because the president's constitutional "Power . . . to make treaties" is only "*by* . . . the Senate." The president's power to make treaties is only derivative of the Senate's power.[91] The Senate's original constitutional authority

[87] This evidence is "conventional" because the federal statutes implement a treaty (*i.e.*, the Constitution).

[88] *Cf.* Restatement, *supra* note 48 at § 103 comment c ("[r]esolutions of universal international organizations, if not controversial and if adopted by consensus or virtual unanimity, are given substantial weight" as evidence of customary international law).

[89] *See* U.S. Const. art. I, § 7, cl. 2.

[90] *Id.*

[91] *Id.* at, art. II, § 2, cl. 2 (emphasis provided). The original plan submitted by the Committee of Detail on August 6, 1787 provided that only "the Senate of the United States shall have power to make treaties . . ." 2 The Records of the Federal Convention of 1787 183 (Max

to make treaties as indicated in the original plan submitted by the Constitutional Convention's Committee of Detail suggests that the Senate has as much – if not more – constitutional authority to make persistent objections to an emerging customary international legal norm reflected in a treaty under the Senate's consideration for approval. Indeed, treaties made by the Articles Congress (which are still supreme law of the land according to the Supremacy Clause) did not require a president to make them or bring them into force.

The Senate constitutionally can make an objection to an emerging customary international legal norm in the treaty by requiring the president to deposit a reservation objecting to the norm in order for the treaty to receive the Senate's approval.[92] Note, however, that the Senate (and president) cannot object to an extant customary international legal norm. An arguable exception to this rule is if the reservation's effect is limited to prohibiting the treaty's constituent tribunal from adjudicating interstate cases addressing the customary international legal norm to which the reservation is subject.[93] Furthermore, the United States cannot make reservations that violate the object and purpose of the treaty or that are prohibited by the treaty itself.[94] Whether a reservation to a specific treaty norm would violate the treaty's object and purpose or would be prohibited by the treaty will turn on the nature of the treaty and the specific norm.

If the president already expressed an objection to an emerging customary international legal norm during the treaty's negotiation that the Senate does not share, the Senate also can condition its consent upon the

Farrand, ed., 1937) [hereinafter FARRAND'S RECORDS]. Not until September 7 (ten days before the Convention's final adjournment) did the Constitutional Convention give the president derivative power to make treaties. *Ibid.* at 538–39.

92 *See* Fourteen Diamond Rings v. United States, 183 U.S. 176, 183 (1901) (dicta) (suggesting that Senate may condition its consent to a treaty); *Treaties and Other International Agreements: The Role of the United States Senate*, A Study Prepared for the Senate Committee on Foreign Relations by the Congressional Research Service, 103d Cong., 1st sess. (Comm. Print) (1993), 96–98 (same); RESTATEMENT, *supra* note 48 at § 314 (same).

93 *See infra* discussion accompanying note 155.

94 *See Vienna Convention*, art. 19 ("A State may, when signing, ratifying, accepting, approving or acceding to a treaty, formulate a reservation unless: (a) the reservation is prohibited by the treaty; . . . (c) . . . the reservation is incompatible with the object and purpose of the treaty.").

understanding that the president will not deposit a reservation objecting to the norm, thereby withdrawing the United States' objection, because the president's authority to make treaties is only derivative of the Senate's authority.

Congressional Capacities

Congress has the constitutional authority under Article I to "define and punish . . . Offences against the Law of Nations."[95] Congress does so through the enactment of legislation with presidential approval or without presidential approval if the legislation subsequently receives two-thirds votes from both the House and Senate.[96] Congress has no constitutional authority under the Define and Punish Clause to object to an emerging customary international legal norm because the clause speaks only of *extant* law of nations norms, of which the customary law of nations forms a part. When the Constitution gives Congress the power to define and punish offenses against the law of nations, this power extends only to the clarification[97] and punishment of such violations[98] through implementing legislation under its Article I, § 8, cl. 18 authority.[99]

[95] U.S. CONST. art. 1, § 8, cl. 9.

[96] Congress arguably also can define such offenses through the adoption of congressional resolutions.

[97] The Framers used the term "define" to mean "clarify" – not create. *See* 2 FARRAND'S RECORDS, *supra* note 91 at 61 ("Mr. Govr: The word define is proper when applied to offences in this case; the law of nations being often too vague and deficient to be a rule."); *cf.* WILLIAM BLACKSTONE, 4 COMMENTARIES ON THE LAWS OF ENGLAND 67 (1769) ("those acts of parliament, which have from time to time been made to enforce this universal law, or to facilitate the execution of [its] decisions, are not to be considered as introductive of any new rule, but merely as declaratory of the old fundamental constitutions of the kingdom; without which it must cease to be a part of the civilized world.").

[98] The term "offenses" meant both criminal and noncriminal "violations." *See* 4 BLACKSTONE, *supra* note 97 at *Of Offences Against the Law of Nations*, ch. 5 (listing both criminal and noncriminal offenses against the law of nations); JOSEPH STORY, 3 COMMENTARIES ON THE CONSTITUTION OF THE UNITED STATES, ch. 3, § 1160 (1833) ("As the United States are responsible to foreign governments for all violations of the law of nations, . . . congress ought to possess the power to define and punish all such offences, which may interrupt our intercourse and harmony with, and our duties to them.").

[99] U.S. CONST. art. I, § 8, cl. 18 (Congress has power "to "make all Laws which shall be necessary and proper for carrying into Execution the foregoing Powers, and all other

However, Congress does have the constitutional authority to signal its objection to an emerging customary international legal norm by enacting legislation and resolutions implementing other clauses of the Constitution. Insofar as James Wilson's observation that the United States could not unilaterally make law of nations norms referred only to *global* norms[100] and this observation was shared by the other Framers, congressional authority under the Define and Punish Clause does not preclude Congress from objecting to emerging American federal customary international legal norms through legislation implementing other constitutional clauses. However, such implementing legislation must be "necessary and proper."[101]

Federal Courts' Incapacity

The concept of a persistent objector suggests that the objector in an inverse way "makes" law by effectively declaring a certain norm to not be legally binding on the objector. If federal courts constitutionally can make law in certain circumstances, do federal courts have a constitutional capacity to make a persistent objection? According to legal formalism, judges can only interpret – not make – law. As Francis Bacon put it, "their office is *jus dicere* and not *jus dare*."[102] Judges are not sovereigns capable of making law. The general constitutional corollaries to this doctrine are that the authority to make law resides only in the Congress and president, and that the federal courts entertain a limited jurisdiction that prevents them from making law.

On the other hand, federal courts sometimes operate as international or interstate courts,[103] and some international tribunals can decide cases

Powers vested by this Constitution in the Government of the United States, or in any Department or Officer thereof.").

[100] *See* 2 Farrand's Records, *supra note 91 at 61 (Wilson: "To pretend to define the law of nations which depended on the authority of all the Civilized Nations of the World, would have a look of arrogance that would make us ridiculous.").*

[101] U.S. Const. art. I, § 8, cl. 18

[102] Francis Bacon, The Essayes 316 (1625).

[103] *See* Kansas v. Colorado, 185 U.S. 125, 14 (1902) (Supreme Court sitting as international tribunal in dispute between Kansas and Colorado). The Supreme Court also has described itself an international court when sitting as a prize court because prize cases were determined by the law of nations. Penhallow v. Doane, 3 U.S. (3 Dall.) 54, 91 (1795) ("A prize

ex aequo et bono[104] in the absence of positive law if the parties to a case so agree. International tribunals cannot pronounce a *non liquet* because of an absence of applicable positive law in a case. The prohibition of a *non liquet* pronouncement is well-established positive law based on "uninterrupted continuity of international arbitral and judicial practice."[105] Accordingly, an international legal construction of federal court jurisdiction arguably would allow federal courts as international courts to decide some purely party-based jurisdiction cases *ex aequo et bono*, and insofar as such decisions provide persuasive precedent for future cases, these decisions reflect law – albeit purportedly natural.[106]

However, the Persistent Objector Rule is only relevant to that part of the positive law of nations that is customary. Therefore, the constitutional capacity of federal courts arguably to make law by deciding cases *ex aequo et bono* is not relevant to whether federal courts have a constitutional capacity to make persistent objections because the application of the Persistent Objector Rule comes into play only when positive law – specifically, customary international law – already has crystallized.

On the other hand, even judicial interpretation of positive law can generate secondary rules that acquire their own legally binding authority. Legal Realists have long argued that judges make law,[107] as evidenced in the common law, and federal courts often are common law courts.[108]

court is, in effect, a court of all the nations in the world, because all persons, in every part of the world, are concluded by its sentences.").

104 *See, e.g., I.C.J. Statute*, art. 28, art. 2 (ICJ may "decide a case *ex aequo et bono*, if the parties agree thereto.")

105 *See, e.g.*, Hersch Lauterpacht, *Some Observations on the Prohibition of "Non Liquet" and the Completeness of the Law, in* HERSCH LAUTERPACHT, 2 INTERNATIONAL LAW: COLLECTED PAPERS 216, 217 (ed. Elihu Lauterpacht, 1975).

106 For example, when the U.S. Supreme Court exercises its original jurisdiction, the Constitution does not say which law to apply. For example, an interstate, diversity case may not involve any federal law claims; therefore, the Court constitutionally could decide the case e*x aequo et bono* without reference to any legal authorities. By contrast, the jurisdictions of inferior federal courts often are limited by Congress because Congress has the constitutional authority to vest jurisdiction in such courts.

107 *See, e.g.*, KARL LLEWELLYN, THE BRAMBLE BUSH: ON OUR LAW AND ITS STUDY (1930).

108 *See* Sosa v. Alvarez-Machain, 542 U.S. 692, 124 S. Ct. at 2764, 159 L. Ed. 2d at 9H (federal courts retain jurisdiction for common law claims notwithstanding *Erie Railroad Co. v. Tompkins*).

Most importantly, there is judge-made law in the law of nations.[109] For example, when an international court interprets a right explicitly guaranteed by a treaty (*i.e.*, positive international law) by applying the right to the facts in a specific case, the meaning that the court gives to the right through its application to the case often is one that the treaty-makers did not consider. For example, the Council of Europe guaranteed the right to freedom from discrimination in 1950 by incorporating it in the *ECHR*. It is unlikely that it occurred to Council members that a case would come up forty-nine years later before the European Court of Human Rights in which a homosexual parent would challenge the state's denial of child custody to him on the basis of his homosexuality and that the Court would interpret the meaning of the right to freedom from discrimination to protect a homosexual parent's right to custody over his child.[110] Such judicial interpretations that, strictly speaking, are only binding on the parties to a case later can become codified in treaties[111] and, hence, clearly positive law. This judicial interpretation serves as evidence of emerging conventional customary international law that later may become binding on states not parties to the original case as a matter of both customary international law and treaty law. Indeed, insofar as such international judicial precedent can serve to bind states that are not parties to the particular case or treaty, this judicial precedent is evidence of extant conventional customary international law binding on such states. Even those judicially made general principles (*e.g.*, principle of subsidiarity, margin of appreciation doctrine, "pressing social need" rule) can be legally binding on states not parties to the original case by their adoption in a subsequently ratified treaty.[112]

[109] *See id.* at 542 U.S. 692, 124 S. Ct. at 2756, 159 L. Ed. 2d at **743 ("The law of nations included a second, more pedestrian element, however, that did fall within the judicial sphere, as a body of judge-made law regulating the conduct of individuals situated outside domestic boundaries and consequently carrying an international savor.").

[110] *See* Salgueiro da Silva Mouta v. Portugal, Appl. No. 33290/96, Eur. Ct. H.R. (1999).

[111] *See, e.g.*, Treaty Establishing a Constitution for Europe, Dec. 16, 2004, art. II-81(1), 47 Official Journal of the European Union (C 310) ("Any discrimination based on any ground such as . . . sexual orientation shall be prohibited.")

[112] *See, e.g., id.* at II-preamble, ¶ 5:

> This Charter reaffirms, with due regard for the powers and tasks of the Community and the Union and the principle of subsidiarity, the rights as they result, in particular, from the constitutional traditions and international obligations common to the Member States,

However, the early conception of the law of nations (to which the Framers adhered) held that judges were only "finding" law through the exercise of their natural reason; therefore, the federal courts cannot lawfully exercise any lawmaking authority that arguably may include the authority to not recognize an emerging legal norm. As a matter of practice, judges (whether U.S. or foreign) never have stated that they have the authority to make a persistent objection. Courts confine the language of their opinions to whether a customary international legal norm already has crystallized or not. If it has not, the court cannot apply it. Therefore, if international courts themselves do not consider themselves to be making persistent objections, then it is difficult to recognize that international courts do have the authority to make persistent objections.

Conflicting Positions between the Political Departments

What if there is a conflict between these political departments of the federal government regarding an objection? Does one department's objection trump another's acceptance of the emerging customary norm? For example, what if the president were to accept an emerging customary international legal norm and the Congress subsequently objects to the emerging norm? The Persistent Objector Rule requires persistency of the objection; therefore, the subsequent objection would be invalid. Or, if the president undertakes an action executing his/her authority under the Commander-in-Chief,[113] Reprieves and Pardons,[114] or Appoint-

the Treaty on European Union, the Community Treaties, the European Convention for the Protection of Human Rights and Fundamental Freedoms, the Social Charters adopted by the Community and by the Council of Europe and the case-law of the Court of Justice of the European Communities and of the European Court of Human Rights.

[113] *See* U.S. Const. art. II, § 2, cl. 1 ("The President shall be Commander in Chief of the Army and Navy of the United States, and of the Militia of the several States, when called into the actual Service of the United States. . . ."), § 2, cl. 2 ("he shall nominate, and by and with the Advice and Consent of the Senate, shall appoint Ambassadors, other public Ministers and Consuls"), and art. II, § 3 ("he shall receive Ambassadors and other public Ministers").

[114] *See id.* at. art. II, § 2, cl. 1 ("he shall have Power to grant Reprieves and Pardons for Offences against the United States").

ments[115] Clauses that signals the acceptance of an emerging customary international legal norm and Congress subsequently makes a law that effectively rejects this emerging norm, Congress' objection cannot stand because not only would such congressional action probably violate the separation of powers principle but it also would unlawfully allow a federal statute to trump a customary international legal norm.[116] Or, if the president were to object to the emerging norm and the Congress subsequently accepts the norm, then the initial objection would no longer be valid because, again, the Rule requires persistency for an objector to acquire exemption from the norm's application. Or, if the president withholds his/her objection to an emerging customary norm until after receiving the Senate's consent to a treaty codifying the norm by later depositing a reservation, then this reservation could not be a persistent objection because the Senate already had endorsed the emerging customary international legal norm – notwithstanding the fact that the president is under no constitutional obligation to bring the treaty as a whole into force.

However, if there is an extant federal statute that represents an objection to an emerging customary international legal norm, the president cannot eliminate the objection by, for example, merely signing a subsequent treaty that is inconsistent with the federal statute because s/he would not be "tak[ing] Care that the Laws be faithfully executed."[117]

State Capacities

Whether states-parties to the Constitution have the constitutional capacity to object to an emerging customary international legal norm also requires one to address first whether these states can contribute to the

[115] *See id.* at art. II, § 2, cl. 2 ("he shall nominate, and by and with the Advice and Consent of the Senate, . . . Judges of the supreme Court, and all other Officers of the United States, whose Appointments are not herein otherwise provided for, and which shall be established by Law: but the Congress may by Law vest the Appointment of such inferior Officers, as they think proper, in the President alone, in the Courts of Law, or in the Heads of Departments").

[116] *See supra* Subsection 6.2.2.

[117] U.S. CONST. art. II, § 3. This presidential incapacity to make a persistent objection is consonant with the conventional law of nations in that the *Vienna Convention* recognizes that states can consider themselves not bound by a treaty if the treaty manifestly violates a fundamental provision of its internal law, in this case, the presidential duty to faithfully execute federal statues under Article II. *Vienna Convention*, art. 46 (1).

formation of customary international law because one of the defining conditions of a customary international legal norm is *state* practice.[118] The United States consists of sovereign states, and states, of course, contribute to the formation of customary international law through, for example, their laws and treaties – or in the case of states of the United States, interstate and foreign state compacts. We already have seen that there exists not only global but also regional customary international law (also called "local custom"). Recall that Vattel recognized the existence of regional customary international law[119] Also, the ICJ in the *Asylum Case*[120] and the U.S. Supreme Court in *The Antelope*[121] recognized the existence of regional customary international law. Indeed, the Inter-American Commission on Human Rights in *Pinkerton and Roach v. United States* appears to have recognized that the laws of states-parties to the Constitution can be evidence of an American federal customary international law.[122] In discussing whether a customary international legal norm prohibiting the execution of persons under the age of eighteen existed, the Commission in *Pinkerton and Roach* made note of not only how many states had ratified the *ICCPR* and the *ACHR* (both of which prohibit such executions[123]), but also how many states in the United States had laws either explicitly or effectively prohibiting juvenile executions. The Commission concluded that although there was no norm, the norm was emerging given that "thirteen states and the U.S. capital[[124] had] abolished the death penalty entirely and nine retentionist states [had] abolished it for

[118] This section only will address the U.S. constitutional capacity of states *per se* – not their branches of government – to provide evidence of a persistent objection. States-parties to the Constitution arguably can express objections through the actions of their political branches (*e.g.*, state laws, executive pronouncements) – like any other foreign state.

[119] Vattel, Law of Nations, *supra* note 19 at *Preliminaries*, § 26 (recognizing regional customary international law).

[120] 1950 I.C.J. at 276–77.

[121] 23 U.S. at 121 (recognizing European law of nations).

[122] *See* Pinkerton and Roach v. United States, Inter-Am. Comm. H.R. No. 3/87, Annual Report of the Inter-American Commission on Human Rights: 1986–87, OEA/Ser.L/V/II.71/doc.9 147 (1987).

[123] *ICCPR*, art. 6 (5); *ACHR*, art. 4 (5).

[124] Indeed, the Supreme Court has held that even the District of Columbia is a "state" under international law.

> Were there no other territory under the government of the United States, it would not be questioned that the District of Columbia would be a "state," within the meaning of

offenders under the age of 18."[125] Here, the Commission effectively is referring to the absence of an American, federal customary international legal norm prohibiting juvenile executions, and we can infer from the Commission's conclusion that states of the United States collectively can make customary international law.

Three evidentiary sources of customary international law are interstate compacts, state-foreign state compacts, and state laws. However, the constitutional capacity of states-parties to the Constitution to make compacts with each other and foreign states is subject to congressional approval[126] and the states' respective constitutional limitations,[127] and state laws cannot violate federal law.[128] Nevertheless, states-parties to the Constitution retain constitutional authority to legislate in areas where federal law has not occupied the field.[129] Therefore, assuming that the federal government has not taken a position on an emerging customary international legal norm (either because of disinterest or constitutional limitations[130]), states-parties to the Constitution can contribute to the formation of cus-

> international law; and it is not perceived that it is any less a state, within that meaning, because other states and other territory are also under the same government.

Geofroy v. Riggs, 133 U.S. 258, 268–69 (1890).

125 Pinkerton and Roach v. United States at § 60.

126 U.S. Const. art. I, § 10, cl. 3 ("No State shall, without the Consent of Congress, . . . enter into any Agreement or Compact with another State, or with a foreign Power. . . .").

127 *See Vienna Convention*, arts. 27 and 46 (Art. 27: "A party may not invoke the provisions of its internal law as justification for its failure to perform a treaty. This rule is without prejudice to article 46." Art. 46: "A State may not invoke the fact that its consent to be bound by a treaty has been expressed in violation of a provision of its internal law regarding competence to conclude treaties as invalidating its consent unless that violation was manifest and concerned a rule of its internal law of fundamental importance.").

128 U.S. Const. art. VI, cl. 2 ("This Constitution, and the Laws of the United States which shall be made in Pursuance thereof; and all Treaties made, or which shall be made, under the Authority of the United States, shall be the supreme Law of the Land; and the Judges in every State shall be bound thereby, any Thing in the Constitution or Laws of any State to the Contrary notwithstanding.").

129 *See* Skiriotes v. Florida, 313 U.S. 69, 75 (1941) ("Congress having occupied but a limited field, the authority of the State to protect its interests by additional or supplementary legislation otherwise valid is not impaired.").

130 Such limitations include the federal government's constitutional incapacity to make compacts or laws that violate the Constitution. *See* Marbury v. Madison, 5 U.S. (1 Cranch.) 137 (1803) ("an act of the legislature, repugnant to the constitution, is void"); Reid v. Covert, 354 U.S. 1 (1957) (United States cannot make treaties that violate Constitution).

tomary international law. However, subsequent federal treaty or legislation constitutionally would supersede this customary international law because both federal statutory and treaty law supersedes inconsistent state law under the Supremacy Clause.

However, do states-parties to the Constitution have constitutional authority to object to an emerging *American, federal* customary international legal norm? The answer to this question is not clear because of the U.S. Supreme Court's consensus inquiry's relationship to the Supremacy Clause in the Court's Eighth Amendment jurisprudence. The Supreme Court has applied a national consensus test in construing the Eighth Amendment by examining the state laws of the United States and "the consistency of the direction of change"[131] in the norm's emergence. If there is a national consensus as to the norm, the Eighth Amendment is to be construed in conformity with this norm. A national consensus is established when the state laws of a bare majority of states (*i.e.*, presently twenty-six states) have accepted the norm.[132] If this national consensus test could extend to the rest of the Constitution and its amendments – and there does not appear any reason why it should not – then the national consensus test has an important implication for states-parties to the Constitution wishing to avail themselves of the Persistent Objector Rule.

This national consensus test suggests that the Court effectively is applying American, federal customary international law for construing the Eighth Amendment – which would be appropriate given that the Eighth Amendment to the Constitution is an amendment to a treaty that must be construed in conformity with the states-parties' customary international legal obligations. However, this national consensus test also sug-

[131] Atkins v. Virginia, 536 U.S. 304, 346 (2002).

[132] *See, e.g.*, Atkins v. Virginia, 536 U.S. 304 (sufficient evidence of national consensus against executing mentally retarded people demonstrated in part by twenty-six states prohibiting practice); Penry v. Lynaugh, 492 U.S. 302, 335 (1989) ("insufficient evidence of a national consensus against executing mentally retarded people" demonstrated by only sixteen states prohibiting practice); Thompson v. Oklahoma, 487 U.S. 815 (1988) (insufficient evidence of national consensus against executing persons committing capital crimes under age eighteen); Tison v. Arizona, 481 U.S. 137 (1987) (death penalty for felony murder held unconstitutional partly on basis that most states did not allow imposition); Edmund v. Florida, 458 U.S. 782 (1982) (same); *cf.* MARTIN, CHALLENGING HUMAN RIGHTS VIOLATIONS, *supra* note 74 at 45–47 (arguing for "Customary International Law 50% threshold test for establishing global customary international legal norm").

gests that states-parties to the Constitution cannot avail themselves of the Persistent Objector Rule in exempting themselves from being bound to this American, federal customary international legal norm because these states are constitutionally bound effectively under the Supremacy Clause to comply with the U.S. Supreme Court's construction of constitutional provisions.

An analogous situation is the European Court of Human Rights' consensus inquiry for construing the *ECHR*. The European Court of Human Rights examines whether there is a sufficient European consensus supporting a norm. If there is sufficient consensus, the Court uses the norm for construing provisions of the *ECHR* – regardless of whether a state-party effectively has expressed a persistent objection to the norm during its emergence through its domestic legislation.[133] However, if the state-party attached a reservation effectively signaling its timely objection to the European customary international legal norm, then the Court cannot use the norm for construing the *ECHR*.[134]

133 For a detailed discussion of the European Court's consensus approach, *see* Laurence R. Helfer, *Consensus, Coherence and the European Convention on Human Rights*, 26 CORNELL INT'L L.J. 133 (1993).

134 The reservation, however, cannot violate the object and purpose of the *ECHR* and the state-party's customary international legal obligations at the time of the reservation's deposit. *See Vienna Convention*, art. 19; *cf.* Issues relating to Reservations Made upon Ratification or Accession to the Covenant or the Optional Protocols Thereto, or in relation to Declarations under Article 41 of the Covenant: 04/11/94, General Comment 24, 52d Sess., ¶¶ 8 and 10, UN Doc. CCPR/C/21/rev. 1, add. 6 (1994) ("provisions in the *ICCPR* that represent customary international law . . . may not be the subject of reservations"). The International Law Commission while commenting on the original draft version of the Object and Purpose Rule under the *Vienna Convention* suggested that the rule is not an independent barrier to reservation acceptance by other nations. *See* Documents of the Conference on the Vienna Convention, A/CONF.39/11/Add.2. During later negotiations, many nations proposed amendments to the *Vienna Convention* to clarify that the Object and Purpose Rule was an absolute bar to reservations, but these amendments were all rejected. Catherine Redgwell, *Universality or Integrity? Some Reflections on Reservations to General Multilateral Treaties*, 64 BRIT. Y.B. INT'L L. 245, 255–60 (1993). Regardless of the Object and Purpose Rule's apparent ambiguity as an independent bar to reservations, the UN Human Rights Committee in addressing the validity of reservations to the *ICCPR* (which expressly authorizes the Committee to issue general comments under Article 40, *ICCPR*) has commented that the Object and Purpose Rule does act as an independent bar. Therefore, it is fair to conclude that the UN Human Rights Committee's unequivocal position provides more persuasive authority than the International Law Commission's ambiguous position because the Committee is an international tribunal unlike

The consensus test of the U.S. Supreme Court suggests that states-members of intergovernmental organizations (such as the United States) sometimes cannot avail themselves of the Persistent Objector Rule when their respective constituent treaties are construed in conformity with their respective regional customary international legal obligations. This conclusion is strengthened in the case of the states-members of the United States because these states cannot make a reservation to the Constitution and/or its amendments.[135]

What about emerging *global* or *other regional* customary international law norms? The states-parties to the Constitution have constitutional authority to object to such emerging rules if federal law has not already fully addressed the norm. Indeed, the Tenth Amendment suggests that states retain the sovereign right to be persistent objectors: "The powers not delegated to the United States by the Constitution, nor prohibited by it to the States, are reserved to the States respectively, or to the people."[136] And, insofar as a state's compact with a foreign state(s) reflects an objection to an emerging global or American nonfederal customary international legal norm, Congress' approval of such a compact serves to constitutionally confirm the objection.

In conclusion, states-parties to the Constitution can avail themselves of the Persistent Objector Rule only in regard to customary international

the Commission and, therefore, the Committee's views carry more legally authoritative weight.

135 The Constitution does not provide for reservations. *See* U.S. CONST. art. V. During the New York Constitutional Convention, it was suggested that New York ratify the Constitution on condition that certain other amendments were added. However, Madison responded:

> The Constitution requires an adoption *in toto* and for ever. It has been so adopted by the other States. An adoption for a limited time would be as defective as an adoption of some of the articles only. In short any condition whatever must viciate the ratification.

5 THE PAPERS OF ALEXANDER HAMILTON 184 (H. Syrett ed. New York: 1962). Madison's argument resonates with the *Vienna Convention*:

> When it appears from the limited number of the negotiating States and the object and purpose of the treaty that the application of the treaty in its entirety between all the parties is an essential condition of the consent of each one to be bound by the treaty, a reservation requires acceptance by all the parties.

Vienna Convention, art. 19 (2).

136 U.S. CONST. amend. X.

legal norms that address areas not occupied by existing federal law.[137] Furthermore, these states cannot avail themselves of the Persistent Objector Rule when the Constitution is construed in conformity with American federal customary international law that has been established by a bare majority of states accepting the norm.

6.2.2. Federal statutes and executive acts cannot trump customary international legal obligations

Are there any limits on federal statutory law and executive orders trumping the United States' customary international legal obligations? If not, the Persistent Objector Rule would not apply to the United States – at least insofar as persistency of objection is required. However, recent federal court practice seems to suggest that federal statutes and executive orders always trump customary international law regardless of when it emerged.[138] However, this recent rule is fraught with insurmountable problems. First, the Constitution does not say that federal statutes or executive orders can trump the United States' customary international legal obligations. Only some federal courts have fabricated this rule. Indeed, if Congress has the constitutional duty only to clarify and punish offences against already existing law of nations norms, Congress does not have the authority to enact laws that violate these norms.

Second, some federal courts have incorrectly paraphrased a dictum in the U.S. Supreme Court's *The Paquete Habana* that has resulted in an

[137] *Cf.* Skiriotes v. Florida, 313 U.S. at 78–79 ("When [a state's] action does not conflict with federal legislation, the sovereign authority of the State over the conduct of its citizens upon the high seas is analogous to the sovereign authority of the United States over its citizens in like circumstances.").

[138] *See, e.g.*, Galo-Garcia v. Immigration & Naturalization Serv., 86 F.3d 916 (federal statute supersedes customary international law); Committee of United States Citizens Living in Nicaragua v. Reagan, 859 F.2d 929 (federal statute supersedes customary international law); United States v. Merkt, 794 F.2d 950 (federal statute supersedes customary international law); Garcia-Mir v. Meese, 788 F.2d 1446 (federal statutes and executive orders supersede customary international law); United States v. Howard-Arias, 679 F.2d 363 (federal statute supersedes customary international law); Tag v. Rogers, 267 F.2d 664 (federal statute supersedes customary international law); *cf.* Sosa v. Alvarez-Machain, 542 U.S. 692, 124 S. Ct. at 2755, 159 L. Ed. 2d at 15A (federal jurisdictional statute can supersede law of nations norm at any time).

interpretation of the dictum that is overreaching.[139] The Supreme Court in *The Paquete Habana* stated "where there is no treaty, and no controlling executive or legislative act or judicial decision, resort must be had to the customs and usages of civilized nations." Some lower federal courts have overreached the dictum's meaning by adding the word "only," as in "only 'where there is no treaty, and no controlling executive or legislative act or judicial decision, resort must be had to the customs and usages of civilized nations.'"[140] The difference is important because the addition of the word "only" transforms the dictum from being a rule designed to *interpret* vague treaties, legislative acts, executive acts, and judicial opinions into a rule that requires the *direct* application of customary international law *only* when there are no such authorities. However, a court need not use customary international law if such authorities are sufficiently specific, that is to say, "controlling." The addition of "only" incorrectly turns what is otherwise a traditional interpretive international legal rule into a rule that subjugates customary international law to these other authorities.

Third, this recent rule fails to recognize earlier potentially conflicting case law and authorities. For example, the U.S. Supreme Court stated in 1812 that sovereigns could not retract their obligations under a treaty. In *The Schooner Exchange v. McFaddon*, the Supreme Court stated:

> In almost every instance, the treaties between civilized nations contain a stipulation to this effect in favor of vessels driven in by stress of weather or other urgent necessity. In such cases the sovereign is bound by compact to authorize foreign vessels to enter his ports. The treaty binds him to allow vessels in distress to find refuge and asylum in his ports, and *this is a license which he is not at liberty to retract.*[141]

Insofar as treaties can reflect a customary international legal norm, the Supreme Court's statement suggests that the United States cannot violate such a norm when it has either explicitly or implicitly accepted it by way

[139] 175 U.S. 677, 700 (1900) (dictum).

[140] In the Matter of the Extradition of Cheung, 968 F. Supp. 791, 803 n. 17 (D. Conn. 1997); *see also* Garcia-Mir v. Meese, 788 F.2d 1446 (same); Tag v. Rogers, 267 F.2d 664 (same); Dimon-Sainz v. United States, No. 97–3117-RDR, 1999 U.S. Dist. LEXIS 18582 (D. Kan. 1999) (same).

[141] 11 U.S. (7 Cranch) at 141 (emphasis provided).

of treaty.[142] Later in the next century, the Supreme Court in *United States v. Macintosh* stated in dicta that Congress under its war powers authority could not violate customary international law:

> From its very nature the war power, when necessity calls for its exercise, tolerates no qualifications or limitations, *unless found* in the Constitution or *in applicable principles of international law*.[143]

Lower federal courts[144] and opinions by the U.S. Attorney General,[145] respectively, have stated that federal statutes and executive acts cannot supersede the United States' customary international legal obligations.

Fourth, the rule appears to be based on the notion of congressional supremacy in lawmaking. As argued earlier in regard to the Last-in-Time Rule,[146] Congress under the Constitution is not the supreme lawmaker, as Parliament is in England, that can make statutes that abrogate common law of which customary international law is part. Therefore, there is no congressional supremacy on which to base the justification of a federal statute abrogating a customary international legal norm.

However, there appears to be one way in which the United States or any state could make a *kind* of objection to an extant customary international legal norm's enforcement. The United States or a

[142] *Id.* at 136 (acceptance of law of nations norm made either explicitly or implicitly).

[143] 283 U.S. 605, 622 (1931) (dictum) (emphasis provided).

[144] *See, e.g.*, United States v. Buck, 690 F. Supp. 1291 (S.D.N.Y. 1988) (customary international law trumps controlling executive acts) (dictum); Rodriguez-Fernandez v. Wilkinson, 654 F.2d 1382, 1385 (noting fundamental international law principle against arbitrary detention), *aff'g*, 505 F. Supp. 787 (D. Kan. 1980) (indefinite detention of excludable alien violative of customary international law, which trumps executive order); The Schooner Jane, 37 Ct. Cl. 24, 29 (1901); The Ship Rose, 36 Ct. Cl. 290, 301 (1901) (customary international law trumps federal statute); The Schooner Nancy, 27 Ct. Cl. 99, 109 (1892).

[145] *See, e.g.*, 11 Op. Att'y Gen. 297, 299–300 (1865) (Congress has no power to abrogate customary international law or to authorize its infraction as "it is binding on all branches of our government and citizens"); 9 Op. Att'y Gen. 356, 362–63 (1859) (public law of nations "must be paramount to local law in every question when local laws are in conflict" and "[w]hat you will do must of course depend upon the law of our own country, as controlled and modified by the law of nations"); *see also* Jordan Paust, *Rediscovering the Relationship Between Congressional Power and International Law: Exceptions to the Last in Time Rule and the Primacy of Custom*, 28 Va. J. Int'l L. 393 (1988), for additional authorities cited therein.

[146] *See supra* Subsection 5.2.

state *arguably* could lawfully make a reservation to an extant customary international legal norm in a treaty if the treaty also creates an enforcement organ and if the reservation is interpreted to mean only that the state-party does not recognize the organ's competence to interpret the norm. This exception was suggested by the UN Human Rights Committee because it was concerned with maintaining the principle of interstate reciprocity that would otherwise be violated if an international tribunal were allowed to interpret a treaty norm to which a state-party had made a reservation.[147] However, the Committee also stated that in human rights cases, this method of exception would not apply – except perhaps in interstate cases – because human rights protections are for the benefit of individuals and not states.[148] For example, if the United States should ratify the *ACHR*, including its provision recognizing the Inter-American Court of Human Rights' competence to adjudicate cases, and deposit a reservation stating that it does not accept a particular *ACHR* right, then the Court would still have competence to interpret the right in a case alleging its violation.

Finally, there is one other arguable way in which federal statutory law could supersede customary international law: the "Subsequent Objector Rule." The Subsequent Objector Rule states that a new state (especially one whose people had been colonized or subjected to oppression by another state) is not bound by customary international law existing before the new state's formation, and a group of states can form new customary international law superseding an earlier customary international law that bound them and other states. The new state or groups of states effectively can object after the crystallization of customary international law.[149] However, it should be noted from the outset that the Subsequent

[147] *See* UN Hum. Rts. Ctte., General Comment No. 24 (52), General comment on issues relating to reservations made upon ratification or accession to the Covenant or the Optional Protocols thereto, or in relation to declarations under article 41 of the Covenant, § 17, U.N. Doc. CCPR/C/21/Rev.1/Add.6 (1994) ("The principle of inter-State reciprocity has no place, save perhaps in the limited context of reservations to declarations on the Committee's competence" to consider inter-state complaints.).

[148] *Ibid.* at § 8 ("Although treaties that are mere exchanges of obligations between States allow them to reserve *inter se* applications of rules of general international law, it is otherwise in human rights treaties, which are for the benefit of persons within their jurisdiction. . . . ").

[149] Ian Brownlie, Principles of Public International Law 11 (4th ed. 1990).

Objector Rule has never been recognized as international law.[150] Although a new state is not bound by previous treaty obligations entered into by its former sovereign, the new state is bound to observe these obligations if they reflect customary international law. Hence, the "Subsequent Objector Rule" has not been accepted in international law. Accordingly, the Supreme Court has stated that "[w]hen the United States declared their independence, they were bound to receive the law of nations."[151]

With the possible above limited exception concerning international tribunal jurisdiction over interstate disputes involving a reserved treaty norm that reflects customary international law of a non-human rights character, the United States does not have the constitutional capacity to exempt itself from an extant customary international law norm to which it explicitly or implicitly accepted.

6.2.3. Emergence and crystallization rules for U.S. federal and extrafederal customary international law

Fortunately, the U.S. Supreme Court effectively has formulated a clear crystallization rule for the purpose of construing the Constitution. As noted earlier, the Supreme Court effectively has articulated a consensus rule that requires an emerging norm to reflect the practices of only a bare majority of states (specifically, twenty-six out of fifty) to be sufficient for establishing the moment of crystallization for the emerging norm. One need only determine when the twenty-sixth state law guaranteeing the norm was enacted for establishing the date of the norm's crystallization. However, for the other twenty-four or less states, they cannot avail

[150] International Law Association, *Final Report of the Committee on the Formation of Customary (General) International Law: Statement of Principles Applicable to the Formation of General Customary International Law* 27, *available at* http://www.ila-hq.org/pdf/CustomaryLaw.pdf (2000) (there is no subsequent objector rule in international law).

[151] Ware v. Hylton, 3 U.S. (3 Dall.) at 281; *see also* 1 Op. Att'y Gen. 27 (1792), *reprinted in* 1 Opinions of the Attorneys General 27 (Dennis & Co., Inc. 1945) ("The law of nations, although not specifically adopted by the Constitution or any municipal act, is essentially a part of the law of the land."). It was hardly controversial to American jurists in the eighteenth and nineteenth centuries that the law of nations was U.S. law – regardless of Article III's failure to explicitly mention it. *See* Stewart Jay, *The Status of the Law of Nations in Early American Law*, 42 Vand. L. Rev. 819 (1989).

themselves of the Persistent Objector Rule once the norm has crystallized as a matter of constitutional law (*i.e.*, treaty law) because all fifty states are legally bound by the Constitution, thereby, effectively waiving their right to avail themselves of the Rule.[152] Furthermore, the Bare Majority

[152] Although both the U.S. Supreme Court and the European Court of Human Rights have established consensus tests for using the state laws or practices in their respective constructions of the U.S. Constitution and the *ECHR*, their tests are different. The U.S. Supreme Court's formulation of the consensus test only requires a bare majority of states whose laws reflect uniformity, whereas the European Court's appears to require more than a bare majority. *See, e.g.*, Dudgeon v. Ireland, 45 Eur. Ct. H.R. (ser. A) at 23–34 (1981) (requiring "great majority" of states for establishing consensus). However, the European Court's consensus test is still vague. *See* Laurence R. Helfer, *Consensus, Coherence and the European Convention on Human Rights*, 26 CORNELL INT'L L.J. 133 (1993) (European Commission and Court of Human Rights have spoken in "vague generalities" about what constitutes consensus). The difference between U.S. constitutional and *ECHR* tests arguably can be justified on the basis that a supermajority is not required in the case of a nation constituted by states (such as the United States), whereas a greater consensus is required in a case where states do not constitute a nation but only an international organization (such as the Council of Europe). On the other hand, national cohesion can be undermined by a consensus that is defined by the state practices of only a bare majority of states.

Europe one day may accept something closer to the U.S. rule as positive law if Europe becomes more unified through its acceptance of the new *European Constitution* because the *European Constitution* rejects the conventional notion that a decision of the European Court of Human Rights is binding only on the parties and incorporates the case law of this court as binding on all EU state members. The Preamble to the *Charter of Fundamental Rights of the European Union* [*European Charter*], which is incorporated into the *Treaty Establishing a Constitution for Europe* [*European Constitution*], states the following:

> This Charter reaffirms, with due regard for the powers and tasks of the Community and the Union and the principle of subsidiarity, the rights as they result, in particular, from the constitutional traditions and international obligations common to the Member States, the Treaty on European Union, the Community Treaties, the European Convention for the Protection of Human Rights and Fundamental Freedoms, the Social Charters adopted by the Community and by the Council of Europe and the *case-law* of the Court of Justice of the European Communities and of the European Court of Human Rights.

Treaty Establishing a Constitution for Europe, Dec. 16, 2004, II-pmbl., ¶ 5, 47 Official Journal of the European Union (C 310) ((emphasis provided) [hereinafter *European Constitution*].

The same can be said for establishing a Caribbean regional customary international law for those Caribbean states who are parties to the *Agreement Establishing the Caribbean Court of Justice* because the *Agreement* establishes that "[j]udgments of the Court shall be legally binding precedents for parties in proceedings before the Court . . ." Agreement Establishing the Caribbean Court of Justice, Feb. 14, 2001, art. 22 (entered

Rule must be used only when the practices of states-parties to the Constitution provide the only evidence of federal customary international law. If the United States already has customary international legal obligations in regard to foreign states, this customary international law must be used to construe the Constitution.

Aside from customary international law that binds the United States as a whole as a matter of federal law, there is (i) American nonfederal customary international law and (ii) customary international legal norms for the United States *vis-à-vis* foreign states. In the case of American nonfederal customary international law, there is no federal law governing the matter, and states can make such customary international law, evidence of which might be provided by state laws, interstate compacts, and state-foreign state compacts. For example, there may be a general state practice governing marriage among the United States having the sense of legal obligation evidenced by state laws that reflect an American nonfederal customary international legal norm. In this case, the emergence and crystallization rules discussed in Subsection 3.2 apply as they also apply to the United States' relations with foreign states.

* * * * *

This subsection should assuage the concerns of some constitutionalists who believe that the enforcement of international law by the federal government – especially the federal courts – will undermine the American people's and individual states' rights to self-determination in that only the *implicit* consent of the American people or states is required for a customary international legal norm to be legally binding on them. The application of the Persistent Objector Rule demonstrates how the United States and its member-states can retain control over which emerging customary international legal norms that they accept as legally binding. As customary international law becomes increasingly used by parties to litigation either directly through, for example, the Alien Tort Statute or through its

into force July 23, 2003) [hereinafter *CCJ Agreement*].

Nevertheless, such European consensus tests still would not apply to the crystallization of customary international legal norms for Council of Europe members *vis-à-vis* other foreign states, or the crystallization of other regional customary international law.

use in construing the Constitution, it will become increasingly important to know exactly which customary international legal norms bind the United States. Knowing who has the constitutional capacity to make a persistent objection under what circumstances is essential to knowing which customary norms would be legally binding and, ultimately, to ensuring the preservation of national and state sovereignty.

6.3. ERODING *ERIE*: GENERAL PRINCIPLES OF LAW RECOGNIZED BY CIVILIZED NATIONS

General principles of law recognized by civilized nations are not mentioned in Article III. They constitute extra–Article III international law. Can federal courts apply such general principles of law in light of its decision in *Erie Railroad Co. v. Tompkins* that held that federal courts cannot apply federal common law,[153] which includes such general principles of law? The Supreme Court already has eroded the *Erie* doctrine by recognizing that federal courts can apply the law of nations in admiralty/maritime and tort cases.[154] Should *Erie* be eroded further by allowing federal courts to apply such general principles of law in diversity cases?

As is well known to students of constitutional law, the Supreme Court in *Erie* overturned its earlier decision in *Swift v. Tyson*.[155] At issue in both cases was the proper interpretation of the federal diversity jurisdiction statute, which in its earlier version stated that:

> the laws of the several states, except where the constitution, treaties or statutes of the United States shall otherwise require or provide, shall be regarded as rules of decision, in trials at common law, in the courts of the United States, in cases where they apply.[156]

[153] 304 U.S. 64 (1938).

[154] *See* Sosa v. Alvarez-Machain, 542 U.S. 692, 124 S. Ct. at 2764, 159 L. Ed. 2d at 9H (federal courts retain jurisdiction for common law claims notwithstanding *Erie*).

[155] 41 U.S. 1 (1842).

[156] Judiciary Act of 1789, § 34, *now codified in different language at* 28 U.S.C. § 1652 ("The laws of the several states, except where the Constitution or treaties of the United States or Acts of Congress otherwise require or provide, shall be regarded as rules of decision in civil actions in the courts of the United States, in cases where they apply.").

The *Swift* Court interpreted the phrase "the laws of the several states" to mean only (i) state statutory or constitutional law, (ii) "long-established local customs having the force of laws," or (iii) the interpretation of such laws and customs.[157] In *Swift*, the plaintiff wanted to take advantage of the favorable New York case law that the state courts had developed to govern negotiable instruments. However, this case law did not interpret either New York law or long-established customs. Consequently, the *Swift* Court did not consider such case law to be part of "the laws of the several states."

Although state case law is considered to be part of state common law, state common law also incorporates the law of nations, which includes general principles of law recognized by civilized nations.[158] For example, both New York and Pennsylvania state courts earlier had recognized that the law of nations was incorporated into state law.[159] Most importantly, this international law includes the *lex mercatoria* (or what the *Swift* Court called "general principles of commercial law"[160]). The New York case law governing these negotiable instruments conflicted with the *lex mercatoria*, and the *Swift* Court used this *lex mercatoria* to hold the negotiable instrument valid. The Court's reasoning conformed to a well-settled canon of statutory construction: statutes in abrogation of common law must be construed strictly to avoid any unnecessary conflicts. In *Swift*, the U.S. Supreme Court construed the federal diversity statute narrowly to exclude New York's case law governing the negotiable instrument at issue because, otherwise, the federal statute would conflict with that part of both New York's and the United States' common law that consisted of the *lex mercatoria*.

The Court's decision in *Swift* sought to discourage forum shopping that could occur by filing a federal diversity action. Diversity easily could be established in cases involving negotiable instruments because these

[157] Swift v. Tyson, 41 U.S. at 18.

[158] *See, e.g.*, Bains v. The James and Catherine, 2 F. Cas. 410, 412–13 (C.C.D. Pa. 1832).

[159] Respublica v. de Longchamps, 1 Dall. 120, 123 (Pa. Oyer and Terminer, 1784), *reported in* 1 U.S. (Dall.) (1784) (law of nations incorporated into Pennsylvania state law to its fullest extent); Rutgers v. Waddington (NYC Mayoral Ct. 1784), *reprinted in* 1 The Law Practice of Alexander Hamilton: Documents and Commentary 392, 414–419 (Julius Goebel Jr. *et al.* eds. 1964) (law of nations incorporated into New York state law).

[160] Swift v. Tyson, 41 U.S. at 18.

instruments could be bought by a citizen from another state. Before *Swift*, a plaintiff could file a diversity claim in a federal court that was located in a state whose case law was more favorable to the plaintiff than the defendant. The *Swift* Court sought to discourage such forum shopping by establishing a uniform federal common law.

Unfortunately, the *Swift* decision did not discourage forum shopping because it did not address removal cases. For example, a diverse defendant seeking protection under the *lex mercatoria* could remove their case from state court to federal court under the federal removal statute.[161] However, state courts could continue to apply nonuniform law because they were not bound by the federal diversity jurisdiction statute. This arrangement resulted in disparate treatment for plaintiffs who were not citizens of the state in which the federal district court was located – an arrangement that the *Erie* Court believed violated the principle of equal protection of the laws.[162]

However, the *Erie* Court overlooked two important issues. First, it failed to recognize that extra–Article III international legal authorities already were binding on state courts. In construing the federal diversity statute to include state case law that violated this international law, the *Erie* Court encouraged state courts to violate their international legal obligations. Instead, the Court should have used the *Charming Betsy* Rule to construe the federal removal statute to not allow removal unless state courts had violated their international legal obligations. The *Erie* Court swept too broadly by prohibiting federal courts from applying extra–Article III international law in diversity cases.

Second, the *Erie* Court mistakenly had criticized *Swift* on the basis that the decision falsely rested on an assumption that there is "a transcendental body of law outside of any particular State but obligatory within it unless and until changed by statute."[163] Although much of state common

[161] *See* 28 U.S.C. § 1441 (a) ("any civil action brought in a State court of which the district courts of the United States have original jurisdiction, may be removed by the defendant or defendants, to the district court of the United States for the district and division embracing the place where such action is pending").

[162] Erie Railroad Co. v. Tompkins, 304 U.S. 64, 74–75 (equal protection of the law "rendered impossible" when noncitizen given privilege of selecting court over citizen).

[163] *Id.* at 79.

law can be abrogated by state statute, a state statute cannot trump a state's international legal obligation. Therefore, insofar as the *Erie* holding could apply to the use of extra–Article III international legal authorities in diversity cases, it is inconsistent with international law, and federal courts must be able to apply general principles of law recognized by civilized nations.

6.4. STICKING TO *STARE DECISIS*: SUBSIDIARY INTERPRETIVE SOURCES

The subsidiary interpretive sources in Article 38 of the *I.C.J. Statute* include "judicial decisions." Although federal court decisions also are not mentioned in Article III, they certainly represent federal law, and they also often represent evidence of other law of nations norms.[164] It is hardly controversial that federal judicial decisions can be used to interpret positive international law. However, what is controversial is whether international courts should ascribe to the *stare decisis* doctrine[165] and what kind of deference should be given to the decisions of other international courts.

The U.S. Supreme Court in *Sanchez-Llamas v. Oregon*[166] recently held that the ICJ's decisions in the *LaGrand Case* (F.R.G.-U.S.)[167] and the *Case Concerning Avena and Other Mexican Nationals* (Mex.-U.S.)[168] did not bind the U.S. Supreme Court, relying upon its earlier decision in *Breard v. Greene*[169] as controlling authority. As demonstrated in Subsection 1.1, the U.S. Supreme Court does not enjoy final and conclusive judicial review authority in many cases, whereas the ICJ does. However, as the U.S. Supreme Court correctly pointed out, the *I.C.J. Statute* establishes that the ICJ's decisions only bind the parties.[170] In *Sanchez-Llamadas*, both petitioners were not any of the Mexican nationals covered by the ICJ's decisions in *LeGrand* and *Avena*. Accordingly, the U.S. Supreme Court's decision on this issue was correct, and the Court held that the ICJ's

[164] *See* United States v. Smith, 5 U.S. (5 Wheat.) 153, 160 (law of nations can be ascertained "by judicial decisions recognizing and enforcing that law").

[165] *See supra* Subsection 3.4.

[166] No. 04–10566, 548 U.S. – (June 28, 2006) (slip opinion).

[167] 2001 I.C.J. 466 (June 27).

[168] 2004 I.C.J. 128 (Mar. 31).

[169] 523 U.S. 371 (1998).

[170] Sanchez-Llamadas v. Oregon, No. 04–10566, 548 U.S. –, 19–20 (citing *I.C.J. Statute*, art. 59).

interpretations deserved only "respectful consideration."[171] This level of deference should come as no surprise. The Supreme Court accords only "respectful consideration" to its own precedents.[172] Although the Supreme Court seeks to stick to the *stare decisis* doctrine, it often overturns its own decisions. This is consistent with the practices of international tribunals.

However, consider the following hypothetical. What if Mexico had sued the United States[173] before the U.S. Supreme Court on behalf of one of its nationals covered by the ICJ's decision in *Avena*? The ICJ's *Avena* decision should represent the controlling authority – not *Breard* – because unlike the ICJ, the U.S. Supreme Court's decisions are not final and conclusive in cases between the United States and foreign states. As federal courts under the Constitution executed decrees issued earlier by the Courts of Appeals in Cases of Capture, which had explicit final and conclusive adjudicative authority under the Articles of Confederation, so too would federal courts (including the U.S. Supreme Court) have to execute the orders of the ICJ.

Although it would be prudent for potential parties to future cases to conform their behavior in accordance with the precedents of the U.S. Supreme Court and other international courts because it is highly likely that these courts will continue to follow their own and each other's precedents, one should recognize that judges do make mistakes. Sometimes the parties do not sufficiently brief the court on the law – especially when their lawyers are not familiar with international law. Strict adherence to precedents sometimes results in far-reaching harms. For example, when judges have construed constitutional provisions without regard to international law because there were no applicable international law norms at the time, later constitutional constructions by judges using these earlier precedents can be wrong in light of new international legal obligations that the United States subsequently has acquired. Therefore,

[171] *Id.* at 18.

[172] *See, e.g.*, Lawrence v. Texas, 539 U.S. 558, 577 (2003) ("The doctrine of *stare decisis* is essential to the respect accorded to the judgments of the Court and to the stability of the law. It is not, however, an inexorable command."), *overturning* Bowers v. Hardwick, 478 U.S. 186 (1986).

[173] Under the *Montevideo Convention on the Rights and Duties of States* (to which the United States is a party), a "federal state shall constitute a sole person in the eyes of international law." Dec. 26, 1933, art. 2, 49 Stat. 3097, TS. 81, 165 L.N.TS. 19, 3 Bevans 145 (entered into force Dec. 26, 1934). Therefore, the United States is the proper party.

federal courts should stick to the *stare decisis* doctrine only to the extent that precedents should be given only respectful consideration in subsequent cases not involving the same parties.

6.5. THE NATURAL LAW OF NATIONS

Let us now turn to the natural law of nations jurisdictions of U.S. federal courts. One of the objects and purposes of the Constitution is to "establish Justice,"[174] and under the conventional law of nations, a treaty – such as the Constitution – must be interpreted in conformity with its object and purpose.[175] Therefore, the federal court jurisdictional provisions in the Constitution must be construed in conformity with the Constitution's object and purpose to "establish Justice." In using the term "Justice," the Constitution's Preamble is not merely referring to "law" and/or "court administration." The Framers implemented their natural law ideology explicitly by incorporating natural equity into the positive law of the Constitution.[176] As discussed earlier,[177] states often have incorporated what they consider to be natural law norms into treaties.

Accordingly, federal court jurisdiction could include the authority to apply the natural law of nations, that is, the authority to decide cases *ex aequo et bono* if the parties agreed to allow the court to do so. For example, consider a case in which a state sues a municipality, and the parties have agreed to have the case decided *ex aequo et bono* because both the state and municipality want to have judicial cover over a potentially controversial outcome. In such a case, the U.S. Supreme Court can exercise its original jurisdiction, and Congress cannot limit how the Court adjudicates the case. The Court could apply extra–Article III international legal authorities or no legal authorities at all in reaching its decision. There is nothing in the Constitution prohibiting the Supreme Court from doing so, and – indeed – the Constitution's object and purpose to

[174] U.S. CONST. pmbl.

[175] *Vienna Convention*, art. 31 (1).

[176] *See*Randy E. Barnett, *A Law Professor's Guide to Natural Law and Natural Rights*, 20 HARV. J.L. & PUB. POL'Y 655, 655 ("founding generation universally subscribed to the idea of natural rights").

[177] *See supra* Chapter 4, text accompanying notes 4–7.

"establish Justice" would justify such an exercise of jurisdiction. Of course, the Supreme Court's exercise of original jurisdiction is discretionary,[178] and the Supreme Court may well be justified in declining such an exercise of jurisdiction given the parties' lack of political backbone. Furthermore, the inferior federal courts also could decide cases *ex aequo et bono* if Congress vests such jurisdiction in these courts. There is nothing in the Constitution preventing Congress from doing so, and again, the Constitution's object and purpose to "establish Justice" would justify such a jurisdictional vestment.[179]

In conclusion, what is important to note about the present international law governing international tribunal jurisdiction is that this law is designed to avoid *non liquet* judgments that could lead to war. The desire to avoid interstate conflicts erupting into war has even led states to allow international tribunals to decide cases *ex aequo et bono*. The old Vattelian positivist international legal principle that required states to comply only with those positive international legal norms to which they had expressly,

[178] *See* Rules of the Supreme Court of the United States, Rule 20 (1) (*effective* May 2, 2005) ("Issuance by the Court of an extraordinary writ authorized by 28 U.S.C. § 1651(a) is not a matter of right, but of discretion sparingly exercised. To justify the granting of any such writ, the petition must show that the writ will be in aid of the Court's appellate jurisdiction, that exceptional circumstances warrant the exercise of the Court's discretionary powers, and that adequate relief cannot be obtained in any other form or from any other court.").

This discretionary authority to not decide a case over which a federal court has jurisdiction also has been exercised in admiralty cases in which federal courts dismiss cases on forum *non conveniens* grounds. *See, e.g.*, The Maggie Hammond, 76 U.S. 435, 457 (1870) (U.S. admiralty courts may decline jurisdiction in case involving "the citizens or subjects of a foreign country, whose courts are not clothed with the power to give the same remedy in similar controversies to the citizens of the United States.").

Particularly relevant to federal courts exercising a necessary law of nations jurisdiction is that the U.S. Supreme Court also has recognized the discretionary authority of federal courts of equity to dismiss cases between aliens or nonresidents on the basis of inconvenience to the defendant. *See, e.g.*, Canada Malting Co. v. Patterson Steamships, Ltd., 285 U.S. 413, 422–23 (1932). Inconvenience is an equitable notion based on notions of natural justice.

[179] However, in cases impacting on *jus cogens* norms, federal courts deciding cases *ex aequo et bono* could not ignore this law because such norms are binding on all states. And, in interstate cases, federal courts deciding cases *ex aequo et bono* cannot reject international human rights law that would otherwise govern the case because such law is not subject to the reciprocity dynamics of general international law.

implicitly, or presumptively acceded, has become outdated in light of both the present availability of many international tribunal systems global and regional, and modern international law that requires states to seek pacific means of settling interstate disputes.[180] Even Vattel's apparent claim that there were no international tribunals for settling international disputes was somewhat inaccurate.[181] As we have seen, the Aulic Council Chamber and Imperial Chamber Court were at least available to settle such disputes – albeit they appear not to have been used for such a purpose. The present interpretive process for positive international law – from treaty law to customary law to general principles to judicial decisions and publicist teachings – reflects an increasing acceptance of natural law adjudication that finds its explicit recognition in necessary law of nations jurisdictional provisions, such as those in the *I.C.J. Statute*[182] and the *CCJ Agreement*[183] and the recognition of *jus cogens* norms.[184] Accordingly, it should come as no surprise that many people would conclude that international legal adjudication encourages judicial activism. However, such purported judicial activism is authorized by positive law.

[180] *See UN Charter*, art. 33 ("The parties to any dispute, the continuance of which is likely to endanger the maintenance of international peace and security, shall, first of all, seek a solution by . . . judicial settlement . . . "). This is not to suggest that there did not exist international law requiring pacific settlements before the *UN Charter*. Many treaties required states-parties to seek pacific settlements to disputes by tribunals. *See, e.g.*, Treaty with the Cherokee, Nov. 28, 1785, art. VIII, *available at* http://www.yale.edu/lawweb/avalon/ntreaty/chr1785.htm (last visited Aug. 8, 2005) ("It is understood that the punishment of the innocent under the idea of retaliation, is unjust, and shall not be practiced on either side, except where there is a manifest violation of this treaty; and then it shall be preceded first by a demand of justice, and if refused, then by a declaration of hostilities."); *Treaty of Westphalia*, art.- XXIII ("all Partys in this Transaction shall be oblig'd to defend and protect all and every Article of this Peace against any one, . . . and if it happens any point shall be violated, the Offended shall before all things exhort the Offender not to come to any Hostility, submitting the Cause to a friendly Composition, or the ordinary Proceedings of Justice.").

[181] *See* VATTEL, 3 LAW OF NATIONS, *supra* note 19 at § 173 ("nations acknowledge no common judge on earth").

[182] *I.C.J. Statute*, art. 38 (2).

[183] *CCJ Agreement*, art. 17 (3) (Caribbean Court of Justice has jurisdiction "to decide a dispute *ex aequo et bono* if the parties so agree.").

[184] Note that this process does not reflect a hierarchical one. The engine behind this process is the need to interpret ambiguous norms.

Nevertheless, when federal courts move away from Article III, international law to extra–Article III international law, federal courts can become susceptible to charges of judicial activism because the federal courts – unlike Congress – do not have an *express* constitutional power to clarify and punish violations of the law of nations – including extra–Article III international legal norms. At first glance, federal courts would appear to be on firmer constitutional ground if they forbear from using extra–Article III international legal authorities when construing federal law or directly applying such international law in non-federal law claims cases or cases decided *ex aequo et bono*. The federal courts should wait until Congress acts. However, if federal courts already have the constitutional authority to use such extra–Article III international legal norms, would not an attack on their constitutional authority to use such norms be premised on legislative activism? In other words, if the federal courts wait until Congress provides legislation expressly allowing the use of such norms, the federal courts are allowing Congress to overreach its own constitutional authority and intrude on their own constitutional authority. The federal courts are not making law. They are exercising their adjudicative authority provided by the Constitution to which the states accepted as law. Therefore, they are not being judicially activist.

7

The General Liberal Construction Rule: Extending *Lynham* to Other Article III and Extra–Article III International Law

As discussed earlier, federal courts exercising their nonfederal law claims jurisdictions (*viz.*, party-based and admiralty/maritime jurisdictions) sometimes can directly apply extra–Article III international legal authorities. Furthermore, federal courts exercising *ex aequo et bono* jurisdiction also can directly apply such norms. Finally, such authorities also can be used in the construction of federal law.

In Subsection 5.2, this book discussed the *Lynham* Liberal Construction Rule that requires states-parties to construe their treaty obligations liberally. The U.S. Supreme Court formulated this rule to avoid interstate interpretive conflicts and wars that might arise from a state-party's narrow construction of its duty to its treaty-partner. Although the liberal construction rule in *Lynham* applied only to treaties with foreign states, there appears to be no reason why this liberal construction rule should not also apply to other international legal sources (*e.g.*, sponsions, customary international law, and general principles of law recognized by civilized nations) given the reciprocal nature of international law in general. Indeed, the *Lynham* Liberal Construction Rule also would apply to the Constitution and federal statutory law implementing the Constitution because of the Constitution's status as a treaty. For example, consider a hypothetical case in which a CIA agent kills a foreign national in Romania. The family of the dead foreign national sues the CIA agent in a *Bivens*[1] action alleging a Fifth Amendment violation on the basis that the CIA agent deprived the foreign national of his life without due process of law.

[1] *See* Bivens v. Six Unknown Named Agents, 402 U.S. 388 (1971) (recognizing availability of damages relief for constitutional violations committed by federal authorities).

The right to life extends extraterritorially under the *American Convention on Human Rights* (*ACHR*).[2] However, the right to life under the *ECHR* arguably does not unless the state exercises "effective overall control" of the extraterritorial area in which the killing took place.[3] In such a case, the federal courts must construe the Fifth Amendment's Due Process Clause (guaranteeing no deprivation of life without due process of law) in conformity with the *ACHR* and not the *ECHR* because the use of the *ACHR* in construing the Fifth Amendment provides the most liberal construction.

As discussed earlier, such nonfederal law claim jurisdictions generally implicate international or interstate relations, and, accordingly, the use of a liberal construction rule is necessary to ensure reciprocity. For example, consider a case in which New York and New Jersey enter into an interstate compact (which does not require congressional approval) that guarantees New York citizens the right to sue New Jersey and the New Jersey citizens the right to sue New York in their respective state courts for pollution originating in the defendant state. Subsequently, New York unilaterally interprets the interstate compact to not include suits for injunctive relief but only for money damages. New Jersey sues New York before the U.S. Supreme Court. New York relies on the regional customary international law reflected in the *ECHR* that generally only provides damages relief for construing the compact.[4] New Jersey relies on the regional customary international law reflected in the *ACHR* that provides not only damages relief but also injunctive relief for construing the compact.[5] The Supreme Court exercising its original jurisdiction would be required to use the

[2] Alejandre et al. v. Cuba, Case 11.589, Report No. 86/99, OEA/Ser.L/V/II.106 Doc. 3 rev. at 586 (1999) (recognizing extraterritorial application of right to life under the *ACHR*); *see also* Saldías de López v. Uruguay, Comm. No. 52/1979, U.N. Doc. CCPR/C/OP/1 (1985) (views adopted July 29, 1981) (recognizing extraterritorial application of right to life under the *ICCPR*).

[3] Bankoviç and Others v. Belgium and Others, Application, No. 52207/99, Eur. Ct. H.R. (2001) (refusing to recognize extraterritorial application of the right to life except in areas under "effective overall control" of state party). However, it should be noted that the *Bankoviç Case* probably was wrongly decided. *See* Francisco Forrest Martin, *The International Human Rights and Ethical Aspects of the Forum Non Conveniens Doctrine*, 35 U. Miami Inter-Am. L. Rev. 101, 106–109 (2003) (discussing problems with European Court's reasoning in the *Bankoviç Case*).

[4] McGoff v. Sweden, 83 Eur. Ct. H.R. (ser. A) at 28 (1984).

[5] Aloeboetoe et al. v. Suriname, Judgment of Sept. 10, 1993, Inter-Am. Ct. H.R. (Ser. C) No. 15 (1994).

ACHR as the controlling interpretation of the New York–New Jersey interstate compact because the use of the *ACHR* provides the most liberal construction of the compact.

However, in some cases, the need to ensure reciprocity may be absent. For example, the parties to an admiralty case may be citizens of the same state. But, as argued earlier concerning the *Lynham* Liberal Construction Rule, the federal government cannot provide aliens greater legal protection to aliens than their own citizens without running afoul of the equal protection principle. Therefore, the *Lynham* Liberal Construction Rule still would apply.

On the other hand, there are other cases in which the parties are nationals of the same foreign state. For example, a foreign consul may sue a fellow national in an Alien Tort Statute action. In such cases, the use of a liberal construction rule would appear not to be mandatory unless their own national law also prohibited alienage discrimination. Furthermore, the use of a liberal construction rule in cases in which a federal court is exercising *ex aequo et bono* jurisdiction also would appear not be mandatory unless the court believed such a liberal construction was required as a matter of natural justice.[6]

One should not underestimate the importance of such liberal construction rules. The failure of judges to use international law as controlling authority has not been merely a failure to apply the United States' international legal obligations but – many times – the failure to construe these obligations properly, that is, liberally. Too many times, litigants properly have raised international legal claims and defenses only to have judges improperly construe the international law narrowly. For example, in *Sosa v. Alvarez-Machain*, the U.S. Supreme Court chose a strict construction of customary international law by holding that nonprolonged arbitrary detention was not prohibited by such law. The Court failed to recognize that although the RESTATEMENT required that arbitrary detention be prolonged to be prohibited by customary international law,[7] other

[6] Indeed, this conclusion would be congruent with a general principle of equity that remedial laws should be construed liberally. *See generally*, Karl Llewellyn, *Remarks on the Theory of Appellate Decision and the Rules or Canons About How Statutes Are To Be Construed*, 3 VAND. L. REV. 395 (1950).

[7] RESTATEMENT (THIRD) OF FOREIGN RELATIONS LAW OF THE UNITED STATES § 702 (1987).

international legal authorities did not require so.[8] For example, Alvarez-Machain cited the *ICCPR* in support of his claim, and the UN Human Rights Committee in *Saldías de López v. Uruguay* earlier had held that nonprolonged, extraterritorial, arbitrary detention (such as in the case of *Sosa*) did violate the right to liberty, which is a customary international legal norm.[9]

The extension of the *Lynham* Liberal Construction Rule to other Article III and extra-Article III, international legal authorities complements and supplements what the Supreme Court began in *McCulloch v. Maryland* when it liberally construed Congress' legislative authority. In the same manner that the *Non Liquet* Prohibition Principle provides federal courts the authority to exercise a robust interpretive power for preventing violent conflicts, the extension of the *Lynham* Liberal Construction Rule to constitutional provisions, federal statutes, sponsions, customary international law, and general principles of law recognized by civilized nations provides congressional, senatorial, and presidential exercises in federal lawmaking to be interpreted liberally while at the same time restraining such power in cases in which violent conflicts (interstate and otherwise) could erupt. Most importantly, the Rule recognizes that it cannot be applied in cases in which individual rights and/or liberties would be violated. The extension of the *Lynham* Liberal Construction Rule fulfills the Preamble's object and purpose of forming a "more perfect Union" and ensuring "domestic Tranquility."

[8] Sosa v. Alvarez-Machain, 542 U.S. 692, 124 S. Ct. 2739, 159 L. Ed. 2d 718.

[9] Comm. No. 52/1979, U.N. Doc. CCPR/C/OP/1 (1985) (views adopted July 29, 1981).

Conclusion

As we have seen, the Constitution as a treaty established a U.S. federal court system that is an international court system with interstate and national dimensions. Accordingly, federal judicial power is enabled and governed by international law. An international legal construction of Article III federal judicial authority enables federal courts to review the compatibility of federal and state law with the Constitution and provides a better justification of such authority. Moreover, an international legal construction of federal judicial authority in conformity the *Non Liquet* Prohibition Principle also ensures that the exercise of such judicial review authority when using both Article III and extra–Article III international legal authorities is not judicial activism.

Most importantly, federal courts often must use those Article III and extra–Article III international legal authorities that provide the most liberal construction to the United States' and its member-states' federal and nonfederal international legal obligations. In doing so, federal courts will further integrate U.S. constitutional law with other international law – an important policy objective in a globalized world that seeks the uniformity of law and the reduction of transaction costs associated with nonuniformity.

One important conclusion about the general nature of international law as a whole appears to be emerging: there is a diminishing space in which international actors – such as federal courts – can act without supervision by international law. Whether there is a positive rule of international law that is binding on a particular state (or international organization) will turn more upon how much specificity and/or unambiguity international actors (*e.g.*, states, international organizations, international tribunals) demand from a norm's articulation than on the existence of the norm itself. A party almost always can claim that some international legal norm exists that imposes a legal obligation on another party, and if, for example, a treaty norm is insufficiently specific or unambiguous, an international actor almost always can construe the norm in light of other international legal norms (such as custom or general principles recognized by civilized nations) to provide the needed specificity or unambiguity. Driving this process is the international community's political and legal objective to resolve conflicts peacefully that otherwise can erupt into war, and enabling the international community to do so in a disciplined manner is the availability of a growing corpus of international legal authorities (*e.g.*, treaties, case law) and international organs and tribunals tasked with settling or adjudicating these disputes. Most importantly, these international tribunals can provide greater definition to those positive international legal authorities that arguably require greater specificity and/or unambiguity by applying those norms to concrete cases. The application of rules to facts "on the ground" provides concrete meaning to arguably nonspecific or vague rules. The international community's objective to peacefully resolve conflicts combined with the *Non Liquet* Prohibition Principle governing international tribunal practice undercuts any arguable disconnect between positive law and applicable facts.

In light of the availability of a great number of international legal norms governing an increasing number of areas in the era of globalization, lawyers increasingly will bring international legal claims in federal courts, and federal judges will find themselves increasingly faced with international legal issues to adjudicate. Federal judges cannot afford to not familiarize themselves with international law. Fortunately, they already have an advantage by being versed in U.S. constitutional law because, as this book has sought to demonstrate, U.S. constitutional law is international law.

As noted in the Introduction, "most constitutional jurists have been doing international legal analysis without knowing it." Accordingly, most of the U.S. Supreme Court cases discussed in this book have been consistent with the ILC approach. With the exception of the Last-in-Time Rule, any departures from international law have been marginal. However, the Supreme Court's continued adherence to the Last-in-Time Rule will make constitutional case law incoherent and internationally illegitimate. It is fortunate that the Supreme Court recently in *Hamdan v. Rumsfeld* held that the president could not violate provisions of the *Geneva Conventions* even during war. The Supreme Court earlier in *United States v. Macintosh* has noted that Congress also cannot violate international law during war – albeit only in dictum. In light of *Hamdan* and *Macintosh*, a rejection of the Last-in-Time Rule should pose neither a constitutional or conceptual challenge for the Supreme Court. As the Supreme Court previously did with *Plessy*,[1] *Stanford*,[2] and *Hardwick*,[3] it should retire this rule, repositing it with the refuse of these other deleterious decisions.

Finally, as it is may be obvious to the reader, the recent internationally illegal practices surrounding the United States' "war on terrorism" (*e.g.*, the U.S. invasion of Iraq, the CIA's practice of renditions and "waterboarding," and the denial of terrorist suspects' access to the courts) has been this book's subtext and a major reason for writing this book. However, I have not dealt directly with these recent practices because it has struck me over the last few years that the failure of federal officials to observe international law oftentimes has resulted from a more fundamental misunderstanding of the Constitution's relationship to other international law. Accordingly, I have attempted to provide a better understanding of this relationship, and it is my hope that the reader has found this book both timely and helpful.

[1] Plessy v. Ferguson, 163 U.S. 537 (1896) (allowing separate but equal treatment of African-Americans), *overturned by* Brown v. Board of Education, 347 U.S. 483 (1954).

[2] Stanford v. Kentucky, 492 U.S. 361 (1989) (allowing execution of persons committing capital crimes under age eighteen), *overturned by* Roper v. Simmons, 543 U.S. 551 (2002) (relying on international prohibition of juvenile executions).

[3] Bowers v. Hardwick, 478 U.S. 186 (1986) (no privacy right to engage in homosexual conduct under the Fourth and Fifth Amendments), *overturned by* Lawrence v. Texas, 539 U.S. 558 (2003) (relying on international law).

Epilogue

In 1952, the Constitution was placed in inert gas-filled casements, hermetically sealed, and transferred into the custody and charge of the National Archives. In the same year, another – albeit subtly symbolic – hermetic sealing of the Constitution was attempted. Members of Congress introduced the Bricker Amendment that would have hermeneutically sealed the Constitution from international law by undercutting the United States' treaty obligations.[1] Fortunately, the proposed Bricker Amendment failed to pass.

Recently, the National Archives unsealed the Constitution's casements, repaired the parchment, and stabilized the ink. However, another preservation project must be undertaken by all of us. We, too, must unseal the Constitution and restore its original meaning whose text was inked in international law and whose courts' competencies are constrained and complemented by such law.

[1] *See* S.J. Res. 1 ("Bricker Amendment"), 83rd Cong. 1st Sess., § 2 (1953) ("A treaty shall become effective as internal law in the United States only through legislation which would be valid in the absence of a treaty.").

Index